Directed Digital Dissidence in Autocracies

Oxford Studies in Digital Politics

Series Editor: Andrew Chadwick, Professor of Political Communication in the Centre for Research in Communication and Culture and the Department of Social Sciences, Loughborough University

Apostles of Certainty: Data Journalism and the Politics of Doubt
C. W. Anderson

Using Technology, Building Democracy: Digital Campaigning and the Construction of Citizenship
Jessica Baldwin-Philippi

Expect Us: Online Communities and Political Mobilization
Jessica L. Beyer

If ... Then: Algorithmic Power and Politics
Taina Bucher

The Hybrid Media System: Politics and Power
Andrew Chadwick

News and Democratic Citizens in the Mobile Era
Johanna Dunaway and Kathleen Searles

The Fifth Estate: The Power Shift of the Digital Age
William H. Dutton

The Only Constant Is Change: Technology, Political Communication, and Innovation over Time
Ben Epstein

Designing for Democracy: How to Build Community in Digital Environments
Jennifer Forestal

Tweeting to Power: The Social Media Revolution in American Politics
Jason Gainous and Kevin M. Wagner

When the Nerds Go Marching In: How Digital Technology Moved from the Margins to the Mainstream of Political Campaigns
Rachel K. Gibson

Trolling Ourselves to Death: Democracy in the Age of Social Media
Jason Hannan

Risk and Hyperconnectivity: Media and Memories of Neoliberalism
Andrew Hoskins and John Tulloch

Democracy's Fourth Wave? Digital Media and the Arab Spring
Philip N. Howard and Muzammil M. Hussain

The Digital Origins of Dictatorship and Democracy: Information Technology and Political Islam
Philip N. Howard

Analytic Activism: Digital Listening and the New Political Strategy
David Karpf

The MoveOn Effect: The Unexpected Transformation of American Political Advocacy
David Karpf

News Nerds: Institutional Change in Journalism
Allie Kosterich

Prototype Politics: Technology-Intensive Campaigning and the Data of Democracy
Daniel Kreiss

Taking Our Country Back: The Crafting of Networked Politics from Howard Dean to Barack Obama
Daniel Kreiss

Media and Protest Logics in the Digital Era: The Umbrella Movement in Hong Kong
Francis L. F. Lee and Joseph M. Chan

Bits and Atoms: Information and Communication Technology in Areas of Limited Statehood
Steven Livingston and Gregor Walter-Drop

Digital Feminist Activism: Girls and Women Fight Back against Rape Culture
Kaitlynn Mendes, Jessica Ringrose, and Jessalynn Keller

Digital Cities: The Internet and the Geography of Opportunity
Karen Mossberger, Caroline J. Tolbert, and William W. Franko

The Power of Platforms: Shaping Media and Society
Rasmus Kleis Nielsen and Sarah Anne Ganter

Revolution Stalled: The Political Limits of the Internet in the Post-Soviet Sphere
Sarah Oates

Disruptive Power: The Crisis of the State in the Digital Age
Taylor Owen

Affective Publics: Sentiment, Technology, and Politics
Zizi Papacharissi

Money Code Space: Hidden Power in Bitcoin, Blockchain, and Decentralisation
Jack Parkin

The Citizen Marketer: Promoting Political Opinion in the Social Media Age
Joel Penney

Tweeting Is Leading: How Senators Communicate and Represent in the Age of Twitter
Annelise Russell

The Ubiquitous Presidency: Presidential Communication and Digital Democracy in Tumultuous Times
Joshua M. Scacco and Kevin Coe

China's Digital Nationalism
Florian Schneider

Networked Collective Actions: The Making of an Impeachment
Hyunjin Seo

Credible Threat: Attacks against Women Online and the Future of Democracy
Sarah Sobieraj

Presidential Campaigning in the Internet Age
Jennifer Stromer-Galley

News on the Internet: Information and Citizenship in the 21st Century
David Tewksbury and Jason Rittenberg

Outside the Bubble: Social Media and Political Participation in Western Democracies
Cristian Vaccari and Augusto Valeriani

The Internet and Political Protest in Autocracies
Nils B. Weidmann and Espen Geelmuyden Rød

The Civic Organization and the Digital Citizen: Communicating Engagement in a Networked Age
Chris Wells

Computational Propaganda: Political Parties, Politicians, and Political Manipulation on Social Media
Samuel Woolley and Philip N. Howard

Networked Publics and Digital Contention: The Politics of Everyday Life in Tunisia
Mohamed Zayani

Directed Digital Dissidence in Autocracies

HOW CHINA WINS ONLINE

JASON GAINOUS, RONGBIN HAN,
ANDREW W. MACDONALD, AND KEVIN M. WAGNER

OXFORD
UNIVERSITY PRESS

Oxford University Press is a department of the University of Oxford. It furthers
the University's objective of excellence in research, scholarship, and education
by publishing worldwide. Oxford is a registered trade mark of Oxford University
Press in the UK and certain other countries.

Published in the United States of America by Oxford University Press
198 Madison Avenue, New York, NY 10016, United States of America.

© Oxford University Press 2024

All rights reserved. No part of this publication may be reproduced, stored in
a retrieval system, or transmitted, in any form or by any means, without the
prior permission in writing of Oxford University Press, or as expressly permitted
by law, by license, or under terms agreed with the appropriate reproduction
rights organization. Inquiries concerning reproduction outside the scope of the
above should be sent to the Rights Department, Oxford University Press, at the
address above.

You must not circulate this work in any other form
and you must impose this same condition on any acquirer.

Library of Congress Cataloging-in-Publication Data
Names: Gainous, Jason, 1971– author. | Han, Rongbin, author. |
MacDonald, Andrew W., author. | Wagner, Kevin M., 1971– author.
Title: Directed digital dissidence in autocracies : how China wins online /
Jason Gainous, Rongbin Han, Andrew W. MacDonald, Kevin M. Wagner.
Description: New York : Oxford University Press, 2024. |
Series: Oxford studies digital politics series |
Includes bibliographical references and index.
Identifiers: LCCN 2023022521 (print) | LCCN 2023022522 (ebook) |
ISBN 9780197680384 (hardback) | ISBN 9780197680391 (paperback) |
ISBN 9780197680407 (epub) | ISBN 9780197680421 | ISBN 9780197680414
Subjects: LCSH: Communication in politics—Technological
innovations—China. | Internet—Political aspects—China. |
Political participation—China—Computer network resources. |
Social media—Political aspects—China. |
Political participation—Technological innovations—China. |
Dictatorship—China.
Classification: LCC JA85.2.C6 G35 2023 (print) | LCC JA85.2.C6 (ebook) |
DDC 320.95101/4—dc23/eng/20230613
LC record available at https://lccn.loc.gov/2023022521
LC ebook record available at https://lccn.loc.gov/2023022522

DOI: 10.1093/oso/9780197680384.001.0001

Paperback printed by Marquis Book Printing, Canada
Hardback printed by Bridgeport National Bindery, Inc., United States of America

Contents

Acknowledgments vii

1. The China Case: Strong State, Popular Contention, and the Internet 1

2. The Chinese Internet: Citizen Awareness of Government Control 17

3. What Does Directed Digital Dissidence Look Like? Critical Information Flows, Trust, and Support for Protest 37

4. Social Media: The Battleground of the Information War 56

5. Jumping Over the Great Firewall: A Threat to the Chinese Strategy 72

6. The Digital Dissident Citizen: Who Are the Wall Jumpers? 84

7. Managing the Information War: Voices Heard from Beyond the Wall Are Lost 98

8. Digital Directed Dissidence in Action: Applications and Its Limits 107

9. Will Directed Digital Dissidence Keep Working? 125

v

vi   *Contents*

Appendix A: Survey Questions   133
Appendix B: Normality of Residuals for All Models   145
Appendix C: Chinese Social Media Posts   147
Notes   149
References   153
Index   169

Acknowledgments

Thanks Bella. Rave on cat shit, I'll bury you later!
—Jason Gainous

To my wife Yi, my daughter Audrey, and my parents. Their unconditional support has allowed me to focus on the research.
—Rongbin Han

To my wife Jodie, and our beautiful children Maddie, Alex, and Harrison. You are my constant source of love, inspiration, and encouragement.
—Kevin M. Wagner

To all those that have helped me along the way in the Covid-19 era, it's been a long ride, and I could not have done it without the kindness of friends and family.
—Andrew W. MacDonald

We would like to thank the Centro de Investigaciones Sociales at Universidad de Puerto Rico for providing resources for Jason Gainous to work on this project. Thanks to Yuchen Cao, Hailey Mattingly, and Jialong Wang for valuable research assistance. Finally, thanks to the University of Louisville's Center for Asian Democracy for funding for this project.

1

The China Case

Strong State, Popular Contention, and the Internet

The Chinese authoritarian state has withstood significant crises since it was founded in 1949. In its earlier years, the instability generated from repeated economic and political campaigns under Mao—from the Great Leap Forward to the Cultural Revolution—proved exhaustive, devastating, and disillusioning (Deng and Treiman 1997; Dikötter 2013; Lee and Yang 2007; MacFarquhar and Schoenhals 2006). Many believed that by the time of Mao's death, the regime was likely to collapse. Yet China's party-state system demonstrated a considerable level of resilience and adaptability through a transformation of its economic system as well as revisions to its political structures (Dittmer and Liu 2006; Montinola, Qian, and Weingast 1995; Nathan 2003; Naughton 1996; 2007; Shambaugh 2008). This is a sharp contrast with other autocratic single-party systems in much of the world.

Despite the more recent success of autocratic leaders, the long, sustained trend has been away from single-party-controlled states. Many have been challenged or even replaced, including almost all of the former communist states and many of the nations in the Middle East during the Arab Spring (Lotan et al. 2011). Yet China's system has proven to be durable. Even when faced with understandable anger over the handling of the COVID-19 pandemic, the Chinese central government has managed, blunted, and directed dissent effectively in online discourse. In this book, we consider the robustness of the Chinese party-state in the digital era. More directly, we add to previous research on the durability of the Chinese state by considering how effective directing and marshaling online discourse can help sustain the system itself.

Although scholars have largely abandoned the rose-colored view of the internet as inherently supportive of diversity and democracy (see, e.g., Barber 2001), it continues to be viewed as positive and politically transformative (Gainous, Segal, and Wagner 2018). The internet has been seen as providing a new

Directed Digital Dissidence in Autocracies. Jason Gainous, Rongbin Han, Andrew W. MacDonald, and Kevin M. Wagner, Oxford University Press. © Oxford University Press 2024. DOI: 10.1093/oso/9780197680384.003.0001

opportunity structure for a freer flow of political information and as a venue that fosters political exchange in a way that challenges closed states. However, the mechanisms and limitations of the internet are becoming more apparent. Some states have effectively blunted the transformative nature of online political discourse by limiting opposition communication, closely monitoring content, and manipulating online expression (Deibert 2015; Deibert et al. 2008; 2010; Gainous, Wagner, and Ziegler 2018; Han 2018a; Roberts 2018; Toepfl 2011). Digital technology makes greater and more detailed surveillance possible, allowing authoritarian states to target dissidents and avoid costlier broad methods of repression or co-option (Hou 2017; 2020; Xiao 2019; Xu 2020). Indeed, autocracies are surviving in this modern digital environment because of the additional power of government to control and use information flows (Gainous, Wagner, and Abbott 2015).

We extend this line of research here further and propose that the internet can be more than blunted. It can be transformed into a key strategic element for maintaining the status quo. Although some states grapple with the internet in blunt and often ineffective ways, more sophisticated state actors can use and manipulate the new medium to support and even buoy the extant governing structure. This approach reverses the democratization or even equalization narrative as the opportunity structure presented by the internet exists for more than just citizens; it provides new tools for the state as well (Creemers 2017; Esarey 2015; Gainous, Segal, and Wagner 2018; King, Pan, and Roberts 2017; Schlæger 2013). Indeed, not only can state actors use digital communications; they may potentially use them with far greater sophistication and efficacy. Beyond just limiting or even narrowly targeting the opposition, now more sophisticated state actors are marshaling the content and directing the conversation (Esarey 2015).

In this book, we will consider the mechanism and impact of this evolving state-led political internet in China. Our theory, *directed digital dissidence* (DDD), explains how autocracies manage critical online information flows and what impact this management has on mass opinion and behavior. Scholars have long found that citizens often resort to "rightful resistance" to lodge complaints and defend rights in the offline world (O'Brien and Li 2006). Increasingly, sophisticated closed state governments, rather than simply suppressing this opposition online and forcing it into less controlled channels, shepherd and direct the opposition narrative. In this way, the central government is complicit in this resistance via "strategic censorship," where they tolerate some public criticism of local officials but suppress criticism of top leadership (Lorentzen 2014).

Directed digital dissidence contends that the expansion of the internet may simultaneously stimulate dissidence while providing the central government an avenue to direct that dissent toward selected targets and away from the central government. This allows the government to give citizens a voice while maintaining its central authority. In this model, the internet dissipates threats to the state by serving as a relief valve rather than a pressure cooker (Hassid 2012b). This is a clearly strategic process in China, where it is centrally directed and part of the regime's legitimation strategy. The internet is stabilizing for these regimes, as it gives a place for anger and dissatisfaction to go while giving the state the tools to limit, control, and direct it.

Our theory of the relationship between internet use and regime support recalls many of the arguments made over the years that seek to explain the resilience of the Chinese government. Many scholars have explored the popular support for (or at least the passive acceptance of) the Chinese authoritarian regime as the primary reason that explains its survival. They argue that the economic reform and liberalization has generally failed to produce demands for democracy, and the party-state has successfully maintained or even enhanced its popularity through institutional adaptions and improved governance (Chen and Dickson 2010; Dickson 2003; W. Tang 2016; Yang and Zhao 2015; D. Zhao 2009). Perceived satisfaction with effective governance reduces the agitations that often stimulate change. Interestingly, this approach differs from the structural theories that see capitalism as a catalyst to democratization.

Indeed, China scholars find that the rise of private entrepreneurs and the middle class has yet to pose any serious political challenge to the party-state. For instance, Kellee Tsai (2007) maintain that economic reform and marketization have not led to substantial democratic reforms in China in part because private entrepreneurs have been able to create adaptive institutions and work within the system. An Chen (2002, 403) argues that China's reform has in effect "submitted the entrepreneurial class and other middle classes to a status of political and economic dependence," so that they do not associate their interests positively with democratization. Similarly, scholars find that the party-state has successfully co-opted social groups such as private entrepreneurs and the middle class, thus not only preventing them from becoming threats to the regime, but also turning them into allies of the state (Chen and Dickson 2010; Dickson 2003).

In effect, democracy in China may have been delayed because the earlier adoption of some major economic reforms, such as the liberalization of foreign direct investment, lessened the need to change the state in order to push for these reforms. The foreign-invested sector serves as a laboratory for the difficult and sensitive reforms, helping increase convergence with capitalism while reducing societal resistance. This has redirected and reformulated the transition debate into one over foreign versus Chinese competition. The influx of foreign direct investment has allowed the state to extricate itself from the socialist contract without losing control (Gallagher 2002; 2011).

The Chinese authoritarian regime still enjoys considerable popular support in the reform era. Studies have repeatedly shown that Chinese citizens have consistently demonstrated one of the highest levels of either political support or political trust across the globe (Jie Chen 2004; Kennedy 2009; Lianjiang Li 2004; 2013; Manion 2006; Shi 2008; 2001; W. Tang 2016; D. L. Yang 2007). Wenfang Tang (2016) attempted to explain the regime's sustained support through the concept of "populist authoritarianism," which incorporates multiple elements of Chinese political culture, including the mass line ideology, strong community solidarity, widespread public involvement, higher rates of political participation, and perhaps most importantly, a responsive government. More directly, it has been theorized that the Chinese party-state has adapted its institutions to vitiate political challenges through improved governance. Despite many persisting problems, measures such as introduction of grassroots democracy (Heberer and Schubert 2008; O'Brien 2001; O'Brien and Han 2009), the push for legal reforms (Diamant, Lubman, and O'Brien 2005; Peerenboom 2001; 2003), enhancement of intraparty democracy (C. Li 2009; Lin 2004), and the accommodation of popular complaints (Cai 2014; O'Brien and Li 2004; Y. Su and He 2010; Weller 2012), as well as other reforms, have, to a certain extent, improved public participation, government accountability, and state responsiveness (Dickson 2021).

However, focusing exclusively on how the party-state has maintained popularity can be misleading, largely because it underestimates the level of popular dissatisfaction regarding the reform process itself. Though major social groups have benefited from the reforms, the process has been uneven and often inequitable. Chinese reforms have favored some groups at the expense of others. The reforms have also been limited by corruption, poor implementation by local governments, and inefficient new bureaucracies (Pei 2009). In effect, reform-era China has produced advances, but it has also generated popular contention among various social groups, including but not limited to peasants, laid-off workers, urban middle class, students, intellectuals, and dissidents (Bernstein and Lv 2003; Cai 2010; F. Chen 2003; X. Chen 2012; Hurst 2009; Kelly 2006; O'Brien and Diamant 2014; O'Brien and Li 2006; Perry 2015; Perry and Selden 2003; Shirk 2007; Sun and Zhao 2008; Yao and Han 2016; D. Zhao 2001). As is the case in many national assessments of public satisfaction, the overall numbers often mask a more nuanced narrative.

Unsurprisingly, the perceived uneven benefits have produced political unrest. The annual count of "mass incidents," such as collective petitions, demonstrations, strikes, and riots, has climbed sharply in China, jumping from about 8,700 incidents in 1993 to more than 200,000 by 2011 (Lee and Zhang 2013, 1476; So 2013, 3; Xie and Shan 2012, 61). Nonetheless, there is little evidence that this unrest has resulted in significant political reforms of the governing structures or stimulated a widespread movement toward more democratic reforms. Indeed, even the political turmoil from cases such as the Tiananmen Student Movement in 1989, and the more recent Arab Spring–inspired Jasmine Revolution, have thus far failed to move the Chinese authoritarian state toward more inclusive democratic structures. The puzzle China poses is one where unrest, as in other authoritarian states, is present, but the sustained and effective push for substantive institutional reform is largely absent.

No doubt part of the answer lies in the consistent strength and capacity of the authoritarian Chinese state. Contentious politics scholars studying China have depicted a mighty state, which possesses formidable coercive power and is ready to exercise it when deemed necessary. This was illustrated during the Tiananmen Square occupation in 1989 and in many other cases of mass protests (Béja 2009; Brook 1998; Davis and Lin 2004; Human Rights Watch 2008; D. Zhao 2001). The Chinese state has developed effective and extensive capabilities to limit social unrest. The party-state has created "a multiagency juggernaut" that sustains the state and maintains stability (Jacobs 2011). Ultimately, as social and political stability are a top priority, the state has adapted by enhancing coercive apparatus for local authorities and by significantly increasing the resources provided to the state security operations (J. Gao 2015; Hassid and Sun 2015; Kan 2013; Wang and Minzner 2015; Xie 2013). The approach has been sophisticated, and increased technology has allowed a greater ability for the Chinese state to surveil the population and target individuals with a precision that avoids the pathologies of more universal repression (Xu 2020).

However, as the East German Communist Party learned, state capacity cannot be the only factor in autocratic regime resilience. More recent studies suggest that the Chinese state has also been highly creative in devising strategies to prevent and demobilize popular protests, in both the real world and the virtual space. For instance, Rachel Stern and Jonathan Hassid (2012) argue that, in addition to heavy-handed repression, the state may deliberately maintain the uncertainty about the limits of permissible political action to encourage self-censorship, thus amplifying silence among active social groups such as journalists and lawyers. Research by Kevin O'Brien and Yanhua Deng (2015) illustrates that when popular mobilization occurs, local officials often resort to relational repression. This includes exploiting activists' social ties, locating individuals who can pacify the protest, and dispatching a work team to conduct thought work to demobilize protesters. Sociologists Ching Kwan Lee and Yonghong Zhang (2013) analyzed Chinese state practices in moments of unrest. They identified protest bargaining, legal-bureaucratic absorption, and patron-clientelism as the micro-foundations of Chinese authoritarianism. Ultimately, these mechanisms adopt the logic of market exchange, rule-bounded games, and interpersonal ties to de-escalate unrest and preserve regime and social stability.

Interestingly, and perhaps counterintuitively, popular contention and unrest can actually contribute to regime stability as part of a governance strategy.

System stability is enhanced where dissatisfaction is managed inside the governing structure. If internal mechanisms are available for protest or challenge, the unrest can be channeled and contained. Aggrieved citizens are allowed to make use of state's own laws and policies in framing their protests using a mechanism coined as "rightful resistance" (O'Brien 1996; O'Brien and Li 2006). In a sense, citizens come to see the state as a necessary means for having their grievance vetted and addressed. This is true in China where citizens often use the state for "rightful resistance" to lodge complaints and defend rights (O'Brien and Li 2006).

Using the current system to effectuate protest is a rational recognition of the internal divides within the authoritarian regime. Protesters use laws, policies, and norms promoted by the central government to justify their claims and to challenge local authorities that fail to live up to central promises. By operating near the boundary of authorized channels, using the rhetoric and commitments of high-level authorities, and actively seeking greater public exposure, protestors are able to effectively exploit institutionalized channels of dissent while avoiding repression. Rightful resistance provides the protesters with the language as well as effective strategies of protest. As a theoretical framework, it offers a strong explanation of how powerless citizens may exploit the slim political opportunity in repressive regimes and negotiate for better governance. Because of its robust explanatory power, the framework has been widely embraced and developed by the scholarly community studying contentious politics in China (Cai 2010; X. Chen 2012; 2009; Sun and Zhao 2008).

From the regime's perspective, rightful resistance can work as a stability maintenance mechanism that turns popular contention into "constructive noncompliance" (L. L. Tsai 2015, 253). First, it confirms and reinforces the legitimacy of authoritarian regime in that citizens engage in rightful resistance precisely because they have some faith and trust in the party-state, or at least the central government. Indeed, scholars have found that China's rural residents tend to differentiate the central government from local authorities and have more trust in higher levels of government (Lianjiang Li 2004). In addition, Chinese citizens also distinguish between the intent and the capacity of the central government. Many believe that the central government has laudable intentions but lacks the capacity to prevent local officials from ignoring or defying its policies.

Further, rightful resistance helps preserve the stability of the regime as it encourages protesters to seek local, immediate, and specific remedies and improvements. In doing so, it keeps popular contention localized in a way that keeps protests from harming the regime's overall legitimacy. It also dissipates dissent before it forms a nationwide movement that can challenge the larger system (Hess 2013). Channeling dissatisfaction into local grievances is effective on two fronts. When local government is the scapegoat for state policy failures, pressure on the regime is not just relieved; the central government gets to showcase its responsiveness and benevolence by imposing discipline on its local agents. In addition, by tolerating and even encouraging rightful resistance, the regime turns popular unrest into a form of political participation that helps fill the policy feedback deficit caused by lack of traditional democratic institutions that would allow for policy input and participation (e.g., see Lorentzen 2013; O'Brien and Li 2006; Reilly 2013; L. L. Tsai 2015; Weller 2012).

Rightful resistance serves as a powerful explanation for the paradoxical coexistence of a resilient authoritarian regime and pervasive popular contention in China. To a large extent, it is an image of contention that, rather than undermining the regime, actually helps perpetuate authoritarian rule. But there are two important prior conditions for rightful resistance to work favorably for the state: the protests need to be localized, and protesters need to stick to the "rightful" framing of their grievances. This is where digital technology has the possibility of disrupting the system. The expansion of the internet and digital media challenges both conditions: Citizens now may learn that they are not alone, and they are exposed to alternative and broader framing that can challenge the state narrative.

By enabling freer flow of information in repressive settings, modern information communication technologies allow citizens to publicly voice their discontent and to mobilize and organize more effectively against authoritarian regimes. In particular, by connecting discontented citizens, information communication technologies help them to communicate about their grievances, to learn protesting opportunities and strategies from one another, and to reach out to each other in solidarity. Moreover, by breaking the state's monopoly over mass media, the expansion of the internet and social media may help citizens to recognize the pervasiveness of certain social political problems and to build up a shared awareness about the necessity of systematic change rather than individualized or localized solutions. In its least form, the expansion of digital media calls into question the credibility of state propaganda and its framing of issues, demanding the state address the difference between its view of events and the public perception (Shirky 2011). Losing complete control over information flow makes it increasingly difficult for the party-state to keep popular contention contained to the "rightful resistance" track. As people discover recurrent, pervasive, and systematic problems beyond their communities, they are likely to see the current state apparatus as ineffective. Ultimately, citizens would lose trust in the regime and demand larger systemic changes beyond their locality.

Indeed, many closed states have failed to adapt to this new environment (e.g., Howard 2010; Howard and Hussain 2013a). However, some closed states have been more effective in limiting and controlling content (Gainous, Wagner, and Ziegler 2018). Indeed, the Chinese state has established a compressive and

8 DIRECTED DIGITAL DISSIDENCE IN AUTOCRACIES

systematic censorship system to control information flow in the virtual space (Deibert et al. 2008; 2010; Han 2018a; Harwit and Clark 2001; King, Pan, and Roberts 2013; 2014; MacKinnon 2009; Roberts 2018). The Chinese censorship regime has been so systematic and effective that some argue that their control of the domestic internet is probably the world's most sophisticated (OpenNet Initiative 2005).

However, limiting or blocking content is not the only avenue open to a state. The internet also provides authoritarian states an avenue to engage citizens and shape public opinion through innovative propaganda strategies. Besides promoting e-government platforms (Lollar 2006; Schlæger 2013), China has actively promoted its own preferred discourses online by engaging on popular social media platforms (Esarey 2015; Schlæger and Jiang 2014), embracing popular cyber culture in online propaganda (Lagerkvist 2008), and deploying internet commentators (a.k.a. the "50 Cent Party") to anonymously fabricate seemingly spontaneous pro-regime voices or to denigrate dissidents and critical expression (Han 2015b; Hung 2010; King, Pan, and Roberts 2017; Miller 2016). Despite the challenges of moderating this new online public forum, the Chinese state has proven quite adaptive and possesses considerable power to influence the information flow in the internet age.

Rightful resistance as an accepted framework provides an opportunity structure for both the state and the protestors. Although it can be an effective protesting strategy for disadvantaged social groups in repressive regimes, the state has some clear benefits as well. The gaps that provide that opportunity were already noted well before the dominant role of the internet in societal discourse. Jürgen Habermas noted that even in states that are largely democratic, the failing public sphere could no longer provide a separate and critical evaluation of the state. In Habermas' (1991) view, political actors are using media to manipulate public opinion to achieve a false consensus. A savvy autocratic state is in a strong position to dominate discourse similarly through effective information control, thereby interfering with rational-critical debate. The internet provides a more nuanced and targeted means to manipulate conversation and consensus far beyond broadcast or print mediums. The internet affects cognitive processing of issues by expanding and quickly replacing the information that can be sampled by users. Careful pruning of the news' flow can shift attitudes (Gainous, Marlowe and Wagner 2013).

The internet has provided a means for the Chinese state to maximize the strategy that began with "rightful resistance." Now the state can do more than just attempt to use local officials as foils; it can inject itself into the online discontent so as to manage and channel opposition, often without having to own its role. We term this "directed digital dissidence." By this we mean that the state adopts a strategy to use the internet to manage, control, and direct dissidence in real time to sustain the regime. This approach allows citizens to believe they have an opportunity to voice their opinions and vent their anger, while steering their efforts so as not to seriously jeopardize the central authority or the regime's legitimacy. Directed digital dissidence as an approach allows the state to maintain or even more actively reinforce the "rightful resistance" mentality among the citizens, thus preserving its rule, while giving the appearance of citizen empowerment. This is very much in line with what Peter Lorentzen (2014) coined as "strategic censorship." By tolerating critical reporting on local officials and other actors but suppressing criticism of the top leadership, the central government, or the regime as a whole, can reap the benefits of free media without risking the chance that regime dissidents will use the technology against the regime itself. Indeed, empirical studies by Gary King, Jennifer Pan, and Margaret E. Roberts (2013; 2014) reveal that the state only selectively censored online content— prioritizing the removal of collective mobilization expression but tolerating general criticism (also see Chen and Xu 2017; K. W. Fu, Chan, and Chau 2013; Qin, Strömberg, and Wu 2017; Tai and Fu 2020).

Admittedly, "directed digital dissidence" describes a similar process that some studies have already articulated in different ways. We build on and add to the burgeoning literature on authoritarian resilience in China, especially studies that focus on how the government channels discontent. Other studies have probed the mechanisms through which Chinese party-state channels discontent, especially through information management. For instance, studies by Christian Göbel (2021), Christoph Steinhardt (2017), and Peter Lorentzen (2013; 2017) have similarly suggested that the Chinese state has responded to social unrest in ways that help "deflect discontent from the regime" and "temper local official and protester behavior" (Steinhardt 2017, 539). We are making a similar argument here. But, instead of just identifying the government strategy, we focus more on testing the effectiveness of such a strategy with empirical data. Indeed, while this attempt to use the internet to control dissent is consistent with earlier offline efforts under rightful resistance, the efficacy of such actions are less clear. Further, in this work, we broaden the notion and consider how the redirection of dissent can be done across a broader range of targets, including non-state actors and other nations.

Besides the efficacy of the strategy itself, what further complicates the issue is that scholars studying cyber politics in China have yet to agree upon the effectiveness of state control over the internet itself, and thus the implications of digital empowerment or the usefulness of any government information strategy for authoritarian rule (Han 2018a; Hobbs and Roberts 2018). Is state control over the internet successful? Does internet and social media usage alter the attitudes and behavior of citizens in authoritarian regimes such as China? To what extent have authoritarian regimes such as China been challenged by the expansion of the internet and social media? Many earlier studies tend to focus on how the regime has been challenged without looking into how the state copes with the challenges. Those exploring state responses, other than a few exceptions (Hobbs and Roberts 2018), only document what the state has done and its immediate observational impact on online expression, but they fall short of gauging the impact of the state's information strategies on citizens' attitudes and behavior, thus the efficacy of state adaptation.

Second, while current studies have explored the different potential mechanisms of the government channeling discontent, they are inconclusive and tend to be speculative regarding what that strategy is (or whether there is such a strategy). For example, King, Pan, and Roberts (2013) argue that Chinese government cares more about collective action than general criticism of the regime. But the strategic censorship model by Lorentzen (2014) suggests that the state would censor criticism of top leaders more while tolerating and even encouraging criticism of local officials. Rongbin Han and Li Shao (2022) find that the Chinese state, instead of scaling up control over citizenry complaints in reaction to mass protests and major disasters, tends to adjust the level of control because of political ceremonies, policy shifts, or leadership changes. While the theories may not be in opposition to each other, they clearly do not go hand in hand either. Our research branches from these works in different ways. King, Pan, and Roberts (2013) note that although the efficacy of the state may vary at the lower levels, its goals are considered to be unitary. Our research and the mechanism of DDD explores how the central-local divide might drive internet public opinion management. Lorentzen (2014) also concerns himself with the issue of the central-local divide. However, although he has several articles elaborating on this central-local mechanism in discontent channeling and information strategy (Lorentzen 2013; 2014; 2017), none presented systemic public opinion data to see whether the strategy is effective, as mentioned above. The research of Han and Shao (2022) shows that state censorship in China can be driven by complicated motives and tests the state's capacity to control online information flow. However, it falls short of revealing whether the state has a specific information strategy, nor does it examine whether citizens' behavior or attitudes are affected. Through our survey data, this project adds quantitative evidence of such a strategy by revealing its effects. Additionally, through added case studies as proposed in these revisions (especially that of COVID-19), we will contribute important qualitative event narration that the previously mentioned authors have not explored.

Overall, this book attempts to bridge the gaps by connecting existing theory on how citizens resist and protest authority in autocracies with a theory about autocratic strategic management of such activity to explain how autocratic states use these protests to sustain themselves. It is in the interaction online between the state, China in this instance, and its citizens, that the power and true impact of the new digital environment becomes clearer. It is on this sphere of interaction that we focus this study and characterize as directed digital dissidence. Our study of the Chinese experience suggests that it is indeed the case that the more citizens use the internet generally, the more trusting they are of the central government. Further, we find support for our theory of directed digital dissidence. Internet use, specifically exposure to critical information there, does appear to encourage activist and protest-centered sentiment focused on dissatisfaction with the local government. These results, taken together, would suggest that the Chinese government is quite successful at channeling the flow of information in a way that solidifies its hegemony while simultaneously providing a sense of empowerment to citizens. Such findings suggest that a strategy of strategic censorship is working for the Chinese state, continuing its successful rightful resistance divide-and-rule strategy. directed digital dissidence is China's effective adaptation to the internet and likely a model for other closed states.

Our Approach and the Layout for This Book

China is, perhaps, the best case to test our directed digital dissidence theory, given its well-known efforts to restrict the flow of digital information. To date there have been no large measures of public opinion research with detailed measures of political social media use centered on the implications in China. In December 2015, we conducted an original large-scale random survey of more than 2,000 Chinese citizens with approximately 75 questions probing their internet use, social media use, political attitudes, as well as their awareness of and efforts to circumvent the firewall imposed by the Chinese government. These data gave us the unique opportunity to build an understanding of how the exchange of digital information in this restrictive context is shaping opinion.

Conducting the survey online allowed us to ask the types of questions that would be difficult or impossible to ask using other approaches. There is no better way to build generalizable measures of citizen use of the internet and social media, consumption of dissident flows of information, and the subsequent impact on their attitudes and behavior. We can effectively capture measures of their online activities, as well as their attitudes about internet use. However, the survey strategy does have some limitations. A survey does not allow us to directly measure the central government's censorship strategies. Given that directed digital dissidence integrates both the rightful resistance and the strategic censorship arguments, it is critical that we measure both citizen activism online and state responses. Although we cannot measure government activity through the survey, we have supplemented our measures with an ample body of literature that evidences that the Chinese central government does, indeed, employ strategic censorship (Lorentzen 2014; also see King, Pan, and Roberts 2013; 2014). This helps us locate citizen attitudes and compare whether the results the state is evidently seeking have been achieved in our survey population. Additionally, we are able to measure in our survey citizen awareness of internet blocking and other strategic tactics, such as the central government's use of the 50 Cent Party. This allows us to examine the scope and effectiveness of tactics and countertactics that the state has employed.

Although we focus on the evidence of directed digital dissidence and its effectiveness in the Chinese context, we begin by building our argument around a few premises based on previous research. We ground this work in the premise that there is an information war, particularly in autocracies. Information is consequential; it shapes attitudes and ultimately behavior. Therefore, the inability to shape the flow of information poses a threat to regime stability. The Chinese government is battling dissident narratives exchanged within the general population. These narratives include both specific, often local, governance problems and narratives that question foundational properties of the regime itself. We propose that in the Chinese case, the central government is winning this war via two primary strategies: (1) The central government allows, if not encourages, a local-level dissident information flow (relief valve), and (2) it also promotes a pro–central government flow of information via the Chinese internet. This directed digital dissidence effectively mitigates potential consequences for the central government of a dissident digital flow on both sides of the walled Chinese internet.

We begin in chapter 2, "The Chinese Internet: Citizen Awareness of Government Control," where we introduce the data, discuss how it was collected, and highlight some of the primary measures used throughout the book. This chapter also provides evidence that many Chinese internet users perceive having a personal experience with motivated hostile internet forces or at least have heard that these forces exist. By hostile forces, we mean any commentator or poster, either pro-government or otherwise, using the cover of anonymity to try to illicitly shape Chinese citizens' political perceptions. This finding lays the foundation for our argument that the Chinese government is actively trying to manage the information exposure of its citizens. Finally, in this chapter, we examine the factors that explain variation in citizens' awareness of forces trying to direct the flow of information. This awareness is driven, largely, by the frequency with which citizens use the internet and their level of political interest. As noted below, these results become important as the empirical story unfolds.

In chapter 3, "What Does Directed Digital Dissidence Look Like? Critical Information Flows, Trust, and Support for Protest," the empirical evidence indicates that there is a consistent flow of critical information. Existing research and the results of our survey support the premise that many Chinese citizens distrust local government. We also have evidence that support for local-level protest is fairly common. It is here we observe the consequences of the state using dissidence for strategic gain. To observe the effect of this directed digital dissidence, we present the results of a mediation model that shows that if the central government is allowing digital dissidence to flow when it is aimed at the local government, their strategy is working. Our results indicate that heightened internet use increases the odds of exposure to dissidence, which lowers trust in local government. Consequentially, it also stimulates support for local-level protest directed at local governments. This keeps the central government insulated.

Chapter 4, "Social Media: The Battleground of the Information War" presents evidence that dissidence is most likely to be located on social media platforms such as Weibo, QQ, Kaixin001, Douban, and WeChat. It is here where citizens are likely to encounter information and forums that contain information critical of local government. The central government actively censors information critical of itself, but our results suggest that they do not actively limit critical information directed at the local level. Further, our results show that social media use is on the rise, which could increase the effect of allowing dissidence at the local level while limiting opposition directed at the central government. This finding is supportive of the directed digital dissidence theory. If social media use is connected to exposure to local-level critical flows and the central government sees this as a useful strategy to help them maintain their authority, social media serves as a tool to maintain autocracy. This contrasts sharply with scholarship that sees social media as a democratizing force. Finally, this chapter provides more evidence that it is the politically engaged who are the most exposed to critical information flows.

The remaining empirical chapters attempt to falsify or present alternative theories to directed digital dissidence as an effective strategic choice. Up to this point, all the analysis and evidence has been centered on describing and documenting the consequences of exposure to information on the Chinese internet. Much of this approach is based on the assumption that online consumption in China takes place in a space that is restricted and filtered by the central government. However, this is not a complete picture of the extant circumstances. Many Chinese citizens are actively circumventing filters to consume and exchange information that can be critical of the central government. These cracks in the *Great Firewall*[1] are potentially letting dissident flows circumvent the filters and threatening the Chinese government's maintenance of "strategic censorship." If this crack continues to widen as a result of the growth in the number of citizens with the technical savvy to evade state filters, resistance could shift to focus more directly on the central government.

In chapter 5, "Jumping Over the Great Firewall: A Threat to the Chinese Strategy," we describe how the Chinese government is addressing and effectively neutralizing this threat. We begin by building the framework for understanding how this development may threaten the Chinese government strategy. Indeed, our data indicates that many citizens are actually jumping the wall to gather sensitive political information. Given the obvious difficulty in measuring such a sensitive activity, we employed several checks on the validity of our measure, all of which generally align with respondents' self-reported behavior. In this chapter, we demonstrate that many citizens do distrust the central government, and that the more internet users jump the wall, the less trusting and satisfied they are with the central government. This is a development that accords with other research on internet use. Other scholars have found that exposure to sustained counternarratives online is damaging to autocratic regime support (Gainous, Abbott and Wagner 2017). As demonstrated earlier, exposure to a critical flow of digital information can shape attitudes about local government. This is not a tolerable outcome for the central government. In this chapter, we present evidence which indicates that there may be consequences resulting from the difficult proposition of trying to control the information flow on the other side of the firewall. The results in this chapter show that this difficulty could counteract or even overwhelm, from the point of view of the regime, the positive effect of the directed digital dissidence strategy.

Given the potential attitudinal consequences of wall jumping, we build a profile of those who do in chapter 6, "The Digital Dissident Citizen: Who Are the Wall Jumpers?" Our data indicate that there are a multitude of reasons citizens jump the wall. One motivation is to seek out political information or consume foreign news media, but these are by no means the only reasons. Citizens may also jump the wall seeking domestically banned foreign entertainment content. US television is popular in China. Further, some in China circumvent the filters to access common foreign social media platforms including Instagram and Twitter. Those seeking political information or foreign news media are, at least implicitly, seeking narratives unapproved by the regime about the central state. Users may just be interested in how foreign press covers certain events or be curious about stories in the Hong Kong / Taiwan presses. However, as other research has shown (Hobbs and Roberts 2018), whether users are seeking alternate news sources, are curious about stories otherwise not covered in the Chinese media sources, or are just interested in the wider variety of content available outside China, once they have jumped the firewall, they are likely to seek out a wide variety of content beyond their initial motivation. Ultimately, wall jumping exposes users to narratives about the Chinese central government that the regime would prefer they not see.

Beyond simply examining the motivation for wall jumping, in this chapter we also explore the relationship between users' censorship avoidance and frequency of wall jumping. We identify a strong relationship between these two responses. The frequency with which respondents use the internet is the strongest estimate of both these responses. We argue in the next chapter that this relationship is key to our claim that, at least in China, the consequences of wall jumping are effectively neutralized. As highlighted below, more frequent internet use not only undergirds censorship avoidance and wall jumping, but it also means that users are highly exposed to regime-approved content on the domestic internet. Indeed, the consumers of unfiltered material are also the significant consumers of government mediated online content as well.

This counter-effect is detailed in chapter 7, "Managing the Information War: Voices Heard from beyond the Wall Are Lost. In this chapter, we contend that directed digital dissidence is an effective strategy even in the face of technologically savvy users. This is true even when the users are both aware of the state's strategy and actively trying to circumvent it. The empirical results of this final data-driven chapter are clear. Although increasing use of the internet results in more wall jumping, increasing internet use also diminishes the negative correlation of that wall jumping. More directly, the more online content is consumed, the greater chance the Chinese government has to mediate and redirect dissidence. We contend that this is a direct result of Chinese government's control of the information flow on their side of the firewall. Simply, those who jump the wall are also more likely to be exposed to the central government's propaganda, thus neutralizing the effect of the counterflow of information beyond the firewall. This characterization is reinforced with further results indicating that those who jump the wall are more attuned to the presence of pro-government posters, and that the positive effect of this awareness on support for the central government is most pronounced among high-frequency internet users.

In chapter 8, "Digital Directed Dissidence in Action: Applications and Its Limits," we explore the application of DDD to actual events in China. Pulling from recent examples, including the COVID-19 pandemic and the government's response to the resulting popular dissent, we explore how directed digital dissidence works and where it does not work as effectively. By reviewing some specific examples of when directed digital dissidence was employed, we can explore the scope and limits of this governing strategy. We explore the power of the strategy and how it operates when the variables are shifting with new events. We also use these examples to see who is targeted in specific cases and how the individuals engaging in online discourse responded to the state employment of directed digital dissidence. Ultimately, this more qualitative chapter allows us to complement the quantitative studies and add context to this research.

In chapter 9, "Will Directed Digital Dissidence Keep Working?," we discuss potential hurdles that may hinder its long-term effectiveness. The internet is not a static medium, and there are always new and potentially significant advances that may alter the ability of states to be the dominant player in the informational space. Indeed, even now many states are likely to lack the level of sophistication and knowledge to employ directed digital dissidence with the efficacy demonstrated by China. Even for China, it is difficult to employ as a mechanism of control and requires sophisticated monitoring and constant adaption. As a result, future control may well be precarious. This method of control is especially challenging considering how the growing digital world is virtually shrinking distance across oceans combined with the process of population replacement that will eventually result in the vast majority of citizens having higher levels of technical savvy. This generation may consume and reshape the flow of information in ways that the state cannot manage successfully. For now, China continues to show that the internet is not beyond the reach of sophisticated closed states.

In this book we explore both the potential and the pitfalls of the growth of the online sphere in China. Our data and examples tell a narrative about the internet's potential to stimulate dissidence and the state's ability to stifle it. Although we did not necessarily anticipate the level of effectiveness the Chinese state would demonstrate, the path that these data led us on tells a story that ends with the Chinese central government, and the authoritarian regime as a whole, largely winning the information war on the Chinese internet. Directed digital dissidence therefore seems to be a successful strategy for the Chinese central government and one that, as we discuss in the conclusion, other autocratic regimes are likely to emulate, if they have not already.

2

The Chinese Internet

Citizen Awareness of Government Control

To the Chinese authoritarian regime, the internet presents both challenges and opportunities. On one hand, the technology has become a crucial strategic sector for economic development and technological advancement. On the other hand, the online sphere has become an important platform for political mobilization and social activism that poses a threat to the control of information that buttresses the central government. As a result, the online sphere must be open enough to generate economic growth but also closely monitored and tightly controlled. These conflicting motivations require the party-state to respond and adapt in different ways. The economic opportunities prescribe a regulatory regime, while the potential for political and social mobilization suggests stricter state-level political controls (Zheng 2008). The quandary of how to navigate these conflicting interests has proven to be difficult. Allowing the freedom for the types of interactions required for economic viability almost inevitably results in space for political discourse with predictable results (Howard 2010). While the economic implications are interesting, if only for being one of the prime catalysts for internet growth in otherwise closed societies, in this book, we focus on the political implications of the expansion of the internet. In particular, we are concerned with how the Chinese party-state has responded to the political challenges it has posed.

Other scholars have recognized the need to assess the political impact of the internet in China. Current studies have provided significant insights, especially concerning how it has served as an empowering tool for citizens living under repressive authoritarian regimes. The internet has enabled freer political expression, promoted civil society, and facilitated sociopolitical activism both online and off (Esarey and Xiao 2008; 2011; Lagerkvist 2007; 2010; Lei 2011; Sullivan and Xie 2009; Z. Tai 2006; G. Yang 2003; 2009; Zheng 2008; for instance, see Chase and Mulvenon 2002; L. Gao and Stanyer 2014). The

Directed Digital Dissidence in Autocracies. Jason Gainous, Rongbin Han, Andrew W. MacDonald, and Kevin M. Wagner, Oxford University Press. © Oxford University Press 2024. DOI: 10.1093/oso/9780197680384.003.0002

internet has significantly transformed Chinese politics in recent years by exposing citizens to public and political discourse and enabling citizens to participate in sociopolitical affairs. This has forced the party-state to adapt itself to address this new reality organizationally, institutionally, and technologically. Scholars have studied the efforts by the Chinese party-state to control and shape the online information flow through a sophisticated process. This includes studies of innovative propaganda tactics such as political astroturfing (deploying internet commentators to fabricate seemingly spontaneous pro-regime comments), ideotainment (wrapping state ideological constructs within more appealing cybercultural elements), and sponsored engagement through e-government sites or official accounts on popular social media sites like Weibo or Tianya to directly engage and guide public opinion (Cairns 2017; Esarey 2015; K. W. Fu, Chan, and Chau 2013a; Han 2015a; 2015b; Hartford 2005; Hassid and Sun 2015; King, Pan, and Roberts 2013; 2017; Lollar 2006, 20; Schläger 2013; Schläger and Jiang 2014).

In this chapter, we contextualize this research by looking at an antecedent issue: What is the Chinese internet, and what does it mean today? Although scholars generally agree that political discourse and social movements are more readily accessible through the internet in China, the larger significance of this new online sphere on the political environment is less clear. If we are concerned about the state response to online engagement, we must focus on how politically relevant the Chinese internet is in practice. Ultimately, before we test the implications of online governance strategies we must assess whether the online sphere reflects the reality of the world in which citizens actually live. This question is crucial as the answer provides the foundation for any research into the effectiveness of the party-state's digital strategy, and the answer is not clear in the scholarship. In her recent work, Bingchun Meng (2016, 811) highlights this exact divide through one of her interviewees, who notes, "If you visit Sina Weibo every day, you'll think there will be revolution tomorrow; if you go to the farmers' market every morning, you'll think a revolution is not going to happen for another hundred years!" This suggests a serious disjuncture between online and offline worlds. Internet "cheap talk" may not have any real-world impact for many less-connected residents.

Indeed, some scholars have questioned the political significance of the internet for even connected citizens. In this view, the Chinese internet is generally nonpolitical or at least not politically significant enough to bring about meaningful civic activism and sociopolitical change (Damm 2007; Leibold 2011). According to James Leibold (2011, 1023), the Chinese blogosphere is producing "the same shallow infotainment, pernicious misinformation, and interest-based ghettos" as elsewhere in the world; thus, one should not overestimate its potential for bringing new forms of civic activism or sociopolitical change. More recent studies show that the rise of the internet has not only enabled regime challengers but has also led to the rise of forces that counter regime criticisms, thus offsetting the threats to the authoritarian regime and neutralizing the internet's political impact on the existing political system in China (Han 2018a; 2018b; Jiang 2016). This is not a new argument or even one confined to the Chinese context. This debate over the impact of digital technology echoes a larger debate about the nature and impact of the internet in autocratic contexts (Gainous, Wagner and Abbott 2015).

With respect to China, the lack of clarity is partially attributable to data scarcity. Scholars have struggled to obtain data with sufficient breadth and depth to explore the political implications of the rise of the internet in a generalizable manner. Many studies are primarily based on case studies, online ethnographic work, or observational data. Others rely on survey data not specifically designed to study the impact of the internet on Chinese politics. For example, Leibold (2011, 1026) uses CNNIC (China Internet Network Information Center) data to argue that the Chinese internet is "chiefly an intranet of playful self-expression and identity exhibition." Reaching this conclusion based on the CNNIC dataset raises some issues. CNNIC is a state organization, and the survey was never intended to focus on political use of the internet. Moreover, even if CNNIC data are valid and reliable, Leibold has based his argument on a questionable assumption that citizens not seeking political information cannot be influenced by political content online, either subconsciously or consciously. A broader approach is needed. It is not enough to merely ask internet users about their primary motives for going online. For measures of the political implications of the internet to be effective, questions have to address netizens' political motives, whether they will be politicized under certain circumstances, or whether online experience may alter their political beliefs, identities, and offline behavior.

Indeed, studies based on other sources suggest quite different results. Leibold may have dismissed the internet's political significance too quickly. For instance, using the 2007 China World Value Survey data, Ya-wen Lei (2011) finds Chinese netizens more politically opinionated, more supportive of democratic norms, more critical of the party-state and China's political conditions, and more likely to be active participants in collective action. Although this is an interesting window into online behavior in China, it too is incomplete. The World Values Survey and other similar instruments provide valuable data but are not dedicated to the study of internet use and its impact. The questions are limited, and thus they allow only limited operationalization of online behaviors by researchers. For instance, the World Values Survey does not allow researchers to differentiate netizens' online experiences. How one uses the internet will often affect its impact on one's political attitudes and behavior (Gainous, Marlowe and Wagner 2013). Interestingly, Ki Deuk Hyun and Jinhee Kim

(2015), who designed their own survey to collect data in China, find that online political expression, facilitated by news consumption, may actually enhance rather than erode support for the authoritarian regime directly and indirectly through nationalism. Their findings are the opposite of what Lei has found based on World Values Survey data.

Differing and incomplete data sources have generated inconsistent results. The larger lesson is that the impact of internet usage is hard to measure in broad terms without digging deeper into the nature and scope of the usage as well as the political and social context. Hyun and Kim (2015), using an original survey, have begun the task of obtaining more specific data and a more nuanced understanding of the internet in China. We take this a step further. Our research attempts to bridge the data divide though a carefully tailored instrument using a larger battery of questions aimed specifically at the effect of the internet on attitudes and behaviors. In this book, we present a broader and more in-depth survey-based data source to give more complete answers about how the internet acts on political attitudes and behaviors in China. This creates a more solid foundation for us to then broach the questions of why and how China attempts to influence online discourse and its larger effect.

Before introducing the data, we think it prudent to offer a discussion, first, about the limitations of survey research in general and, next, about the drawbacks of survey research in the Chinese context. Although it is important to be very clear about the limitations of our methods here, we also want to stress the point that our data, even if getting a bit dated, are very valuable because it has become increasingly difficult to conduct surveys with questions on political opinions and political participation in China.

The Limitations of Our Data

Since *The American Voter* (Campbell et al. 1960) scholars have relied, largely, on survey research to shape our collective understanding of political behavior. For decades, though, the majority of this research has been dominated by studies focused on the United States and other Western contexts. This has largely been a product of the limited availability survey data outside the Western context (with a few notable exceptions).[1] As such, most behavioral and public opinion theory is born out of Western samples. This clearly limits both behavioral theory in general and, most definitely, behavioral theory outside the West. We hope to contribute in a modest way to remedying that shortfall here. To be clear, though, theory development is not limited only by lack of data but also by the limitations of survey research itself. We stand by our data but are cautious about how far we extend our inferences, or at least in the confidence we have in those inferences.

Before we start getting into the data, we outline here exactly what we think are the most prominent limitations of these data.

To begin, perhaps the most consequential shortcoming of survey research is the fact that they are blunt measurement tools; the indicators often fail to capture the nuance of the concepts they attempt to measure. Our survey does not completely escape this shortcoming, as none can. Rather than working with the precision of a scalpel, slicing out the curves and shape of attitudinal/behavioral concepts, oftentimes they work more like a hatchet—just cutting out the general shape. Attitude strength, direction, importance, ambivalence, certainty, and the like are not easy to capture precisely or completely. Survey researchers, including us, combat this shortcoming by adding multiple indicators of single concepts that can be looked at individually or built into indices. This is the strategy we employ here. Although it is certainly true that in-depth interviews offer the kind of nuance in assessing individual level attitudes that surveys do not, interviews are not particularly helpful at drawing inferences about large populations. Ideally, putting the two methods together is most informative, but unfortunately doing so was beyond the scope of the funds for this study. Given that we were particularly careful about including multiple indicators of our primary concepts, we have nearly 20 different indicators of digital media consumption, we are confident that we have sufficiently countered this weakness of survey research.

Next, our survey data are no different from other cross-sectional one-shot survey studies when it comes to the hurdles in using it to make causal inferences. It is extremely hard to find approaches adequate to eliminating the potential for endogeneity in survey models (Sande and Ghosh 2018). For the most part, they are correlational only. First, without random assignment any number of exogenous factors could explain away observed relationships. Of course, we do our best to account for this possibility by including theoretical controls in our models. Decades of political behavioral theory was developed this way and has held up to additional methodological tests (see Robison et al. 2018 for examples). Nonetheless, as methods have developed, scientists have become more cautious about drawing causal inference from correlational models—even in controlled models. Second, identifying the causal direction in survey models is difficult; there are limited options to rule out the possibility that y causes x instead of the other way around (Iacus, King, and Porro 2012). Here, too, we employ some of those options to increase our confidence, such as structural equation models that fit our theoretical expectations (Mulaik 2009; Pearl 2014). We also fit a series of regressions changing the specification (removing and adding variables) to see the effect on the relationship between those variables left in the model and our dependent variables as a form of a mediating model to help isolate a causal variable. We want to be perfectly clear here, though. The fact is that making causal inference with survey data has real limitations regardless of the methods employed to help remedy this shortcoming. Nonetheless, we make an effort here by employing such methods.

Still, though, we also include numerous regression models that employ neither structural nor mediation modeling. There is much to be learned from regressing variables on other variables. Although it is true that the certainty one can ascribe to causal inferences drawn from doing this has its limits, we want to be clear that correlation is the first, and necessary, component to make a causal claim. The necessary elements are (1) correlation between variables, (2) non-spuriousness or another variable or combination of variables cannot explain away the observed correlation between variables, and (3) time order—the cause must precede the effect (Babbie 2021).

Certainly, correlation is not sufficient to make a causal claim, but it is necessary. Regression analysis of survey variables does not employ random assignment; that said, it can, when executed with attention, address each of the first two necessary components of causal inference, and well-developed theory can address the last. Obviously, regression methods are outstanding at identifying correlations between variables: as one variable moves, so does the other. Here we show numerous examples of correlations between digital media consumption and various outcomes. Next, as abovementioned, adding important control variables to models helps increase confidence that the observed correlations are not spurious. Finally, we believe that taking into consideration all the data and analysis laid out here, the results contribute to our theory of directed digital dissidence doing a solid job of accounting for time order. It makes sense intuitively and theoretically that the Chinese government is actively diverting criticism of the central government toward local governments to both prevent negative perceptions of the central government and promote positive perceptions by coming in and taking action against local governments to satisfy citizens' complaints. The central government action to manage the digital environment precedes the effect—Chinese support for the central government.

Introducing the Data

As stated earlier, our survey is original, and it is the primary data for this study. These data are based on a random internet survey conducted by Qualtrics from November 25 to December 2, 2015. We designed the instrument, content, and structure. Arguably, the most significant contribution of this project is these data, as there is a dearth of available large-N survey data measuring political opinion in the Chinese context. Second, and perhaps equally significant, is the uniqueness of the scope of these data. There are nearly 20 different indicators centered on measuring digital information consumption. Additionally, a battery of indicators addresses a slate of political attitudes from trust in institutions to attitudes about protest. Instead of noting the question wording in each of the analyses where we utilize these indicators, we include the entire survey instrument in appendix A. However, for clarity we exclude those questions that we did not utilize for our analysis in the present research. As we discuss our findings, we will note in the text the respective question number for any analysis involving that question.

These indicators centered on digital information consumption range from measures focused on general internet use, social use, political use, social media use, perceptions of digital media information, to indicators of both the awareness of and estimated frequency of pro-government internet posters and those perceived to be net-spies or hostile posters. Central to our examination here, these data even include indicators of both the frequency and reasons why citizens circumvent the well-documented filtering mechanisms imposed by the Chinese government.

The breadth of Chinese information technology–related concepts covered in these data is unmatched by any other data of which we are aware. For that matter, the wide range of topics addressed in these data is expansive even relative to other well-known cross-sectional surveys researchers around the globe rely on (e.g., Pew Internet & American Life Project). Further, because we controlled the design of the instrument, we were able to incorporate multiple question-design formats including standard Likert scaling, continuously distributed response options, and even a series of list experiments (all of these design formats are available in appendix A). Using multiple formats contributes to our ability to make more nuanced inferences and to alleviate concerns about the potential for social desirability effects.

After we designed the instrument in English and translated it into Chinese, we entered the questions into a graphical interface from our survey provider, Qualtrics. We were careful at this stage to make the formatting clear and to distribute the questions across numerous pages to prevent overwhelming respondents with too many questions at once. This helped us achieve a high completion and response rate. Additionally, we were particularly attentive to the possibility of question order effects. Many of the questions are sensitive and could cue responses to subsequent questions. We grouped and placed questions strategically to limit any such potential for response bias. The instrument in appendix A is in the sequential order we asked the questions but, as noted above, there are questions missing there because we include only those indicators we used in the present research. Once we settled on the design, Qualtrics administered the survey in November 2015. They recruit a large pool of respondents for various survey projects through online advertising on websites such as local portals, search engines, social networking services, and online shopping services. Panelists who update their profiles at least once every six months are randomly invited to participate in surveys for which they qualify. Online points are awarded to the corresponding panelists, which they may accumulate and exchange for cash or various other country-specific gifts to serve as an incentive for completion. This number of points is based on the length of the survey. Ours had more than 50 questions, so respondents received a relatively high number of points.

The data collection had two phases. For the first phase, Qualtrics collected and submitted to us a trial run of 286 cases. We checked the data for reliability and adjusted the instrument before proceeding with the second phase, the final data collection. We made only three adjustments, all of which turned out to be central to our analysis. For the trial run, we asked respondents only about pro-government internet posters and not about potential net-spy or hostile posters. We amended this oversight, and it became central to the analysis that follows. In addition, much of our theory focuses on the impact of Chinese internet users circumventing government filters on the internet. We initially had a question about whether citizens had jumped the wall to read sensitive political information (see appendix A, Q25) but decided to add whether they had done so for entertainment purposes as well (Q26, to watch foreign movies, television shows, etc.). Finally, we also included an attention filter question as part of a battery of institutional trust questions where respondents were simply told to select the "None at all" response (Q13H). If they did not select this response, we could assume they were not paying attention to the questions, and the survey ended for these respondents and the data were not collected for them. In the end, the full sample included a total of 2,292 respondents. This sample size provides for a roughly ±2 margin of error.

Although our sample was randomly selected, the sampling frame was based only on internet users whom Qualtrics can access. Qualtrics recruits their frame subjects through online advertising on websites such as local portals, search engines, social networking services, and online shopping services. We do not contend that our sample is representative of the Chinese population, as the method of obtaining respondents obviously mostly excludes those citizens with little or no access to the internet. That said, we are comfortable that our sample is generally representative of Chinese internet users. Given that our research focuses on internet effects, a sample that centers on internet users is appropriate and a sampling frame including the entire Chinese population would have been overbroad for this research. Half of the population do not regularly access the internet according to World Bank and CNNIC data as of late 2015 when we conducted our survey.[2] Using a sample of the entire population could potentially limit the degrees of freedom in our models, and the marginals of nuanced measures of digital media use would likely become too small to have any value. Thus, the large sample of internet users adds to our confidence in the inferences throughout the book.

Nonetheless, we think it is useful to compare our sample of internet users to the Chinese population as well as its internet population. The results presented in table 2.1 compare demographic statistics from our sample to population parameters obtained from 2015 Chinese population data. The results suggest that our sample is comparable on income and gender, but it is slightly younger

Table 2.1 **Comparing Our Sample to Population Demographics**

	Our Sample	*Chinese Census*
Income		
1st Quintile	0–6,000	0–5,000
2nd Quintile	6,000–10,000	5,000–11,000
3rd Quintile	10,000–15,000	11,000–18,000
4th Quintile	15,000–25,000	18,000–27,000
5th Quintile	>25,000	>27,000
Age		
1st Quintile	<27	<28
2nd Quintile	27–31	28–37
3rd Quintile	32–35	38–45
4th Quintile	36–42	46–57
5th Quintile	>42	>58
Education		
No Primary	0.2%	5.3%
Primary	0.2%	24.5%
Middle	2.1%	43.6%
High	11.6%	15.4%
College	79.2%	10.8%
Postgraduate	6.6%	—
Sex		
Male	52.5%	50.6%
Female	47.5%	49.4%

Note: Census data were obtained from the 2015 *China's E-Government Yearbook.* Our sample comes from a random selection of internet users obtained via Qualtrics. Quintile cell values represent the cut points. Income is in yuan. Postgraduate is excluded in the *Statistical Yearbook* data because they do not report this category. It is grouped into college or higher.

and clearly more educated. These sample frame characteristics are not surprising. In truth, they are consistent with what we would expect given the global digital divide, particularly in the developing world (Chen and Wellman 2004; Norris 2001).

Specifically, notice in table 2.1 that the differences between our sample and the census data are small on income and gender. However, our sample is generally younger than the population as a whole. We organized the data by quintiles, and the cutoff points clearly show we have a younger sample. The lower bound of the fifth quintile is 16 years younger in our sample relative to the population. That said, the lower quintiles are not as disparate. The difference in education is more noticeable. Our sample is nearly 86 percent college educated, while the population is only roughly 11 percent college educated. Conversely, less than 3 percent of our sample has only middle school education or below, while around 73 percent of population falls into those collapsed categories. These differences make it difficult for us to make generalized statements regarding the entire population of China on the indicators in our survey. However, our focus is on how digital media consumption is shaping perceptions, so we believe our sample is robust here, especially when it comes to the most active internet users. As described below, we are confident that it is generalizable to this population of Chinese internet users.

Demographic statistics from our sample are also generally comparable to survey data collected by the CNNIC. Although we cannot draw too firm a conclusion by comparing our data to those of the CNNIC, because the CNNIC survey covers a much younger age group (those below 19 make up about 24.1 percent of their entire sample), it is to our knowledge the only other large-scale sample of internet users only, so the comparisons are still worth making.[3] As China's national administrative agency currently under the direct leadership of top internet-governing state agency Cyber Administration of China, CNNIC conducts biannual surveys through a computer assisted telephone interviewing system and publishes the results in the *Statistical Reports on Internet Development in China*. The CNNIC reports, based on a stratified random sampling in China's 31 provincial units (provinces, municipalities, and autonomous regions, excluding Taiwan, Hong Kong, and Macao), provide summary demographic statistics of China's internet population. The *37th Report*, published in January 2016, collected data from 60,000 respondents (30,000 via landlines and 30,000 via cell phones) in December 2015, falling close to the time frame of our survey.

According to the report, 53.6 percent of Chinese netizens are male and 46.4 percent were female. This is close to gender distribution in our sample. In terms of age distribution, the CNNIC 2015 report shows a similar, but slightly younger, internet population than what our sample finds. In the CNNIC survey, 24.1 percent of netizens are below the age of 19, 29.9 percent fall between 20 and 29, 23.8 percent between 30 and 39, and 22.3 percent are above the age of 40. Our respondents are also more educated than those CNNIC has reported. As of December 2015, the 2015 CNNIC report shows that 19.6 percent of Chinese netizens have college or higher degrees; though much lower than the education attainment rate of our sample, it is significantly higher than that of the general population. In addition, it is worth noting that the level of education attainment is lower in the CNNIC survey than our sample in part because the former covers a much younger age group. More than a quarter are not old enough to have even obtained a college degree. Since we asked our respondents to report monthly household income, we cannot directly compare that to the CNNIC data, which asks respondents to report their personal monthly income. We believe that household income is a better measure because students, who constitute a significant portion of China's internet population, tend to report a zero or low monthly personal income. This is why CNNIC data shows that 20.4 percent of their respondents only have an income of 500 RMB (which is about $77) or less.

Describing the Chinese Internet

Although about half the population of China has access to the internet, there is quite a bit of variation in the frequency with which citizens use it. The marginal distributions on six general use items in our data are presented in figure 2.1— daily hours of use (Q1), years of use (Q3), weekly political use (Q4), and visits to government websites for various reasons including using services, policy-related reasons, and filing complaints (Q10–Q12). Considerable variation on each individual item is immediately evident in these distributions. Chinese internet users are not a homogenous group. This bodes well for our tests and expectations. If the internet is consequential in shaping political belief, such an outcome would also mechanically require key independent variables to demonstrate significant variance.

It is clear in the graph in the upper left-hand corner of figure 2.1, that many Chinese internet users spend a considerable amount of time on the internet each day. Around 20 percent of those sampled spend six hours on the web daily. Use falls somewhere between three and six hours daily for more than 57 percent, and only 23 percent use the internet for two hours or less daily. The graph in the middle of the top row of figure 2.1 indicates that a sizable proportion of the population were early adopters of the internet. A little more than 10 percent claimed to have been using the internet for more than 16 years, and about 29 percent said they have been using the internet for somewhere between 11 and 16 years. Roughly 50 percent indicated that they have been using the internet for about

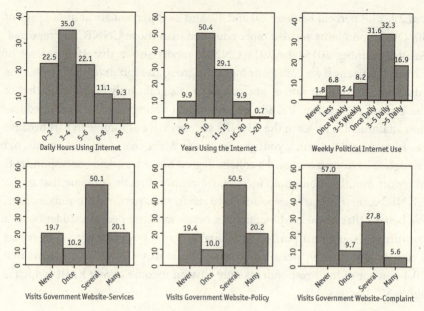

Figure 2.1 Distributions across General Internet Use Items (Percent)

6 to 10 years. Only about 10 percent say they have been using the internet for 5 years or less.

Particularly pertinent to our research is the question of whether Chinese internet users are getting exposure to political information online. This answer is clear in the graphs. In the upper right-hand corner of figure 2.1, and across all three graphs in the bottom row of figure 2.1, the results show that the Chinese internet offers access to politically centered information and that Chinese users are capitalizing on this opportunity. Frankly, we were surprised that nearly 78 percent of those sampled claim to gather political information at least once a day or more. Further, more than 70 percent claim to have gone to government websites to gather information about local services and government policy frequently. Citizens are less likely to lodge a complaint via a government website, with 57 percent indicating that they have never done so. Nonetheless, this leaves 43 percent who have used this digital function at least once. Close to 10 percent say they have done so once, nearly 28 percent have done so several times, and approaching 6 percent have lodged many complaints. It is important to remember that this indicator focuses on complaints about local government, not the central government. As described in chapter 1, this distinction is central to our theoretical claims. This initial descriptive evidence suggests that clearly there is some local level dissidence.

In addition, we posit in our theory of directed digital dissidence that there are multiple flows of digital information. In particular, there is a pro–central government flow and a counterflow that contains politically dissident ideas. Before getting into the measurement of the potential consequences of these channels, we look at citizens' perceived awareness of forces attempting to influence the digital flow of information and at some of the factors shaping such perceived awareness. Finally, we measure what factors underlie how prevalent citizens think the pro–central government flow and counterflow are. There are many direct and indirect pathways through which the pro-government flow enters the Chinese internet. One much-commented-upon channel is via government-sponsored trolls, also known as the 50 Cent Party, who try to defuse criticism of the regime and its policies in comment forums and other popular discussion sites such as Weibo and WeChat (Han 2015b; Hung 2010; King, Pan, and Roberts 2017; Miller 2016).

These internet commentators are supposed to pass themselves off as ordinary internet users in order to manipulate public opinion without being associated with the government. In reality, their astroturfing efforts oftentimes prove ineffective and counterproductive among politically active netizens, as they give themselves away with identifiable traces that can be picked up by more savvy netizens (Han 2015b). Employing these paid commentators can have a negative impact on government aims even beyond their agents being occasionally caught in the act. Often earnest pro-regime commentators are accused of being paid shills and their opinions discounted rather than sincerely considered in online debates. However, it is unclear whether less sophisticated internet users are generally aware of the existence of the 50 Cent Party and its activities.

Our survey asked respondents directly about their awareness of people paid by the government to post positive messaging about the central government via social media and other digital avenues (Q17). The distribution of their responses is displayed in table 2.2. Nearly 37 percent claim to have seen these posts, around 39 percent say they have heard of them, and only about 24 percent claim to never have heard of such posters. Conversely, respondents were also asked directly whether they were aware of posts sponsored by net-spies or other hostile forces (Q18), because of the popular belief that much of the online criticism targeting the Chinese government has been supported or even sponsored by foreign countries or hostile forces. Interestingly, our survey results show that respondents were more aware of the pro-government flow than this counterflow. Roughly 46 percent claimed they had never heard of such posters, while about 36 percent said they had, and only about 18 percent claimed to have seen such posts. This may be due to several reasons. First, it is simply more natural for netizens to criticize the government than praise it, especially given that the Chinese party-state has lost the war of position online (Tong and Lei 2013). As a result, netizens are generally more suspicious of positive information about the government. Second, it is highly likely that the 50 Cent Party is, in fact, much more numerous than any real or imagined net-spy forces.

Table 2.2 **Perceived Awareness of Forces Attempting to Influence the Digital Flow of Information**

	Government Posters	Net-Spy Posters
Never heard of them	23.7%	46.3%
Heard of them	39.4%	36.1%
Seen posts	36.9%	17.6%
N	2,279	1,994

Note: The N is lower for the Net-Spy Posters sample because we added that question to the survey after our pilot of 286 cases.

We know this in part because of the large amount of information that scholars have collected regarding pro-government posters. Leaked official documents also show the mobilization of internet commentators to engage in online crises, promoting central and local propaganda initiatives, and cheerleading for leaders (Han 2018a, chap. 5; King, Pan, and Roberts 2017). Even the state propaganda system itself sometimes openly acknowledges the deployment of internet commentators by reporting on their recruitment, training, and rewards (Han 2018a, chap. 5). Aiding in netizen identification of government-directed internet commentators, they often show consistent identifiable traits. These posters are constantly pro-regime, focusing exclusively on political topics, using official language codes, often publicizing a large number of comments within a short time span to fulfill their assigned tasks, and sometimes even showing direct linkage to government accounts or IP addresses. Dissidents and foreign media/governments are generally believed to be motivated to shape public opinion through online expression, and there are cases showing that at least some of the dissident groups are using the same astroturfing tactics as the 50 Cent Party (Bolsover, Gillian, and Howard 2019; Han 2018a, chap. 6).

However, evidence for the existence of significant net-spy activity is considerably scarcer, and the interest groups supporting net-spies significantly more homogenous. Taken together, even with the difference in awareness of the two flows, what is clear is that many Chinese internet users are well aware (or believe) that there are forces, both positive and negative, trying to shape their perceptions about the Chinese government. This perception is significant because it suggests large numbers of engaged netizens see the online sphere as one in which competing and contested flows of information are available. Further, users are critically viewing and interpreting information online rather than serving as passive sponges of online information.

Our next step was to examine the variations in awareness of perceived attempts to influence the digital flow of information in table 2.2. Our strategy here was to model both awareness of government posters and net-spy posters, respectively, as a function of a host of general behavioral, attitudinal, and demographic indicators and look at these estimates to get a sense of the profile of the people who are noticing these flows. These indicators include general internet use,[4] traditional media trust,[5] political interest (Q19), whether the respondent is a member of the Chinese Communist Party (CCP, Q29), urbanicity (Q27), socioeconomic status (SES),[6] gender (Q28), and age (Q31).[7] Our expectations were that the frequency of internet use would increase awareness of these flows, simply because the probability of exposure to them is heightened as citizens spend more time consuming digital information. We expected those with more trust in the traditional media, which is much more tightly controlled by the state, to be less perceptive of deceptive forces. We expected those with higher political interest to be more aware of both because they are more likely to be privy to the pertinent, and perhaps public, discussions of how these forces are shaping political perspectives. As for the relationship between awareness of posters, pro- and counter-government, and the demographic indicators, we had no overwhelming theoretical expectations here. That said, in the quest to get a sense of the profile of those who are aware of posters, we thought it important to control for, and test for, demographic differences.

Because both of the awareness items are distributed ordinally, we decided to model each using ordered logit. Before doing so, though, we tested (as we do with all the ordinal outcome models) whether treating the outcome variable as continuous and modeling it with ordinary least squares (OLS) would be suitable, making the resultant coefficients more interpretable. This test involved estimating the model using OLS and then plotting the kernel density estimates against the normal density plot to examine whether the residuals of the model distributed normally. If not, this violates OLS assumptions, and a multivariate normal distribution is not the appropriate maximum likelihood link function. When this is the case, we employ the ordered logit link function and rely on odds ratios to estimate the magnitude of the independent variable correlation. Using OLS on each model, in this case, produced residuals that were not distributed normally. The density plots for these models, and all other models where we employ this test, are in appendix B, labeled with the associated tables. A quick examination of the plots labeled table 2.3 Government Posters and table 2.3 Net-Spy Posters clearly indicates the nonnormality of the residuals.

The ordered logit estimates which measure how aware users are of the motivations of the posters are presented in table 2.3. The first observation that we make is that, generally, our chosen set of independent variables is statistically

DIRECTED DIGITAL DISSIDENCE IN AUTOCRACIES

Table 2.3 **Modeling Perceived Awareness of Forces Attempting to Influence the Digital Flow of Information**

	Government Posters (50 Cent Party)				
	Estimate	*S.E.*	*95% CI*		*OR*
General Internet Use	1.95	0.26	1.44	2.46	11.76
Traditional Media Trust	−1.47	0.23	−1.92	−1.02	0.23
Political Interest	0.86	0.19	0.48	1.23	2.35
CCP Member	0.00	0.10	−0.18	0.19	—
Urbanicity	−0.04	0.17	−0.38	0.29	—
SES	2.33	0.35	1.65	3.01	10.30
Female	−0.24	0.08	−0.40	−0.07	0.79
Age	−0.60	0.28	−1.14	−0.06	0.55
Pseudo R^2 = 0.05					
N = 2,176					
	Net-Spy Posters				
General Internet Use	2.03	0.29	1.46	2.59	7.60
Traditional Media Trust	−1.18	0.24	−1.66	−0.70	0.31
Political Interest	0.80	0.21	0.38	1.21	2.22
CCP Member	0.11	0.10	−0.09	0.31	—
Urbanicity	0.02	0.19	−0.35	0.39	—
SES	2.54	0.38	1.79	3.30	12.74
Female	−0.31	0.09	−0.49	−0.13	0.73
Age	−0.55	0.31	−1.16	0.05	—
Pseudo R^2 = 0.06					
N = 1,901					

Note: Estimates are derived using ordered logit. S.E. = standard error, CI = confidence interval, OR = odds ratio (odds ratios are displayed only when 0 is not bounded in the respective CI).

significant, and the correlations are reasonably consistent across both the aware-ness of government posters model and the awareness of net-spy posters. General internet use is a statistically significant positive estimator (0 is not bound in the 95 percent confidence interval) of both awareness of government posters and of net-spy posters, and is the largest estimated relationship in the government posters model. The coefficient should be interpreted such that every one-unit increase in general internet use increases the odds of going up one response category on the government posters scale by nearly 12 times. Likewise, while not the strongest relationship in the model but nonetheless substantively significant, a one-unit increase in general internet use increases the odds of being higher on the net-spy posters scale by almost 8 times. As expected, traditional media trust is negatively related to both outcomes (again, 0 is not bound in either confidence interval). Although the estimate is statistically significant, the magnitude of the relationship is small. The odds ratio is less than 1 in both the government and net-spy posters models. That said, the magnitude of the significant positive relationship of political interest is larger in both models, where a one-unit increase in political interest is associate with a 2-point increase in the odds of being higher on both awareness scales.

The demographic variables in the models do not perform as well as the behavioral/attitudinal variables. This is perhaps not surprising, as there are less theoretically driven expectations for these relationships. They are included to address the possibility of a spurious correlation and to help build a profile of these internet users. Neither CCP membership nor urbanicity are statistically significant in either model. Age is negatively related to awareness of government posters, but this correlation is modest. The odds ratio is less than 1 in the model, indicating that, as age increases, users are less aware of government posters. The positive relationship of SES is statistically significant, as the low end of the positive confidence interval is well above 0. Further, the magnitude of this positive relationship is quite large in both models. A one-unit increase in SES raises the odds of being higher on the awareness of government posters by about 10 times. It increases to nearly 13 times for awareness of net-spy posters. This is in accordance with current studies that show better-educated Chinese citizens tend to be more politically active (Kennedy 2009; Wang, Wu, and Han 2015). Finally, the models show that women are slightly less likely to be aware of either type of poster. The odds ratio is less than 1 for both models.

Taken together, these results suggest that many internet users are aware of people in the digital sphere attempting to influence their perception of the state and of political discourse in general. However, there is some variance in awareness across different demographic groups. The profiles of those most aware generally have some common characteristics. These digital consumers are frequent internet users of higher SES who are particularly interested in politics and slightly more suspicious of traditional media. They are more likely to be male and younger.

Our next set of models uses some of the same independent variables to estimate what percentage of online posts internet users believe come from political actors. We use indicators for the government on the one hand (Q17a) and from net-spies on the other (Q18a). Because percentages are normally distributed, we were able to rely on OLS for both models. Converse to the model estimates presented in table 2.3, these presented in table 2.4 are not consistent across the type of poster. Perhaps an even more striking departure is that the models over-all do not seem to predict the percentage of posts estimated to be from hostile sources. This is true despite the fact that the awareness models did find most independent variables to be statistically significant.

In the models presented in table 2.4, many of the independent variables are statistically significant, meaning that 0 is not bounded in the majority of the respective confidence intervals. There are only two significant variables in the model of the estimated percentage of government-generated posts, political interest and gender. The former is quite a sizable relationship, and the latter, while not as large, is apparently consequential as well. For every one-unit change in political interest, respondents estimate the percentage of posts coming from the government to be 10 points higher. The model also shows that women estimate the percentage to be 4 points higher than men do. Interestingly, in the next model, the correlation of general internet use is substantial. Every one-unit increase in internet use is associated with a 14-point increase in the estimated percentage of posts coming from net-spies or other hostile forces. Much the same as the first model in table 2.4, women estimate the percentage of posts coming from net-spies to be 3 points higher. These findings seem sensible given that most of the 50 Cent Party posts and, if they exist, net-spy posts, would be focused on forums where political issues are discussed.

Conclusion

In this chapter, we introduced our data and took our first look at the empirical results. The data demonstrate that many Chinese internet users are aware of, or at least believe that there are, forces, both pro- and anti-government, who are trying to shape Chinese citizens' political perceptions online. We also examined the factors that explain variation in citizens' awareness of these forces. Perhaps the most substantial finding in these data is that citizen awareness of the existence of these forces tends to be driven primarily by the frequency with which they use the internet. This is an important building block for our theory. Indeed, this finding will become important as the empirical story unfolds in the rest of this book and when we more fully present our theory of the directed digital dissidence. Ultimately, we test whether the flow of information, of which a portion is clearly believed to be coming from motivated actors, has consequences for citizen behavior and attitudes. As noted in chapter 1, we do find evidence of such consequences, which we will detail in the following chapters.

The Chinese Internet 35

Table 2.4 **Modeling Estimated Percentages of Posts from Government and Net-Spies**

	Government Posts			
	Estimate	*S.E.*	*95% CI*	
General Internet Use	0.01	0.03	−0.06	0.08
Traditional Media Trust	−0.06	0.03	−0.12	−0.00
Political Interest	0.10	0.03	0.05	0.15
CCP Member	0.01	0.01	−0.01	0.04
Urbanicity	−0.02	0.02	−0.06	0.03
SES	−0.04	0.05	−0.13	0.05
Female	0.04	0.01	0.01	0.06
Age	−0.03	0.04	−0.11	0.04
$R^2 = 0.02$				
$N = 1{,}663$				
	Net-Spy Posts			
General Internet Use	0.14	0.04	0.06	0.22
Traditional Media Trust	0.05	0.03	−0.01	0.12
Political Interest	0.02	0.03	−0.05	0.08
CCP Member	0.02	0.01	−0.01	0.05
Urbanicity	−0.01	0.03	−0.06	0.04
SES	−0.10	0.05	−0.21	0.01
Female	0.03	0.01	0.00	0.05
Age	0.03	0.05	−0.06	0.12
$R^2 = 0.03$				
$N = 1{,}015$				

Note: Estimates are derived using ordinary least squares (OLS).

Understanding the importance of the findings in this chapter requires us to place them in the context of the larger narrative of the book. Digital information consumption (particularly social media) is increasing the likelihood of being exposed to a flow of information that is critical of the local government. That in turn lowers trust in local government and stimulates supportive attitudes about local-level protest. Notably, our data show that this is all true regardless of how frequently respondents escape the firewall; nonetheless, critique of the central government, as opposed to the local government, is more prevalent among those who venture to the other side of the wall. The final development reincorporates the frequency of use. Users who jump the firewall often face competing effects. They tend to be heavy internet users, which is correlated with favoring the central government, while at the same time the firewall, ceteris paribus, decreases trust in the central government. Therefore, it would appear that the efforts of the Chinese government to structure the flow of information on their side of the firewall are effective. Heightened use of the internet increases the likelihood of exposure to content that presents the government's narrative and limits the effect of counterflows of critical information. Thus, the results in this chapter are the foundation for what the concluding empirical measures show in chapter 7.

In the next chapter, we present primary evidence indicating that exposure to a flow of information critical of local government is consequential for both attitudes and behavior. We demonstrate that exposure to this flow deters trust in the local government and ultimately encourages support for protest-centered action.

3

What Does Directed Digital Dissidence Look Like?

Critical Information Flows, Trust, and Support for Protest

Despite generalities about the impact of online communications on the political sphere (see, e.g., Gainous and Wagner 2014), the immediate and long-term effects can vary by context. In some nations, few people are online; in others there are only nascent domestic platforms for political exchange. Variables such as internet penetration, as well as social and political context, do matter when attempting to assess the internet as a vehicle for change (Gainous, Wagner, and Abbott 2015). In this chapter we consider the context of China and, particularly, how that context shapes the influence and importance of the internet. The Chinese experience is not divorced from those of other nations, but it is informed and shaped by idiosyncratic domestic political, economic, and social conditions. In this chapter, we look at what the internet means in China and begin to consider the role it can play in fermenting dissidence in this tightly controlled state-run system.

Initially, a look at the pattern of adoption of digital communication through the internet in China presents two interesting factors. The internet is a relatively new addition to the public sphere in China, but the rate of adoption in the population is extremely rapid and expansive. According to CNNIC reports, China's internet population has grown from 0.62 million in October 1997 to 731 million in December 2016 (China Internet Network Information Center 1997; 2017). Today, more than 53 percent of Chinese citizens are connected to the internet either via personal computers or mobile devices. Every day, millions of Chinese citizens get online to obtain information, to do business, to communicate with each other, to entertain themselves, and to participate in public affairs through expressing their opinions and interacting with government agencies

---

Directed Digital Dissidence in Autocracies. Jason Gainous, Rongbin Han, Andrew W. MacDonald, and Kevin M. Wagner, Oxford University Press. © Oxford University Press 2024. DOI: 10.1093/oso/9780197680384.003.0003

on e-government platforms or social media sites. Table 3.1 shows the most frequently used online services in China in 2015 and 2016.

As we noted in chapter 2, in China, the internet is not only an economic and technological opportunity but also a sociopolitical challenge. The internet has become a vehicle for China to develop online services that can benefit its economy in many ways. Most notably, the nation is promoting the development

Table 3.1 **Most Frequently Used Online Services in China (2015–2016)**

Applications	2016		2015		
	Population (millions)	Penetration Rate (%)	Population (millions)	Penetration Rate (%)	Growth Rate (%)
Instant Messenger	666.28	91.1	624.08	90.7	6.8
Search Engine	602.38	82.4	566.23	82.3	6.4
News	613.90	84	564.40	82.0	8.8
Video	544.55	74.5	503.91	73.2	8.1
Music	503.13	68.8	501.37	72.8	0.4
Payment	474.50	64.9	416.18	60.5	14.0
Shopping	466.70	63.8	413.25	60.0	12.9
Gaming	417.04	57.0	391.48	56.9	6.5
Banking	365.52	50.0	336.39	48.9	8.7
Literature	333.19	45.6	296.74	43.1	12.3
Travel Booking	299.22	40.9	259.55	37.7	15.3
Email	248.15	33.9	258.47	37.6	-4.0
Forum/BBS	120.79	16.5	119.01	17.3	1.5
Finance	98.90	13.5	90.26	13.1	9.6
Trading Stocks/Funds	62.76	8.6	58.92	8.6	6.5
Weibo	271.43	37.1	230.45	33.5	17.8
Maps	461.66	63.1	379.97	55.2	21.5
Eating	208.56	28.5	113.56	16.5	83.7
Education	137.64	18.8	110.14	16.0	25.0
E-medical Services	194.76	26.6	152.11	22.1	28.0
E-government	238.97	32.7	—	—	—

Source: *The 39th Statistical Report on China Internet Development*

of digital commerce platforms and information technology industries. Indeed, some of the most financially successful internet companies are linked to China. Chinese IT giants such as Baidu (China's counterpart to Google), Alibaba (e-commerce conglomerate comparable to Amazon and eBay), and Tencent (owner of popular online messengers QQ and WeChat) are among the most profitable companies in the world (Economist 2017). However, in easing restrictions on the internet to support commercial opportunities, the Chinese government has inadvertently connected people in a way that allows for greater opportunities for political exchange. Chinese citizens, with the help of the internet, are now able to better communicate with each other, more freely express themselves on public affairs, and more actively engage in the governing process. The Chinese party-state now has to face a more engaged and informed population.

This presents a particularly daunting challenge for the Chinese state, which has sustained itself, in part, through monitoring and restricting the flow of information to and among its citizens. The internet has brought freer information flow that challenges the state's monopoly over media. As information consumed shapes attitudes and opinions (Zaller and Feldman 1992), alternative flows of dissident information should weaken the state's ability to influence the attitudes and behaviors of its citizens. As Clay Shirky (2011a, 36) argues, with the expansion of the internet, authoritarian states such as China that are accustomed to having a monopoly on public speech now will find themselves "called to account for anomalies between its view of events and the public's." The quandary is that the economic growth tied to the digital sphere requires interpersonal interaction that can be repurposed for political exchange. This is a particularly thorny issue in China as the state has largely controlled the flow of information by limiting and controlling the legacy media outlets.

Indeed, despite marketization and commercialization, traditional media in China are still subject to tight state control either directly or through monitoring and correction (Brady 2008; Repnikova 2017; Stockmann 2013; Stockmann and Gallagher 2011). Although traditional media in China does contain limited and selective exposure of corruption and official misconduct (X. Li 2002; Liebman 2012; Zhou 2000), it is generally considered a space to shore up regime legitimacy as critical investigative journalism is largely suppressed (Bandurski and Hala 2010; Brady 2008). This is possible because the traditional media is either owned or controlled by the state. Most mass communication media outlets are supervised directly by the state, and the number of private media enterprises that need monitoring is small enough that the task is entirely manageable.

In contrast, the internet is much more difficult to control, freeing the information flow in China by enabling ordinary citizens to express themselves publicly or, at the least, allowing them to access information other than state propaganda. Although the number of popular platforms for public expression in China may be even smaller than the number of traditional media sources, the number of commenters and opinions that have to be monitored has exploded. Internet users in China, compared to nonusers, have more opportunities to express critical view of state officials, government agencies, or the regime in general and are exposed voluntarily or passively to more negative information about the government (Lei 2011; Tong and Lei 2013).

The Role of Citizens in China's Central-Local Relations

Initially, it appears that the Chinese government fits well into the group of authoritarian regimes that early scholarship suggests are highly vulnerable to the opportunity structure that the internet provides for political dissidence (Wagner and Gainous 2014). Expansion of internet access has significantly enabled and amplified freer expression as well as criticism of the Chinese party-state, which in turn may have an impact on netizens' political beliefs and practices (Esarey and Xiao 2008; Hyun and Kim 2015; Lei 2011; Tang and Huhe 2013; Tong and Lei 2013; Xiao 2011; G. Yang 2009; Zheng 2008). Indeed, despite the state's efforts to control and shape online information flow, one may easily observe critical expression on almost all major online platforms, particularly popular social media sites such as internet forums (e.g., Tianya Club and Baidu Tieba), the Twitter-like Sina Weibo, and WeChat. China's approach was an attempt to embrace the economic gains of internet-fueled growth while managing the social and political implications by attempting to censor and manipulate information, with mixed success.

The activity on Tianya (tianya.cn) is an apt window into the growing online activism. As China's most popular internet forum, the site boasts more than 130 million registered users as of July 2017. During its peak hours every day, more than a million users are simultaneously online reading and commenting on all sorts of topics. Many of its message boards, including the second–most popular board, Free (Zatan), are dedicated to discussing public affairs, which often incurs criticism of the government and even the regime in general. In fact, Tianya also hosts a board titled Grassroots Voices (Baixing Shengyin) that was launched in 2009 specifically for citizens across the country to voice their grievances and complain about perceived injustices. Despite constant state censorship, tens of thousands of citizens have utilized this board to expose and condemn the malfeasance of local governments or officials with the hope to attract attention from the public, the media, or state officials at higher levels (Han and Shao 2022). This rarely leads to a satisfactory solution. There are so many complaints on the board, and most of them attract only dozens of reads and a few replies. Nonetheless, netizens sometimes have successfully turned their issues of concern into online spectacles. This forces the government to respond, occasionally by punishing the officials in question (Gao and Stanyer 2014; Wang and Han 2023). In fact, even complaints that fail to generate a significant online response can be helpful as the government, local authorities in particular, may attempt to resolve the problem to pacify the petitioner and prevent the potential escalation of the protest (Chen, Pan, and Xu 2016; Han and Jia 2018).

Complaints on Tianya's Grassroots Voices are primarily targeting local governments and local officials. Although the board features the theme of local criticism, the absence of criticism directed at higher levels of the government is not solely a product of the local focus of Grassroots Voices. The implication of a locally oriented message board is that there is an alternative forum for critiques of the central government. However, there is no board devoted to complaints against the central government or top leaders on Tianya. There are some less ominous possible explanations for this local focus. It may be that senior officials and governments are distant from citizens and often do not directly interact with them. Thus, they are less likely to become the targets of complaints.

However, state design is the more likely explanation. If fact, it is not just Tianya. The party-state itself also runs a Local Leader Message Board that allows citizens to lodge petitions targeting local authorities and officials (Jiang, Meng, and Zhang 2019; Su and Meng 2016). Under the rightful resistance logic, higher levels of the government, especially the central government, are seen to be benevolent allies to protesters. Indeed, protesters may even intentionally avoid attacking higher levels of authorities or the regime to justify their claims and avoid suppression. Such a "rightful resistance" perspective not only explains the absence of a board focused on the central government; it explains why complaints directed at local officialdom are tolerated while criticism of top leadership and the regime is not (Lorentzen 2013; 2014; O'Brien 1996; O'Brien and Li, 2006). Further, the empirical evidence supports the rightful resistance explanation. Chinese citizens have demonstrated differential trust in various levels of governments. There is more trust in higher levels of the government and less trust in lower levels of the government (Kennedy 2009; Lianjiang Li 2004; 2008; 2013). The rightful resistance explanation, which is of particular interest here, presents the best window into the current literature on Chinese politics as well as the actual experience on the ground.

Rightful resistance serves two important functions. By sanctioning critique, the central government is able to manage opposition and mediate the dissident behavior. Yet, equally important, the rightful resistance framework allows the state to create a venue for opposition, rather than simply suppressing it. This release valve eases the pressure on the government and creates at least the illusion of an interactive relationship between the people and the state. Without democratic institutions such as competitive elections, free press, and vigorous civil organizations, authoritarian regimes such as China suffer from inadequate policy feedback and face a serious principal-agent problem of controlling local officials. Owing to the lack of proper policy input mechanisms, rampant corruption, official misconduct, and governance deficits at the local level often go unnoticed and are thus not corrected by the central government, which in turn will not only weaken the central government's capacity to rule but also erode the regime's legitimacy basis as citizens can directly observe the malfeasance of local authorities and officials (Seligson 2002). To overcome this obstacle, high-capacity authoritarian regimes such as China often install policy input and anti-corruption institutions and make serious efforts to control malfeasance and discipline their local agents (X. Chen 2008; Clark 1993; Li, Liu, and O'Brien 2012; Manion 2004; Minzner 2006; Wedeman 2012).

The rightful resistance framework is consistent with Chinese policies. In China, top leaders have stressed the importance of responding to citizens, fighting corruption, and controlling local agents' misconduct over and over again, linking it to the survival of the regime. Under this structure, the people are naturally allied with the state against corruptible officials, especially at the local levels. This sentiment directs the opposition away from the state itself and focuses it on individuals' flaws. Since President Xi Jinping came into power in 2013, the new administration has undergone an unprecedented anti-corruption campaign, which thus far has brought down thousands of officials, from petty cadres at the grassroots level to top spots in the Politburo such as Politburo Standing Committee member Zhou Yongkang and former party chief of Chongqing Municipality Bo Xilai. The motivation for the crackdown, although still debated (C. Li 2012; Ling Li 2019; Y. Zhao 2012; Zhu, Huang, and Zhang 2019), is almost certainly at least in part an attempt to make the regime more appealing to the masses, who have long complained online and off about corruption. The Chinese party-state has also tolerated or even encouraged citizen participation in supervising state agencies and officials, either to control its agents more effectively or to build an image of benevolent and responsive authoritarianism (Chen, Pan, and Xu 2016; Su and Meng 2016). Citizen participation is well in accordance with an important organizational principle of the Chinese Communist Party (CCP): the "mass line" (*qunzhong luxian*) (Kennedy and Shi 2015). The mass line requires the party and its cadres to consult the masses and incorporate their views, opinions, and suggestions in policy making and implementation.

Mass line is not a new idea. This organizational principle is not only emphasized in Maoist time but also continuously repeated throughout reform era by the party, either sincerely or instrumentally (Kennedy and Shi 2015; W. Tang 2016). The current Chinese Constitution (Article 41) also explicitly states that citizens have the right "to criticize and provide suggestions to any State organ or functionary" and "to complain, charge against, and expose any State organ or functionary for violation of law or dereliction of duty."[1] In practice, since the revolutionary era and especially during Mao's rule, the CCP has mobilized the people to participate in massive campaigns that often target party officials. In the reform era, the state has solicited public participation through a series of institutions such as the letters and visits system (*xinfang zhidu*), administrative litigation, media supervision (*yulun jiandu*), mass supervision (*qunzhong jiandu*), and even grassroots democracy such as village elections (Bandurski and Hala 2010; X. Chen 2008; Hassid 2015; X. Li 2002; Minzner 2006; O'Brien and Han 2009; O'Brien and Li 2004; Repnikova 2017; Zhou 2000).

To some extent, the Chinese state may have even instrumentally regulated riots by permitting small-scale, narrowly economic, often local protests to gather policy feedback, discipline local agents, and ease some social pressure (Lorentzen 2013). Although the abovementioned institutionalized channels have provided Chinese citizens with opportunities to engage in state politics, provide policy feedback about local conditions, and check official behavior, such opportunities are almost exclusively restricted to local levels. As an autocracy, what the Chinese central state desires is citizen participation under its auspices rather than allowing the people to direct their criticism upward. Regime stability is still the state's primary desired outcome. By allowing citizen participation at local levels, the state effectively regulates and uses dissidence as well as localizes citizen dissatisfaction. In addition, the state protects the image of higher levels of the government and projects a picture of a benevolent state that cares about its citizens and responds to their needs and complaints. The success of this approach is fairly clear. Unrest in China has generally been localized. Citizens tend to trust higher levels of the government more than the local government. As a strategy, tolerating or even encouraging "rightful resistance" has been productive.

The larger and subsequent question we tackle in this research is how the internet may have altered this strategy and affected the viability of the rightful resistance framework. The arrival of the internet age has further expanded both formal and informal channels of citizen participation, making it more challenging for the Chinese party-state to manage public participation and popular criticism of the regime. However, it is not pure speculation that the party-state may be selectively tolerating online criticism because it, like other illiberal or authoritarian regimes, has shown both a strong desire and formidable ability to control and manipulate online content to its own advantage. Numerous studies show that the Chinese state has established a highly sophisticated, comprehensive, and rigid censorship system that controls the network infrastructure, a national Great Firewall that blocks access to websites and services deemed threatening to the regime, and both automatic and manual surveillance of online expression by state agencies, service providers, and peer reporting (for instance, see Deibert et al. 2008; 2010; Han 2018a; Harwit and Clark 2001; Y. Li 2009; MacKinnon 2011; OpenNet Initiative 2005; Roberts 2018; Walton 2001; Zuckerman 2010).

Recent studies show that the regime has been selectively censoring online expression, prioritizing content that has collective mobilization potential over general criticism (King, Pan, and Roberts 2013; 2014) or attacks on top leadership over local officialdom (Lorentzen 2014). Moreover, the regime has also attempted to shape online expression by feeding its preferred information and discourses to Chinese cyberspace. This is done both overtly and covertly. Overtly, the state has demanded state media outlets set up online outposts to conquer the high ground of online propaganda, launched thousands of e-government platforms, and encouraged state agencies and officials to engage citizens on social media platforms (Esarey 2015; Hartford 2005; Schlæger 2013; Schlæger and Jiang 2014). Today, all major state mouthpieces such as China Central Television (CCTV) and the *People's Daily* have established a significant presence online. Moreover, according to CNNIC (2017) as of December 2016, government agencies at different levels and in different sectors had 53,546 official websites;[2] the state also ran 164,522 official accounts on the popular Weibo platform—125,098 of which represent state agencies, 39,424 individual officials. Some of these official microblog accounts such as the Chinese Communist Youth League Central Committee (CCYLCC) and several Ministry of Public Security accounts have millions of followers. Moreover, there are more than 34,083 governmental accounts on the trending news aggregator, Jinri Toutiao, attracting millions of clicks daily. On the popular instant messenger platform WeChat, the government had set up more than 83,000 accounts by August 2015, allegedly covering 84.7 percent of government agencies at provincial and prefecture levels (China E-government Council 2015). Covertly, the state has deployed internet commentators (such as the 50 Cent Party) to guide public opinion in online crises and state propaganda campaigns. In particular, the entire propaganda system and the Communist Youth League system have been mobilized to increase the number of internet commentators.

This approach has become much more visible since President Xi Jinping came into power in 2013. For instance, the CCYLCC issued a circular, urging all higher education institutions in China to set up a nationwide internet propaganda troop (*wangluo xuanchuanyuan*). The circular set minimal quota of 350,000, which is then assigned to different provinces and ultimately different universities and colleges.[3] Sporadic evidence suggests that the state may have also attempted to co-opt spontaneous nationalist cyber-forces (Han 2019). The regime has demonstrated it has both the incentive and the capacity to strategically control and shape information flow. The state may tolerate and even encourage criticism of local officialdom, but not the top leadership. It allows the state to reap the benefits of freer expression while avoiding or reducing its disruptive effects (Lorentzen 2014).

Information Flows, Trust, and Support for Protest

Understanding the importance of state intervention on the digital flow of information starts with understanding the influence of information flows on public opinion. We start with the well-studied connection between information and attitudes. People's opinions are formed in part by the information available to them (Zaller 1992). Controlling the availability and consumption of information influences attitudes and opinions (Gainous and Wagner 2011). The information war is about shaping attitudes, opinions, and ultimately political behaviors. As observed above, we know that there is an information flow that is critical of local government in China. Further, as outlined above, we believe that the central government is, at the least, passively responsible for this flow by creating channels for it and allowing it to persist while other broader criticisms are blocked. In this chapter, we seek to measure whether this differential flow of critical information is substantive and its consequences for attitudes and behaviors.

The results presented in table 3.2 provide supportive evidence on both counts. Respondents were asked how often they see digital posts that are critical of local governments or government officials (Q8) and how often either they or their friends post such comments (Q9). The marginal distributions indicate, not surprisingly, that seeing such posts is more common than making them, but nonetheless, both occur relatively frequently. Roughly 83 percent of respondents said they saw posts critical of local government at least occasionally, often, or very often, and of those categories nearly 32 percent chose the often response.

Table 3.2 **The Prevalence of a Critical Flow of Information about Local Government**

	See Critical Stories	Post Critical Comments
Very often	12.2%	4.8%
Often	31.9%	16.6%
Occasionally	38.8%	33.2%
Never	17.2%	45.4%
Total N	2,286	2,276

As for making critical posts (or knowing a friend who has), well over half have done so at some point, with about 33 percent only occasionally doing so, nearly 17 percent often, and almost 5 percent very often. Taken together, these numbers suggest that exposure and contribution to critical flows of information are quite common among our respondents.

The fact that our respondents are more exposed to a critical flow of information than they post critical comments online themselves, though quite intuitive, is worth remarking on for two reasons. First, it likely reflects the nature of online information production and consumption, as netizens in general tend to read/view more than post. Second, and more importantly, it suggests that a significant portion of our respondents who are exposed to negative information about local government are not actively seeking to contribute to the critical discourse. This is important to our analysis later because it shows that these respondents are not self-selecting to be exposed to critical information as a product of their own grievances. Generally, when citizens feel aggrieved by government action, they are more likely to take it to the internet to garner public support, attract media attention, and invite intervention from higher levels of the government (regardless of their odds of success) (Diamant and O'Brien 2014). One possible causal model is that these agitators, if they believe in the power of the internet to effect change, are likely to be more frequent internet users. They are also more likely to be exposed to negative information about the government as they try to find the proper platform to express their grievances and connect with fellow agitators. More directly, negative attitudes toward the government lead to more online engagement and to more exposure to negative information about the government. However, our data suggest that although this causal process might be at work, a significant portion of our respondents do not fit this model. Passive users are exposed to critical information, rather than seek it out. Thus, we propose an alternate model, in which heavy internet use causes critical attitudes toward local government.

This critical information exposure is consequential for both trust in local government and, ultimately, attitudes about the legitimacy of protest against the state. We begin to establish the basis for this model by looking at the marginal distribution of our attitudinal measure of citizen trust in local government (Q13C). We follow this by examining our list experiment so as to gauge the level of distrust in local governments (Q14a1 and Q14a2). Figure 3.1 displays the distribution of the former, which is relatively normal with a slight skew toward trust in local government. Roughly 45 percent have some trust, and about 10 percent have a great deal of trust. This means that about 55 percent have some degree of trust in local government, leaving close to 45 percent with some degree of distrust (about 37 percent with not very much trust and 7 percent with none at all). This suggests that a sizable chunk of the public is dissatisfied with their local government.

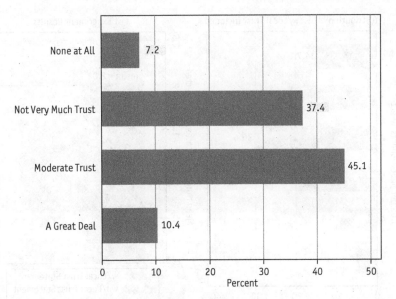

Figure 3.1 Distribution of Trust in Local Government

We included the list experiment to control for social desirability bias among our respondents. Social science researchers have long been concerned as to whether respondents in autocratic settings are comfortable answering questions honestly. If social desirability bias exists, it could potentially lead to an overestimation of government trust. To help alleviate concerns over bias, a list experiment can serve as a validity confirmation for our meta-attitudinal measure. The list experiment asked half of the respondents (randomly assigned) to record how many statements that they agreed with from a list of institutions they trust (such as the media), plus our sensitive item, whether they trust their local government. The other half of the respondents were presented with the same list minus our sensitive item (local government trust). By comparing the mean of the two response groups, we can judge the percentage of respondents who did not trust their local government. This list experiment allowed us to measure aggregate-level trust without asking respondents to explicitly state their response.

The result of the list experiment suggests that a significant number of respondents included the local government statement in their calculations. The distribution of responses on the question including the test statement and the experiment results are both presented in figure 3.2. One interesting observation is that a significant proportion of the respondents selected all five statements. Strategically, one would expect respondents concerned with revealing their true preferences to avoid responding that they agreed with all five questions, as it would clearly indicate that they also agreed with the sensitive list item. Thus, our respondents either did not understand that it would be obvious that they

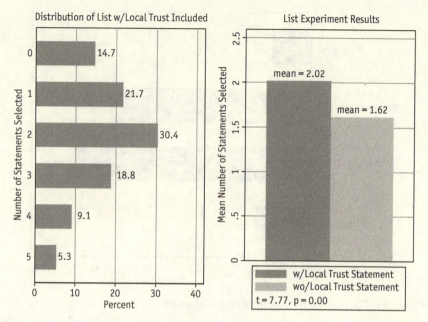

Figure 3.2 Local Government Trust List Experiment

distrusted local government, or they did not care whether that fact was known. This would suggest that a social desirability effect is not that strong.

The next important observation is that the modal response was two. Thus, generally speaking, most respondents distrusted around two of these institutions. Looking at the graph on the right side of figure 3.2, it is clear that there is a fair amount of distrust, as was evidenced in figure 3.1. The mean number of statements selected when the test statement was included was 2.02, while it was only 1.62 when it was not. This is a substantial difference given that the range is only from 0 through 5. In fact, the difference is so large that a t-test resulted in an extremely high t-score (7.77, $p = .00$). Taken together, our meta-attitudinal and list experiment measures of distrust in local government suggest that such distrust is fairly common and respondents are probably not afraid to reveal their true level of distrust.

The point of our list experiment was to determine whether there was a sizable social desirability effect happening in our direct questions about trust. If there is not much difference in the distributions on these variables, the direct questions and the list experiment, then we can assume that there is not much of a social desirability effect manifesting in the direct questions. That is the case here. This is fortunate because if there had been a sizable difference, we could not have confidently relied on the direct measures, and we could not use the list experiment much beyond its univariate application. This is a real limitation of list experiments. The problem is that we have no idea who selected the treatment statement (except, of course, those who selected all of the statements). Thus, we cannot model whether someone selected it. That is part of the reason for a list experiment: it gives the respondent cover, so they can select the treatment statement without the researcher knowing. Again, our point here was to show that the distributions on the list response and the direct question were comparable and, in doing so, provide evidence that people were not lying on the direct question. This makes us confident that the direct questions are usable.

What adds to our confidence is that our findings are generally in accordance with existing studies. In a nationwide representative survey jointly implemented by Texas A&M University and Peking University in 2008, 3,989 respondents were asked to rate their level of trust in central, provincial, and county leaders at a four-level scale: (1) "trust very much," (2) "trust somewhat," (3) "do not trust much," and (4) "do not trust at all." About 63 percent of the respondents trust the county-level cadres very much or somewhat, while 37 percent show a general inclination of distrust (Lianjiang Li 2016). There are a few factors that may explain the differences between our results (55 percent trust and 45 percent distrust) and this 2008 survey. First, we sampled internet users who were exposed to freer flow of information and thus were more likely to be critical of the government. Second, we asked respondents to report their trust in local government in general, rather than specifically the county-level cadres. In general, Chinese citizens demonstrate a pattern of hierarchical trust that increases as the levels of the government go up (Lianjiang Li 2004). It is likely that in our survey, respondents understood local government as the level of government that is closely related to them. County cadres, though considered local, are still somewhat distant from citizens' everyday lives. Third, timing of the two surveys might have affected the results. In 2008 the Chinese government was probably at its peak of political support in recent years because of a number of events such as the Beijing Olympics. In 2015, popular trust in the government, especially local authorities, may have been negatively affected by growing dissatisfaction in governmental handling of socioeconomic issues such as pollution, rising housing prices, and President Xi Jinping's anti-corruption campaign that exposed thousands of corrupt officials at all levels.

Our data support the existence of a relationship running from critical digital information exposure to distrust in local government to support for protest against the government. But, before fully describing our hypothesized relationship, it is important to look at the distribution of our measure of protest acceptability. We asked a total of seven questions regarding citizen attitudes about various protest strategies (Q20A–Q20G). They included attitudes about the following methods of expressing discontent with the government: public protests, ignoring laws, refusing to pay taxes, signing petitions, joining groups seeking to influence government, going to the press, and suing the local government.

We did not directly ask whether respondents had engaged in such activities but rather the degree to which they found each respective activity acceptable if a citizen has a grievance against the state. By asking for their attitudes as opposed to behavior, we are able to get a sense of how the flow of information is shaping perception rather than focusing on rarely performed acts of resistance. There is likely much more variance in attitudes as opposed to behavior with most of these items. Marginal differences in actual engagement would likely have been low on many response items.

The distributions on each of the items measuring attitudes about local government protests are presented in table 3.3. According to our results, there is a considerable level of support for local government protest. There is some variation in response pattern across items, but by and large, the distributions are normal. The bulk of responses for each item (public protests, ignoring laws, refusing to pay taxes, signing petitions, joining groups seeking to influence government, going to the press, and suing the local government) are centered on believing these acts of protest were either sometimes acceptable or acceptable only in extreme cases. The percentages across all items within these response categories range from 16.4 to 45.5.

That said, several items are slightly skewed, though the direction of the skew varies. Attitudes about ignoring laws is the only item that a sizable number of respondents (46 percent) believe is never acceptable. Nonetheless, a majority still considers it acceptable at least in some cases (only roughly 20 percent as sometimes or always acceptable, though). Many (35.5 percent) of our respondents think that refusing to pay taxes is a protest option that is never acceptable. Only about 27 percent think it is always or sometimes acceptable, while the remaining 37 percent deem it acceptable only in extreme cases. Respondents

Table 3.3 **Distribution of Responses on Attitudes about Local Government Protest**

	Public Protests	Ignore Laws	Refuse Taxes	Sign Petition	Join Group	Contact Press	Sue Government
Always acceptable	8.9%	4.2%	5.2%	14.9%	6.2%	21.3%	20.9%
Sometimes acceptable	41.0%	16.4%	21.9%	45.5%	32.2%	43.7%	42.6%
Only in extreme cases	39.4%	33.5%	37.3%	30.6%	31.4%	27.6%	28.4%
Never acceptable	10.8%	46.0%	35.5%	9.1%	30.0%	7.5%	8.1%
Total *N*	2,285	2,281	2,274	2,281	2,277	2,278	2,270

also tend to disapprove of joining groups seeking to influence government, with 30 percent saying never, but nonetheless, a supermajority believe it is an acceptable behavior in some cases (though only roughly 38 percent grouped in sometimes or always acceptable). Both items measuring whether it is acceptable to go to the press or to sue the local government are skewed in the other direction—toward being supportive. In fact, more than 20 percent on both items said they believed this act was always acceptable. Altogether, the results here suggest, even in fairly extreme cases, Chinese citizens are relatively supportive of acts of protest against local government.

Overall, the results on grievance redress questions are in line with our expectations. Respondents tend to show more support to options that are more tolerated by the authoritarian state, including public protests, signing petitions, resorting to media, or suing the government directly. Those are the common strategies employed by Chinese protesters and often reported by traditional and online media. Respondents prefer such options either because they believe them to be more effective and less risky or because they might have been exposed more to such protests directly or indirectly. For instance, according to Yongshun Cai (2010), three factors may effectively bring about intervention from upper levels of the government to address protesters' problems: size, media exposure, and casualties. In other words, staging them publicly and contacting the media will increase the effectiveness of protests. Signing petitions and suing the government, though they might not be as effective, are much less risky. In particular, China introduced the Administration Litigation Law that further enables and legitimizes citizens' efforts to bring local governments and officials into court, although it does not guarantee their success (Diamant, Lubman, and O'Brien 2005; O'Brien and Li 2004; Pei 1997).

By contrast, ignoring or violating laws, refusing to pay taxes, and forming groups to influence government policies are less legitimate and often more risky options. The former two clearly do not fit in rightful resistance, as they are not sanctioned by state policies or the upper levels of the government. The last option is generally deemed politically sensitive and is more harshly suppressed by the government. Groups such as the Falun Gong and the New Citizen Movement, led by law Professor Xu Zhiyong advocating civil rights and constitutional rule, have been brutally repressed. Even in rural protests, which are normally rightful, with only concrete goals that are sanctioned by the state and without a threatening political agenda, most protest leaders "are careful to avoid politically-loaded terms like 'leader' (*lingxiu*) or 'organization' (*zuzhi*), to dispel suspicions that they might be fomenting revolution" (Lianjiang Li and O'Brien 2008, 15–16).

Thus far, the largely descriptive foundation laid out in this chapter indicates that there is a digital critical flow of information, that many Chinese distrust local governments, and that many support acts of protest against them. We then developed a model to measure the relationship between the distrust and protest behavior. This allows us to test our assertion that the Chinese authoritarian regime's digital information management strategy appears to be largely working. The Chinese state strategy, implicitly if not explicitly, directs dissidence away from the central government by pointing it at local government. The more citizens use the internet, the more they are exposed to a flow of information critical of the local government. This negative information exposure is tolerated, if not directed, by the central government. The consumption of this dissident information will have some attitudinal influence, ceteris paribus—in particular, it should lower trust in the local government. These two links (exposure to critical information and lower trust), taken together, should then encourage positive attitudes regarding the acceptability of protests against the local government. This model is represented in figure 3.3.[4]

The structural equation model represented in figure 3.3 is a mediation model. We employ this mediation model to determine whether the total effect of internet use on trust in local government is partially accounted for by exposure to critical information. In addition, we measure whether the effect of exposure to critical information on positive attitudes toward protest is partially accounted for by trust in local government. If general internet use is significant in the first and second levels of the model (critical flow ← general internet use, and trust in local government ← critical flow, general internet use, and controls), then the former is substantiated, and if critical information is significant in both the second and

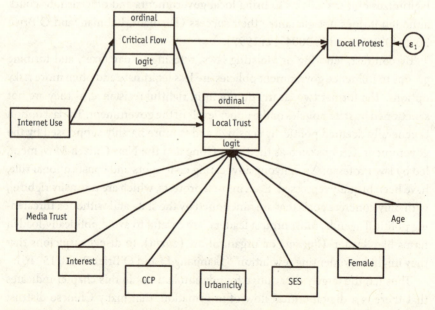

Figure 3.3 Modeling the Effects of a Critical Information Flow

third levels of the model (protest ← critical information, trust in local government), then the latter is substantiated. Path models such as the mediation model we specify here are inherently causal. They treat a variable as a mediator. Both critical information and trust in local government are influencing support for protest through their effect on these mediators.

A mediation model does not, however, completely eliminate the possibility that causality runs in the other direction. One could hypothesize that people who encountered local cadres or local government in a negative manner may go online to actively complain, petition, and protest. Alternatively, people who are at odds with local authorities and cadres may be selectively exposing themselves to negative information about local governments. But based on the evidence in our data, this alternative causal pathway is unlikely. Mediation models are a statistical approach to testing a causal path. They add complexity that makes the test a higher hurdle to clear than a simple single-dependent-variable multivariate model. As a result, we have relatively higher confidence in our proposed linkages. Philosophically, structural equations such as this mediation model assume that causality is often more complicated than a simpler model suggests. Empirically, our causal claim also echoes those of existing studies that show that access to new information, especially from the internet, significantly modifies Chinese citizens' political attitudes, beliefs, and activism inclination (Lei 2011; Zhu, Lu, and Shi 2012).

The estimates for the model in figure 3.3 are presented in table 3.4.[5] The positive effect of general internet use is a significant estimator of both exposure to the critical flow of information and trust in local government (0 is not within the 95 percent confidence intervals). Thus, the more people use the internet, the more likely they are to be both exposed to a critical flow of information and to be trusting of the local government. As stated above, this indicates that the total effect of internet use on trust in local government is partially accounted for by exposure to a critical flow of information. Specifically, it is the next level that lets us know whether the effects of this critical flow on support for local government protest can be accounted for, in part, by trust in local government. The model suggests this linkage is the case. Exposure to the critical flow of information is negatively related to trust in local government and positively related to attitude about protest (0 is not within the confidence intervals). Also, in accordance with earlier studies (Shi 2001), we find trust in local government is negatively related to attitude about protest.

We also ran versions of the model that controlled for multiple alternative explanations of trust in local government and support for protest. We add as independent variables traditional media trust, political interest, CCP membership, urbanicity, socioeconomic status (SES), gender, and age. As expected, the model estimates a significant positive effect of traditional media trust on local

Table 3.4 A Mediating Model of Digital Effects on Attitudes about Protest against Local Government

	Estimate	S.E.	95% CI	
Critical Flow				
General Internet Use	4.96	0.23	4.51	5.41
Trust Local Government				
Critical Flow	−0.86	0.19	−1.24	−0.49
General Internet Use	1.49	0.29	0.92	2.05
Traditional Media Trust	5.83	0.27	5.30	6.36
Political Interest	−0.17	0.20	−0.56	0.22
CCP Member	0.40	0.10	0.20	0.59
Urbanicity	0.37	0.18	0.01	0.73
SES	−0.40	0.36	−1.11	0.31
Female	0.09	0.09	−0.08	0.26
Age	−1.05	0.29	−1.62	−0.48
Attitude about Protest				
Critical Flow	0.26	0.02	.22	0.29
Trust Local Government	−0.09	0.02	−.12	−0.06
Log Likelihood = -5,371.74				
N = 2,270				

Note: Model estimates are based on a generalized structural equation where critical flow and trust local government are estimated using an ordered logit link and attitude about protest is estimated assuming a normal one. S.E. = standard error, CI = confidence interval, OR = odds ratio (odds ratios are displayed only when 0 is not bounded in the respective CI).

government trust. This is perhaps expected, as current studies generally find that exposure to state media—all traditional media outlets are subject more state influence than the internet—is positively correlated with trust in the regime as a whole (Kennedy 2009; Lianjiang Li 2004; Shi 2001). CCP members tend to be more trusting, as do urban residents and younger people. This is interesting, as some previous studies have found that demographic factors such as age and party membership often do not have statistically significant impact on political trust in China (Lianjiang Li 2004; Shi 2001). The other control variables are not statistically significant.

Conclusion

In this chapter, we demonstrate three major effects. The critical flow of information regarding the local government is common on the Chinese internet. Many Chinese citizens distrust the government. Finally, support levels for various means of protest are higher among internet users. This chapter set out to examine how the former two work together to shape the latter. This took us to the mediation model presented in this chapter. The results of this model were consistent with the theoretical foundation we laid out about directed digital dissidence. If the central government is allowing digital dissidence to flow if it is aimed at the local government, the model suggests this strategy has consequences for local-level attitudes and perhaps behavior. Heightened internet use increases the odds of exposure to dissidence, which lowers trust and, consequentially, may stimulate support for protest directed at local governments. This would keep the citizenry from pointing their distrust, and even resistance, at the central government.

Given that the critical flow of information appears to be consequential for citizen attitudes, it is important to know the source of this critical flow. Chapter 4 directly addresses this question. The results suggest that critical information in Chinese cyberspace is primarily flowing through social media. Further, citizens' social media use is extremely common and continues to increase, suggesting that the potential consequences of digital exposure to critical information may also rise in the future. We conclude the next chapter by profiling social media users. Interestingly, the data suggest that they are politically interested, urban, wealthier, female, and younger.

4

Social Media

The Battleground of the Information War

As we explored in the previous chapter, digital media exposure is consequential for Chinese citizen attitudes. It is not just using the internet but the type of content one is exposed to that shapes opinion. In particular, exposure to a critical flow of information seems to be the impetus behind distrust in local government and, ultimately, support for the legitimacy of protest against local governments. In this chapter, we unpack the process and consider where this critical information is available and how it affects behavior. If exposure to dissident information though online platforms is driving support for protest, understanding the sources and the distribution of that information is essential to understanding the relationship between digital media exposure and dissidence. To begin, we explore the movement of critical information through social media as an alternative channel to traditional government-controlled media.

According to the China Internet Network Information Center (2016), about 82 percent (564.40 million) of Chinese netizens used the internet for online news in December 2015, the time when we conducted our survey. By December 2016, the total of Chinese netizens using online news services had increased to 613.90 million, or 84 percent of the internet population (CNNIC 2017). However, this is a broad categorization. Some of the internet content is the digital product of traditional media. As the Chinese state has firm control over traditional media (Kennedy 2009; Lianjiang Li 2004; Repnikova 2017; Stockmann and Gallagher 2011), their digital output is typically non-oppositional. In fact, the Chinese government has pushed state-run media to set up online outlets to define and control the flow of information in the virtual space (e.g., Han 2018a; Roberts 2018). The result is a highly controlled sector of online news services that often reinforces rather than challenges the state's propaganda machine (Guo 2018).

In December 2000, the State Council Information Office (SCIO) designated nine key national and 24 key regional internet news providers. All of these

Directed Digital Dissidence in Autocracies. Jason Gainous, Rongbin Han, Andrew W. MacDonald, and Kevin M. Wagner, Oxford University Press. © Oxford University Press 2024. DOI: 10.1093/oso/9780197680384.003.0004

were either directly run by state media outlets such as the *People's Daily Online*, Xinhuanet.com, CCTV Online, or controlled by local (provincial) propaganda offices. Moreover, in 2005, the SCIO and the Ministry of Information Industry (MII, later merged into the Ministry of Industrial and Information Technology, MIIT) jointly issued the *Administrative Provisions of Internet News Information Services* specifying the news publication qualifications of internet service providers (SCIO and MII 2005). The regulation categorizes online news service providers into three groups: those run by news organizations (e.g., traditional media outlets, mostly under direct state control or subject to state influence, despite commercialization of the media industry in China), those run by non-news organizations, and those established by news organizations to carry content that is already published or broadcasted (e.g., wire services). Internet news providers in three categories are subject to examination and approval by the SCIO (those in category 1 and 2) or have to register with the SCIO (those in category 3). Moreover, only internet news service providers in the first category are allowed to conduct news reporting on "public current events" (e.g., political news), while those in the other two categories, especially the second category, can only reprint news from designated national and provincial level state-run media sources (Han 2015a; 2018a, chap. 2).

With such heavy-handed regulation, it is not surprising that social media has become a viable alternative and has challenged the state hegemony over digital news and information. Social media applications provide a platform that allows the users to generate, share, and consume content. In a very real sense, each individual can potentially be a media outlet, resulting in a news sphere that is far more diffuse and difficult to regulate, though the Chinese government has tried. Despite the state's efforts to penetrate and control expression on popular social media platforms such as Weibo and WeChat and major internet forums like Tianya and Baidu Tieba, citizens generally have more room to initiate topics, set the agenda, and frame online events in ways not possible with previous technologies. As such, social media is more open to the dissemination of critical information and allows citizen journalists to advocate for dissident agenda (Hassid 2012; Penney 2017). Unsurprisingly, Chinese state crackdowns have tried to limit online expression on popular social media platforms such as internet forums and Weibo.

The problems generated by open digital forums were not unknown to the Chinese state and did not arise with the adoption of social media. The state has long been aware of the potential threat of user-generated content. Internet forums, especially campus forums, which were the earliest form of social media type of platforms that feature user-generated content and social networking functions, experienced severe state repression in early 2000s when influential bulletin board systems (BBSes) were either forced to shut down, as in the case of YTHT, the most popular campus forum at the time, or were taken over by university authorities, as in the case of SMTH of Tsinghua University, BDWM of Peking University, and LILYBBS of Nanjing University (Han 2018a; Yang and Wu 2018).

However, the scope and scale of social media are far more extensive. Where message boards were largely limited to a small, fairly elite circle, social media has reached near-complete penetration of the population. With a far larger reach, social media has become a stimulus for the creation of political attitudes and a driver of increased political participation (Wagner, Gainous, and Abbott 2019). In a closed state, social media is more than an alternate form of discourse; it is the only broadly accessible space for political exchange that may differ from the dictates of the state. The social media space is dynamic and volatile and will have information and opinion that is not otherwise available. The less predictable and asymmetrical structure of the online venue, along with speed of transmission, creates an opportunity structure for the dissemination and exchange of information that is often difficult to eliminate entirely or to control constantly (Gainous, Wagner, and Abbott 2015).

As an open communication platform, the internet presents a challenge to closed states and requires states to engage in more sophisticated controls to limit this new sphere. People's attitudes are a product of the knowledge and information available to them (Zaller 1992). Ultimately, as a new channel of information, social media can affect what people know and how they form attitudes and opinions. Because people's attitudes are a construct based on the information cognitively accessible, and since social media increases exposure to dissenting and otherwise unavailable information, going online should stimulate more negative attitudes about the status quo and the current regime. Altering the scope and breadth of accessible information and allowing access to infinite networks of competing flows of information is a stimulus for a change in the perception of politics, governance, and attitudes (Gainous and Wagner 2014). More directly, when Chinese citizens are able to obtain information that is inconsistent with the state narrative, some are going to form less-accommodating attitudes.

Highlighting the impact of this relatively new form of interaction, social media is not only a threat to political control in both China and elsewhere; it has also proven a threat to social norms and traditional controls. The Chinese state has recognized the danger and attempted to act against it, while still preserving the commercial viability of the internet. In China, numerous online campaigns target content undesired by the state. The dissemination of pornography, rumors, and political opposition can result in the punishment of a social media platform. In early 2012, during the struggle that ended the political life of Politburo member, party chief of Chongqing, and princeling Bo Xilai, a rumor was spread on two major microblogging platforms, Sina Weibo and Tencent Weibo, about Bo's allies staging a coup in Beijing. As a result, the comment function of both platforms was suspended for three days (Chao 2012).

However, historically, the preferred approach is more targeted and calculated. While not the sole information shaper online, the Chinese state has been aggressive in attempting to limit and control online content. In 2013, the government launched a massive campaign to enforce the so-called Seven Baselines. The proposal by the then-director of Cyber Administration of China Lu Wei. Lu, who met with a number of internet celebrities, prescribed that netizens cannot violate the baselines of the state. That includes the baseline of laws and regulations, the baseline of the socialist system, the baseline of national interests, the baseline of citizens' legal rights and interests, the baseline of public order, the baseline of social morals, and the baseline of information accuracy. Subsequently, the state limited popular opinion leaders and tightened control over major social media sites. Sina Weibo, in particular, was under government pressure to silence its vocal "big Vs," or verified accounts with tens of thousands or even millions of followers. Charles Xue, an American Chinese venture capitalist and Weibo celebrity with 12 million followers, was detained in the campaign. In response, the platform suspended or permanently banned 103,673 accounts for offenses like personal attacks, harassment, privacy violations, piracy, spreading rumors, and profanity online (Millward 2013).

The massive state repression reportedly caused opinion leaders on Weibo to reduce their activities on the platform by 40 percent compared to the previous year (Cheng 2014). Such continuous repression efforts show the Chinese party-state's ability to exert influence over online expression, but it also confirms the state's fear and belief that the information on the internet, and on social media platforms in particular, poses a threat to state stability if it loses control over the information flow. Social media poses a more serious threat to autocratic rule than just regular internet usage. The evidence for this heightened threat is relatively robust not only from direct scholarly research but also from the revealed information provided by the extensive and vigorous policing of the social media space with which many nondemocratic regimes often engage. Hence, the social media exposure of our respondents is worth exploring independent of general internet usage.

Measuring Social Media Use and Its Impact

We included multiple measures of social media use in our survey. First, we simply asked respondents about how many hours a day they estimate they spend using only social media (Q2). This question also listed examples of various social media, including Weibo, QQ, Kaixin001, Douban, and WeChat. Weibo, which literally means "microblog" and often refers to Sina Weibo specifically, is a Twitter-like microblogging platform launched in August 2009.[1] QQ and WeChat, both of which belong to the Tencent Group, are instant communication apps that offer a wide variety of social media functions including instant messaging, blogging, gaming, and so forth, with the former initially developed and more customized to PCs and the latter a complete redesign for mobile devices. Kaixin001 is more like a Facebook replica, though it does not come close to matching Facebook's popularity and penetration rate. Douban, launched in 2005, is a platform that attracts primarily urbanites and college students who share reviews and discuss lifestyle and cultural topics such as films, books, music, and all sorts of other activities in Chinese cities. We single these specific social media sites out as examples primarily because of their popularity to clarify to our respondents what we mean by social media sites.[2] Although there could be differences in the way citizens use these various platforms, for the sake of parsimony, and because our theory is not centered on platform variation, we grouped them together in one question. That said, we also asked other social media questions in attempt to capture other dimensions of usage, including both how often respondents read news stories about political events posted on social media (Q5) and whether people use social media now more than they did five years ago (Q6).[3]

The distribution on each of these social media items is presented in figure 4.1. First, general social media use is quite frequent: about 28 percent of those sampled use social media one to two hours daily, and nearly 30 percent claim to use social media two to three hours daily. The results on the high end of the scale are perhaps most surprising: nearly 20 percent claim to use social media somewhere between four hours and more than nine hours daily (collapsing the top response categories). If social media were the most likely place to be exposed to a critical flow of information, this degree of use would certainly contribute to developing negative attitudes about the government. The same can be said for the consumption of political news via social media. Roughly 30 percent of those who claimed to read news stories about political events posted on social media multiple time daily, almost 35 percent said they did so at least once daily (everyday), and only approximately 10 percent said they never get political news from social media.

If we compare this result to the total frequency our respondents reported gathering news online, it appears that social media use is skewed toward nonpolitical purposes. As discussed in chapter 2 (figure 2.1), only about 1.8 percent of our respondents claimed that they have never used the internet to gather political information, and more than 78 percent gathered political information at least once a day. This difference in political use does not necessarily mean that social media is not a vector for critical information; it may simply reflect the fact that social media users in our sample are exposed to a lower amount of general

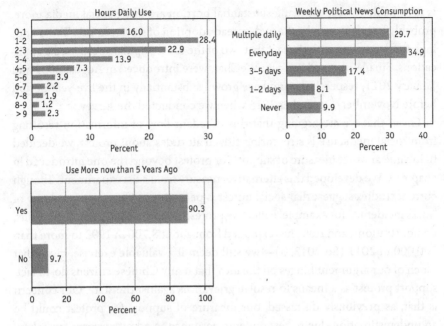

Figure 4.1 Social Media Use Distributions

political information but more critical political information on social media sites compared to other online services. This possibility is important to note because if social media sites are the most likely places for citizens to expose themselves to critical information, the fact that Chinese citizens also use other online sources (rather than social media platforms) for political information may mean that, conditional on receiving more news from non–social media sources, these users are subject to more indirect influence from the authoritarian state. This possibility agrees with our finding presented later in this volume that social media does not in and of itself stimulate support for protest. What really matters is the type of information that netizens consume on social media platforms and on the internet in general. This is why, as our theory reasons, directed digital dissidence as an authoritarian information management strategy is feasible in the first place. The information shapes the attitude (Zaller 1992).

We are interested in two additional factors. First, whether social media is a conduit for the flow of dissidence and, second, whether use of these platforms has increased over time. This could give us a sense of whether we should expect the impact to increase over time, assuming continued growth. Although we expected most would respond affirmatively to using social media more now relative to five years ago, it is a little surprising that approximately 90 percent agreed. Clearly some of this tilted distribution can also be accounted for by the more general use of the internet captured in the question, but nonetheless, it is reasonable to suspect that a substantial portion are using social media more, probably largely driven by the widespread adoption of smartphones. These findings are also in line with the fact that two of the most popular social media applications, Sina Weibo and Tencent WeChat, were introduced in August 2009 and January 2011, respectively, and have grown substantially in the five-year period before November/December 2015 when we conducted the survey.

Given that we are arguing that this dissident flow of information resulting from social media use is structuring citizen attitudes about protest, we decided to include another measure of support for protest beyond the one introduced in chapter 3. We developed this alternative measure from a list experiment. Though current studies suggest that social unrest is pervasive in China—the volume of "mass incidents," for example, collective protests such as strikes, group petitions, demonstrations, and riots, has exploded from about 8,700 in 1993 to more than 200,000 in 2011 (So 2013, 3)—we still deem it a valuable exercise, given that much of our argument hinges on the idea that many Chinese citizens do, in fact, support protest as a means to resolve grievances against the state. Our concern is that, as previously discussed, our measure of support for protest could be an underestimation due to respondents hesitance to admit support for behavior that is heavily repressed in China. Our list experiment here was structured the same way as the trust list experiment in chapter 3. All of the respondents read a statement asking them how many of the following strategies they would use if they felt wronged by the local government: work through their personal network, speak with a local government official, write to a higher level of government about the problem, offer a bribe to a local official, and the test statement, participate in a protest against the local government (Q14b1 and Q14b2). Again, only half the respondents were randomly assigned inclusion of the test statement in their version of the question. Thus, if no one was willing to protest, the mean stated number of strategies for the group of respondents receiving only four statements should not be significantly different from that of the group receiving all five statements. As was the case in chapter 3, our results indicate that many respondents are supportive of protests as an acceptable grievance strategy.

The results of this list experiment are presented in figure 4.2. The first observation worth commenting on is that a significant number of the respondents selected all five statements (see the graph on the left side of figure 4.2). Similar to the trust list experiment presented in chapter 3, these results suggest that either respondents did not understand that it would be obvious that they supported protest against the local government, or they were not concerned about this fact being known. We believe, as was the case with the trust list experiment, that respondents did not seem influenced by a social desirability effect. As seen in figure 4.2, the modal response here was two, indicating that most respondents thought two of these activities were suitable responses to being

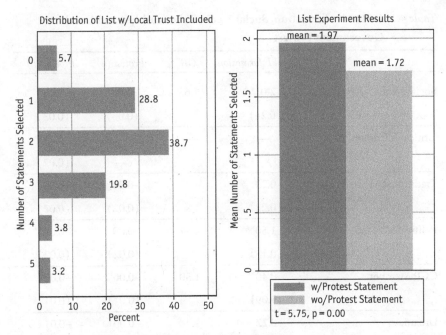

Figure 4.2 Local Government Protest List Experiment

wronged by local government. Looking at the graph on the right side of figure 4.2, the evidence suggests that a significant proportion of respondents included the test statement—participate in a protest against the local government—in their calculation. The mean number of statements selected when this statement was included was 1.97 while it was only 1.72 when it was not. This difference in means is both statistically significant, as evidenced by the t-test (t-score = 5.75, p = .00), and substantively significant. Combined with the distribution of protest activities presented in table 3.2, this list experiment suggests that support for protest against local government is quite prevalent.

In our model, we treat support for protest against the local government as a consequence of attitude formation processes. We demonstrated in chapter 3 that such support might be rooted, at least partially, in exposure to a critical flow of information. The results presented in table 4.1 provide evidence that one of the primary sources of the critical flow is, in fact, social media. Further, the results also demonstrate that this flow accounts for the observed correlation between social media and support for protest against the local government. This latter distinction is important. It clarifies that social media does not in and of itself stimulate support for protest. Rather, it is the type of information one is being exposed to or consuming on one's social media platforms that generates support for more extreme grievance strategies. Instead of social media (the technology) being the primary generator of anti-government sentiment, we hypothesize that

DIRECTED DIGITAL DISSIDENCE IN AUTOCRACIES

Table 4.1 **Critical Information, Social Media Relationships, and Local Government Protest**

	Critical Information	OR	Protest (a)	Protest (b)
Social Media	2.03**	7.63	0.06*	−0.01
	(0.24)		(0.03)	(0.03)
Critical Information	—	—	—	0.25**
	—		—	(0.02)
Traditional Media Trust	−0.23	—	−0.04	−0.03
	(0.22)		(0.02)	(0.02)
Political Interest	1.50**	4.47	−0.00	−0.06**
	(0.18)		(0.02)	(0.02)
CCP Member	0.40**	1.50	−0.00	−0.02#
	(0.09)		(0.01)	(0.01)
Urbanicity	0.22	–	−0.00	−0.01
	(0.16)		(0.02)	(0.02)
SES	1.38**	1.24	0.17**	0.12**
	(0.32)		(0.04)	(0.04)
Female	−0.30**	0.74	−0.04**	−0.03**
	(0.08)		(0.01)	(0.01)
Age	−0.58*	0.56	−0.06#	−0.03
	(0.26)		(0.03)	(0.03)
R^2	0.04		0.02	0.11
Total N	2,156		2,129	2,127

Note: Model estimates are based on ordered logit (with pseudo R^2) for the critical information and ordinary least squares (OLS) for the protest models, with standard errors in parentheses. $p^{**} \leq .01$, $p^* \leq .05$, $p^\# \leq .10$. OR = odds ratio (only displayed when $p \leq .05$).

it serves as a helpful conduit for spreading anti-government sentiment. Users still need to be exposed to dissident information flows and not just use the social media apps—a distinction we view as crucial. The importance of social media given this context is that while technology lowers the cost of both consuming and exchanging such information, it increases the potential for citizens' exposure to the critical flow. Moreover, social media sites may also enable the formation of virtual communities, protesters, and potential protesters. Even average citizens may be emboldened by other community members' emotional, organizational, tactical, and resource support. Thus, they are more likely to voice discontent and protest against the state.

This model results in table 4.1 support this line of reasoning.[4] First, it is clear that the more Chinese citizens use social media, the more likely they are to be exposed to critical information. In fact, every one-unit increase in our measure of social media use increases the odds of being one unit higher on our critical information exposure index by more than seven times.[5] This is quite substantial, as evidenced by the fact that this odds ratio is the largest among the other significant estimators in the model, of which there are quite a few. The model indicates that every one-unit increase in political interest increases the odds of being one unit higher on the critical information index by 4.47 times, which is the second-largest estimated relationship in the model. This is an interesting result, as it seems to suggest that politically interested netizens are either actively seeking or passively exposed to more critical information on social media. It is even more interesting when dovetailed with the third-largest estimated relationship in the model, being a CCP member (odds ratio = 1.50). Therefore, politically interested party members are more likely to be looking for, or exposed to, critical information compared to uninterested nonparty members, ceteris paribus. Of course, exposure does not necessarily result in changing behavior, or even necessarily a uniform impact across groups, but nonetheless this finding is interesting—it suggests that the internet is not entirely cleansed of anti-regime content and that, in fact, users are often exposed to it on social media.

For the purposes of this chapter, the most important result is that the social media estimate holds up when controlling for relevant covariates, particularly political interest. Without doing so, our confidence that social media had an independent relationship would be low. It could be just that those who are politically motivated, often dissidents or citizens with grievances (thus are critical toward the state or the local government) or at least with higher political interest, who are more likely to be exposed simply because they actively seek out more critical information generally. The model suggests that these confounders are not likely contributing to our finding.

There was nothing surprising about the results of our significant demographic controls in the model of critical information exposure (table 4.1). Those with higher SES, as measured by a one-unit change on our index, were 1.24 times more be one unit higher on the critical exposure index. Women were 0.74 times less likely to be higher on the same index, and as expected age was negatively associated with critical exposure. The odds of such exposure decreased by 0.56 times for every one year older respondents were, roughly. However, the most important point to be gleaned from these demographic controls, as with the

66 DIRECTED DIGITAL DISSIDENCE IN AUTOCRACIES

other controls, is that the estimate for the relationship between social media usage and critical exposure is still statistically significant with their inclusion. We believe the fact that most of the control variables are significant reinforcers to our finding regarding social media, allowing for meaningful comparisons of the size of the correlations—comparisons that strongly suggest that social media use has a larger influence on exposure to critical information compared to alternative explanations.

Our next set of models reinforces our contention that social media matters primarily through its role as the transmission agent of critical information. Specifically, models a and b in table 4.1 test whether the relationship between social media and support for protest is completely mediated by digital exposure to information that is critical of local government. Again, the evidence here is clear: the variance in support for various modes of protest related to social media exposure is actually a result of digital critical information exposure. It is important to clarify here that this does not mean that social media is irrelevant. Rather, it suggests the model estimates presented here are consistent with our theoretical argument that social media is consequential for the politics in China but chiefly because of its role as a conduit for the critical information flow that exists largely outside the traditional media environment.

One of the first things to note under the Protest (a) header is that the estimate for social media's relationship with protest support is positive and significant. The coefficient can be interpreted as a 0.06 increase in support for protest for every one-unit increase in social media use when excluding a control for digital critical information exposure and holding all other variables constant. However, the social media estimate is not statistically significant once the control for digital critical information exposure is introduced to the model, as seen in the Protest (b) column. Further, the positive correlation of critical information exposure is statistically significant ($p < .01$), and the magnitude is large: every one-unit increase in critical information exposure is associated with a 0.25 increase in support for protest. While R^2 statistics should be interpreted with significant caution, we also find it encouraging that adding critical information exposure to the model increases the R^2 by more than five times (from 0.02 to 0.11) as compared to model (a). We also estimated a model in which we moved support for protest to the right side of the equation, as an independent variable, and general social media use to the left side, as the dependent variable, to rule out that the causal direction runs counter to our theoretical expectation. Potentially, those who are supportive of protest are more likely to use social media. The protest estimate is not significant when controlling for critical exposure in this reversed model, suggesting that our causal model is most likely. There is some variation in the control variable relationships across the protest models in table 4.1. There are three statistically significant variables in model (a): SES, gender, and age (at the 0.10 level for this last variable). The coefficients of these variables can be interpreted as every one-unit increase in SES is associated with a 0.17 increase in support for protest, being a woman is associated with 0.04 decrease in support for protest, and for every one year older respondents were, the model estimates a 0.06 decrease in support for protest.

Model (b) adds critical information exposure to the model, which finds significance while social media loses significance. We interpret this change as supporting our hypothesis that social media is the pathway through which critical information impacts political attitudes. Moreover, the addition of critical information also improves the overall performance of the control variables—there are a total of four statistically significant control variables in the Protest (b) model. As before, SES and gender are significant in the same direction (0.12 and -0.03 estimates, respectively). The difference in this model is that age is not significant, but political interest and CCP membership are (at the 0.10 level for this variable). The model estimates that every one-unit increase in political interest is associated with a 0.06 decrease in support for protest, and that being a CCP member is associated with a 0.02 decrease in such support. Although it is perhaps expected that CCP membership may reduce one's inclination to support protest against the local government, it is interesting to see that people more interested in politics are also less likely to support various modes of protest. There are three potential explanations. First, it seems probable that politically interested citizens who actively seek news online are also exposed to more state propaganda spread by traditional state media outlets, which in turn counteracts the impact of social media. Though our model does not provide any direct evidence for this explanation, we deem this is possible because our previous analysis shows that a significant portion of our respondents seek political information from sources other than social media. It is also consistent with later results showing that the dissident effects of potential exposure to a critical information flow when jumping the firewall may be effectively dampened by pro-government information flow on the Chinese internet.

Second, it is possible that politically interested citizens have been exposed to critical information of the party-state, but such increased exposure has, over time, made them more cynical about what can be done in the face of critical information. This mechanism is similar to what Haifeng Huang (2015) argues—although state propaganda today can hardly indoctrinate the population, it signals to Chinese citizens the power of the party-state, thus reducing their tendency of resist or protest (also see Wang 2018). Third, politically interested netizens, though they might be exposed to negative news about local government and local cadres, tend to see the entire political system as the root of their problems; thus, they do not support protest against local government. They may

68   DIRECTED DIGITAL DISSIDENCE IN AUTOCRACIES

have more interest in protesting against higher levels of the government or the party-state as a whole, though, given previous research on how politically active Chinese citizens view the state (O'Brien and Li 2006; Saich 2007), we deem this explanation to be unlikely.

The Social Media User Profile

With the models suggesting that social media is consequential in spreading critical information of the party-state, we next turn to developing a profile of social media users. The correlation coefficients and associated p-values presented in table 4.2 begin to fill in this profile. In our analysis, we rely on different statistical tests based on the distributions of the variables. The only insignificant relationship is between CCP membership and social media use. The strongest relationship in the model is between political interest and social media use (p = .00).[6] Those who were more politically interested were also more likely to be exposed to critical political information (see table 4.1), and there is a relationship between general political internet use (Q4) and interest, but that relationship is not as strong as that with social media use ($\rho = 0.08$, p = .00). Using Spearman's rank-order estimation, we found that those who live in more urban settings are more likely to use social media (0.10, p = .00).

The second-largest relationship identified in table 4.2 is the positive Pearson's r estimate for the relationship between SES and social media use (0.20, p = .00). Not surprisingly, those with higher SES are more frequent users of social media. The smallest identified relationship is the point-biserial

Table 4.2 **Correlates of Social Media Use**

	Coefficient	P-Value
Political Interest	0.25	.00
CCP Member	0.03	.17
Urbanicity	0.10	.00
SES	0.20	.00
Female	0.06	.00
Age	−0.10	.00

Note: Coefficient is based on a Pearson's r for SES and age, a point-biserial correlation (Pearson's product moment) for CCP member and female, and a Spearman's rank order for political interest and urbanicity.

correlation (Pearson's product-moment correlation) between gender and social media use (0.06, p = .00). Women are slightly more likely to use social media, which is the only result here that is a bit surprising. Again though, this is only a modest relationship. Social media use encompasses a range of activity beyond political use. This is not to say that social media users tend to show less political interest compared to nonusers; in fact, our finding shows that the opposite is true. Rather, social media users can be more polarized in terms of their political interest. Although a portion of users are motivated strongly by their political interest, another portion are less political interested, even compared to the general internet population. Finally, as one would expect, the Pearson's r coefficient indicates that those who are older are less likely to use social media (-0.10, p = .00).

Our profile of social media users in China is fairly consistent with other measures. For instance, according to the 2016 *Weibo User Development Report* (Weibo Data Center 2017), active Weibo users tend to be young (70 percent are between 18 and 30), from relatively well-developed urban centers (about 67 percent are from third-tier or higher cities),[7] and well educated (77.8 percent have college level or higher degree). In terms of gender, the report shows that there are more active male Weibo users than female users, which is one of the differences from what we find in our data. However, this difference has a likely explanation. Studies have shown that male users are more active on Weibo (Wang, Qu, and Sun 2013).

Taken together, our sample demonstrates that social media users in China tend to be politically interested, urban, younger, and of higher SES. These results seem intuitive, though they still provide a useful picture of the attributes of a typical user. This user portrait is therefore an important piece of context when considering that, as we demonstrated in this chapter, digital media, and particularly social media, shape the potential for protest and, ultimately, political change. This user segment (politically interested, urban, young, high SES) is also important in the sense that it is the segment of the population most likely to shape politics in the future—the civically engaged class. Thus, social media may guide the political attitude formation of the civic class as they age into positions of responsibility. This could be especially meaningful if we are correct that social media is a vehicle for dissonant types of information. As some studies suggest, the Chinese authoritarian regime is still resilient and may even enjoy considerable amount of popular support (Nathan 2003; Shambaugh 2008; Tang 2016). In particular, the emerging middle and entrepreneur classes are not pursuing political change because they benefit from the current regime (A. Chen 2002; Chen and Dickson 2010; Dickson 2003). But our findings here suggest that the civic class in China may be exposed to significantly more informational counterflows than the current main base of party support.

Conclusion

The analysis in this chapter assessed the role social media plays in the dissemination of critical information and how it shapes Chinese citizens' support for modes of political protest. Before presenting our results, we first used descriptive analysis to demonstrate that social media use is quite prevalent and has grown in recent years. Next, we presented our analysis suggesting that (1) critical flows of information affect attitudes on protest, and (2) this flow of critical information is primarily spread via social media. Finally, we then looked at the general profile of social media users: they are more politically interested, more likely to live in an urban setting, tend to be of higher SES, and are more likely to be women and younger.

We also find that the implications of social media as a critical information vector is quite complicated. Though social media sites offer the potential for critical information flow, it does not mean that, in China, political information or criticism of the government is prevalent on such platforms, given the harsh state censorship and the proliferation of nonpolitical entertainment and consumerist and lifestyle topics. In fact, we find that a significant portion of social media users are not pursuing political goals most of the time, echoing earlier studies by scholars such as James Leibold (2011) and Jens Damm (2007). Moreover, it is also likely that social media users are subject to state influences in two ways. First, they may be exposed to traditional media and other online sources when they seek political information. Second, the Chinese party-state has tried to control and shape information flow on social media sites. They have set up thousands of official accounts representing both state agencies and individual officials on popular social media sites such as Weibo and WeChat. Such government microblogs allow the state, including the local governments, to engage in rapid information management and win the hearts and minds of citizens (Esarey 2015). It also allows them to experiment with ways to interact and negotiate with the public as well as the service providers, aiming at improving both social management and political legitimacy (Schlæger and Jiang 2014). Nevertheless, the space available on social media is broad enough that critical information does appear on these platforms. Moreover, despite the relative rarity of this content, its appearance does shape political attitudes.

The potential political effects of social media, and the internet in general, appear to be centered on shaping consequences for local government in China, with a far lesser focus on the central government. If the central government is not particularly concerned about this kind of protest, they may either actively or passively permit more of this content to flow and accept its potential consequences. This strategy seems to be an effective management of digital dissidence.

It allows an outlet of citizen dissatisfaction while deterring threats to the ruling government. Our next chapter examines the possibility of a weakness in the strategy, or a crack in the Great Firewall. In particular, we examine whether attitudes about the central government are influenced by a possible anti–central government information flow happening outside the Chinese internet, where the Chinese government has less control over information. What happens when people circumvent government filtering of the internet?

5

Jumping Over the Great Firewall

A Threat to the Chinese Strategy

The previous chapters have focused on the Chinese internet. By that we mean the digital information flow situated within the firewall. Inside the wall the central government has an active strategy aimed at managing a digital flow that paints the state in the most positive light. We have seen up to this point that this management, at least passively, permits dissidence aimed at local government. However, there are significant numbers of Chinese internet users who are able to, and do, access the internet outside of China, where information critical of the central government or the regime as a whole is readily available. In this chapter, we examine the impact of wall jumping on Chinese users and find, unsurprisingly, that access to a wider internet is associated with lower trust in both local and central governments.

Chinese authorities have been aware of the potential destabilizing possibilities afforded by new technologies. The website of the Cyberspace Administration of China reflects such concerns in the mantra that sets forth a fairly aggressive mission statement. It reads in part, "Without internet safety there can be no national safety" (Schneider 2018, 197). The Chinese experience with the destabilizing influence of technology predates the internet. During the Tiananmen Square demonstrations, the government attempted to end the demonstrations by blocking traditional communications channels in an attempt to isolate the demonstrators. Students used fax machines to organize the demonstrations and to continue communicating even after the government crackdown began (Ma 2000). The fax machine was also the means by which worldwide support was conveyed to the demonstrators, and they may have actually been partially responsible for the demonstrators' resolve to face the government directly. It may well be that the now largely discarded fax machine played a role in emboldening the young man who famously faced down a tank.

Directed Digital Dissidence in Autocracies. Jason Gainous, Rongbin Han, Andrew W. MacDonald, and Kevin M. Wagner, Oxford University Press. © Oxford University Press 2024. DOI: 10.1093/oso/9780197680384.003.0005

Autocratic states have long been familiar with the danger of open communication and the power of information platforms. The history of autocracies can be told through the efforts to control the flow of information. From attempts to control the printing press up through Soviet repression of the underground samizdat, authoritarian regimes have generally placed strict limits on how citizens can use communication technologies. Indeed, President Harry S. Truman once referred to the heart of the Cold War conflict as "a struggle for the minds and loyalties of mankind." (Spalding 2006, 44). However, there are repeated historical examples of regimes misjudging the potential impact of new mass media technologies or finding themselves unable to counter the development of technology, as the Eastern Bloc autocrats found out the hard way with Radio Free Europe, which is credited with fueling opposition to the Soviet Union (Granville 2005). Digital communications took much of the Middle East by surprise and played a substantial role in the Arab Spring (Howard 2010; Howard and Hussain 2013) and even subsequently in Russia's Snow Revolution (Gainous, Wagner, and Ziegler 2018).

This experience is mirrored in part in China. During the 1980s, the Chinese government was slow to address the political possibilities afforded by the expansion of digital technologies. This inattention was mixed with a general sense of optimism and opening up of new intellectual spaces afforded by the change in direction of Chinese development brought on by the reform-minded Deng Xiaoping. There was an intellectual current within the Chinese government that viewed the new technologies as way to catch up economically and technologically (Harwit 1998; Mu and Lee 2005; Qiu 2004; Zheng 2008). This combination of circumstances meant that telecommunications remained essentially unregulated during the 1980s.

As with the rest of the nascent intellectual openness of the 1980s, this laissez-faire attitude ended with the events of Tiananmen Square in 1989. While much of the world was transfixed by the television broadcasts of students demonstrating in the square, students were busy using fax machines to communicate with each other and with the outside world (Ma 2000). Alerted to the potentiality of information technology to serve as a means of counter-regime mobilization (and, perhaps, also alerted to the fragility of the party's rule), introduction of the internet in China came paired with strict controls on its use. In particular, the government formed a working group in 1996 to divide the internet in two: an internet internal to China and another, more limited internet for accessing sites outside of China (Qiu 2004). From this small administrative stroke developed one of the most sophisticated regimes of cyber-control, in which government monitors block and prevent Chinese netizens from accessing any content outside of China that they deem harmful and also heavily censor and police domestically controlled internet services (OpenNet Initiative 2005; Qiu 2004; Roberts

2018; Walton 2001). The result, as discussed in chapter 4, is that the domestic digital sphere is increasingly monitored and controlled, though not as tightly as traditional media platforms.

Measures of Effectiveness: Simply Preventing Wall Jumping?

There is sizable scholarship considering the importance of the internet in general to political engagement and discourse in China. The areas that is less well studied is how access to materials outside the Chinese sphere is influencing the discourse. In this chapter we explore how many Chinese internet users are escaping the walled garden of the Chinese internet and how that experience is affecting their political attitudes about the state. We know based on the access restrictions that the Chinese state is wary of the influence of Western platforms and the information they contain, but there is actually little research on whether that fear is well grounded. Nonetheless, if we extend the logic of attitudes being a product of the information available (Zaller 1992), then it is reasonable to assume there should be differences for consumers of information outside the closely tended Chinese internet.

The situation in China presents an interesting test of the importance of the internet in allowing access to dissident information in an otherwise controlled information state. This is not unique in practice, though it is strikingly large in scope. As noted above, there is a history of states attempting to gain the commercial advantages that broad access to the internet provides, while trying to limit the political implications of this new online forum (Howard 2010; Zheng 2008). Other authoritarian regimes also play a cat and mouse game with internet users as monitoring agencies attempt to limit access to platforms and news outside of the control of the regime. Some states have proven fairly effective, at least in the short term. Russia's crackdown on opposition voices in 2016 proved to be fairly effective at reducing overt dissidence when compared with the fairly open domestic internet in 2011 (Gainous et al. 2018).

However, few nations could even attempt to limit and control information at the level that China currently does, with one of the more sophisticated and extensive internet control schemes in the world. Most other regimes tolerate some level of internet freedom and, when faced with a major crisis, simply shut off the internet altogether to prevent its use as a site of mobilization. In a recent example of this approach, Iran responded to popular protests in just this way (Kadivar 2019). A complete shutdown is a blunt instrument and often the solution of last resort when the state lacks the knowledge or sophistication to otherwise suppress dissident information. Russia's effective crackdown in 2016 was targeted and left the internet functional but limited (Gainous, Wagner, and Ziegler 2018). China's internet controls are sophisticated. China has the ability to not only limit information online but to direct and manage it in ways that serve the greater state. The domestic internet in China is a far more curated and limited vehicle for dissidence than is often seen in countries that lack the sophistication and ability of the Chinese state.

Hence, there are two different cyber spheres in China that are worth exploring. There is the existing walled domestic internet that is tightly curated and controlled and the more open internet that Chinese citizens can access if they escape the constraints imposed by the state. For clarity and consistency, we will define bypassing the online censorship as wall jumping. From existing research, we know that wall jumping in other regimes can lead to mobilization potential for those able to overcome the controls. The Arab Spring riots were significantly aided by Western social media platforms that allowed protesters to exchange information and organize against the state. While the impact of the internet appears to have been uneven across nations, many Egyptians and Tunisians used Facebook to organize protests and spread awareness (Howard and Hussain 2013). External outlets often provide information and perspective that form the basis for shifting attitudes and behaviors.

Although we agree that wall jumping can supply energy to a protest movement, in this chapter we seek to expand the inquiry beyond the immediate utility of outside social media platforms and their otherwise restricted dissident information. While China has had its share of short-term digitally fueled protests, the larger question is whether outside information can create a more sustained and stable opposition to the state and its informational narrative. Our question is broader: Does long-term exposure to foreign websites and platforms shift how users see the state? On one hand, perhaps it is obvious that seeing unrestricted content should influence political views away from support for the government. There is certainly proof the state believes this to be the case, as they are motivated to stringently limit access (Roberts 2018).[1] On the other, there are a number of issues with this assumption. Initially, there is a reverse causation issue with this analysis. Netizens might jump the wall because they are already dissidents. The information seeking might be the result of preexisting attitudes. Though, that may not be the case either. Users may be jumping the firewall for access to games, software, and entertainment as well (Yang and Liu 2014). It is difficult to arbitrate between the possibility that users who already hold anti-regime views are the most likely to jump the wall from the possibility that wall jumping itself has an independent correlation.

Yet, even if we presume that attitudes are being influenced by information outside the state-curated internet, the correlations might be smaller than anticipated for technical reasons like language barriers and limited understandings of outside information platforms. While translation software continues to improve, content is often not in the native language of outside users on platforms that are blocked within a country. These structural restrictions align with China's efforts to guide users. In China, the firewall is often porous, and blocking uses the natural desire for ease of access to guide users to preferred content rather than completely walling off some types of non-preferred content (Roberts 2018).

Hence, there is a fair amount to understand and unpack about the effect of wall jumping on users motivated enough to do it. The answer is in our data, and the influence of wall jumping depends primarily on what the users are being exposed to when they do wall jump, but this answer is premature at this point, as we lack the foundation. In this chapter, we will drill down a bit deeper to see whether we can answer the basic questions concerning the people who are dodging government restrictions on information consumption: Who are the wall jumpers? How large is this group? What are they seeking when they evade the government controls of the internet? What is the nature of the information consumed? Once we establish the characteristics and behavior of this group, we will return to the questions of effect and changing attitudes.

We begin our exploration by testing how many users actually seek to evade the internet controls. Next, we try to estimate just how frequently they do so, and, when they jump the wall, whether they do so to tap into a flow of politically sensitive information or for other reasons. As in the previous chapter, those answering questions related to wall jumping may be tempted to provide answers the respondents deem safe because of concern that they are being monitored. It is additionally possible that respondents are also afraid to provide accurate answers because of a deeper form of preference falsification, in that they may find it personally convenient to underestimate the amount of subversive behavior they engage in. Therefore, to more accurately assess our research questions, we first employed a list experiment to test whether people are jumping the wall (Q15a1 and Q15a2). From the existing research (Hobbs and Roberts 2018), we know that many Chinese internet users do use tools like virtual private networks (VPNs) to get around content blocks, but the list experiment allows us to assess the degree to which this occurs in the aggregate by allowing respondents to indicate this without explicitly admitting it. Because of how crucial wall jumping may be in observing alternative critical information flows, we believe, of the list experiments that we include in this book, the one examined in this chapter may be the most important. Overall, we suspect that respondents might be more reluctant to admit jumping the firewall than admit their distrust of the local government or support of protest against local governments.

The results presented in figure 5.1 are clear. Many Chinese citizens are actively circumventing digital filters and blocks to seek sensitive political information. Respondents were all told they would be given a list of things that people often

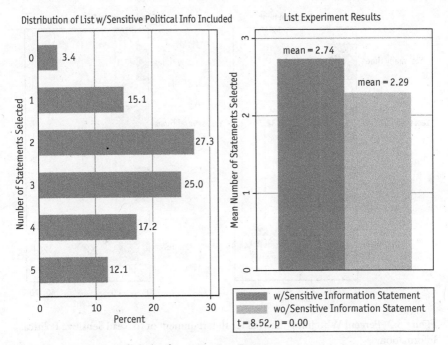

Figure 5.1 Sensitive Political Information List Experiment

see on the internet and then asked to state how many they have seen. The list included these four items for all respondents: dating website advertisements, an angry debate between netizens, religious or spiritual information, and negative news about a celebrity. Then half the respondents were randomly selected for inclusion in their list the fifth item: politically sensitive information. The modal number of items selected under the treatment condition was two (27.3 percent) followed closely by three items (25 percent). The result that is quite remarkable here, though, is the fact that slightly more than 12 percent of the respondents selected all five statements. This is significantly higher than the proportion of respondents who selected all five items in the trust and protest list experiments in chapters 3 and 4, respectively. As such, it is not surprising that the results of the list experiment test here were positive. The mean number of statements selected under the treatment condition was statistically significantly higher than the mean number for those not given the treatment item (2.74 relative to 2.29, p = .00). Clearly, many Chinese citizens are jumping the firewall to get politically sensitive information.

This point is further demonstrated by the results of non-list experiment questions presented in figure 5.2. Respondents were asked whether they had tried to access blocked websites or other blocked internet services to read sensitive political information (Q25) or to watch foreign movies, television shows, and

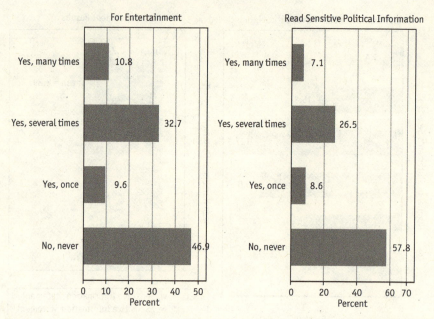

Figure 5.2 Percent Who Jump the Wall for Entertainment or to Read Sensitive Political Information

other entertainment content (Q26). We asked about jumping the wall for entertainment purposes to allow us to compare the distribution to doing so to read sensitive political information. This gives us a sense of motivation. We expected in these questions that citizens would indicate that they were more likely to jump the wall for entertainment than to tap into a dissident flow of information, and although this expectation is borne out in the results, the difference is not large. Nearly 47 percent claim to never jump the wall to seek out entertainment, and roughly 58 percent say that they never do so to get sensitive political information. That said, nearly 32 percent and 27 percent, respectively, say they have jumped the wall several times for these purposes. This latter result is quite substantial. A sizable proportion of our sample of Chinese internet users are peeking over the wall to tap into a dissident flow of information.

In summary, there is strong evidence that Chinese internet users routinely skirt internet controls, in part to view sensitive political content but also to view entertainment programs such as the *Big Bang Theory* that are not permitted to be shown by central government censors. These results dovetail with recent research by William Hobbs and Margaret Roberts (2018), showing that internet users, once past the firewall, explore more than whatever initially motivated them to evade the internet controls. However, that leaves open the question of what, if any, impact wall jumping has on netizen's political opinions.

Does Jumping the Wall Matter?

The question here is whether jumping the wall exposes some of the Chinese internet users to dissonant flows of information that include criticism of not only their local government but also, crucially, the central government. To review, the existing literature and the information we presented in previous chapters strongly suggest that within the Chinese domestic internet, to the extent that there is a dissident flow of information, it is largely aimed at critique of the local government. Our initial assumption was that exposure to a freer internet on the other side of the Great Firewall would expose users to a flow of information critical of the central government. As with all our sensitive questions, we had to be careful about asking questions centered on critique of the central government because we were concerned about both a reluctance to answer honestly and potential difficulty in clearing the Institutional Review Board, Qualtrics, and Chinese government censorship in implementing our survey. Our strategy was to bundle our question about the central government (Q13A) with questions about other institutions and ask another question regarding overall government satisfaction (Q7), a strategy that we believed would lead respondents to feel comfortable answering honestly, though admittedly we are a little more cautious in interpreting results based on these questions than for other subjects. The analysis below primarily focuses on differences in central government satisfaction rather than overall levels of satisfaction—we are not confident enough in our results to make definitive statements about absolute opinion levels on the central government.

The distribution of each of these items is presented in figure 5.3. They are both skewed toward favorability of the government. This runs counter to the results regarding trust in the local government (figure 3.1), where the bulk of respondents fell on the distrusting side of the scale. This result is consistent with what we would expect if there is both a reluctance to admit distrust or support for the central government, and if the central government's control of the flow of information—digitally and traditionally—is influential. The results indicate specifically, first, that significantly more than half of the respondents expressed either quite a lot of trust or a great deal of trust in the central government (more than 83 percent when these categories are collapsed). Second, consistent with those results, the majority of respondents are either fairly satisfied or very satisfied with the way government works in China (nearly 70 percent when collapsed). Clearly, the distribution of the former is slightly more skewed than the latter; perhaps this is a product of respondents mixing their evaluations of the central and local government in the latter. Taken altogether here though, a sizable proportion of respondents express some degree of distrust and dissatisfaction.

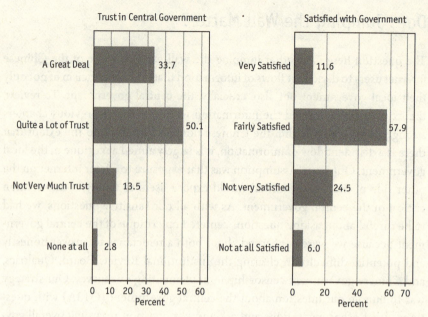

Figure 5.3 Percent Who Trust the Central Government and Are Satisfied with Government

More than 16 percent indicate that they do not have very much trust or none at all in the central government, and nearly 30 percent say that they are either not very satisfied or not satisfied at all with the way government works in China. However, our primary interest is in the differential level of satisfaction with the central government created by wall jumping: Does going over the wall lead to users experiencing enough different content that it affects their trust and satisfaction levels?

The results presented in table 5.1 are estimates of the relationship of wall jumping to both trust and satisfaction, ceteris paribus.[2] We constructed an additive index of the two wall-jumping indicators (Q25 and Q26),[3] and then specified models of each of these outcomes as a function of said index while controlling for general internet use, traditional media trust, political interest, CCP membership, and the other basic demographics we have been relying on throughout. The results here are clear; wall jumping is negatively related on both counts while holding these other factors constant. The odds ratios suggest that every one-unit increase on our wall-jumping index increases the odds of being one category lower on the trust in central government measure by 0.37 times, and by 0.49 times on the satisfaction with government measure.

It is important that these estimates hold up while controlling for alternative explanations of trust and satisfaction. On that front, the model results remain

Table 5.1 **The Wall Jumping Relationship with Trust in the Central Government and General Satisfaction with Government**

	Trust in the Central Government				
	Estimate	*S.E.*	*95% CI*		*OR*
Wall Jumping	−0.99	0.16	−1.31	−0.67	0.37
General Internet Use	1.86	0.31	1.25	2.47	6.40
Traditional Media Trust	5.48	0.29	4.91	6.06	240.09
Political Interest	1.44	0.22	1.01	1.87	4.23
CCP Member	0.39	0.11	0.18	0.60	1.48
Urbanicity	−0.44	0.20	−0.83	−0.05	0.65
SES	−1.32	0.39	−2.09	−0.55	0.27
Female	−0.26	0.10	−0.45	−0.07	0.77
Age	−1.03	0.32	−1.67	−0.40	0.36
Pseudo R^2 = 0.16					
N = 1891					
	General Satisfaction with Government				
Wall Jumping	−0.71	0.16	−1.03	−0.39	0.49
General Internet Use	2.62	0.32	2.00	3.24	13.71
Traditional Media Trust	4.82	0.28	4.27	5.37	123.50
Political Interest	1.04	0.22	0.61	1.47	2.83
CCP Member	0.38	0.11	0.16	0.60	1.46
Urbanicity	0.04	0.20	−0.35	0.43	—
SES	−0.92	0.40	−1.71	−0.13	0.40
Female	0.19	0.10	−0.01	0.38	—
Age	−1.27	0.33	−1.91	−0.63	0.28
Pseudo R^2 = 0.06					
N = 1901					

Note: Estimates are derived using ordered logit. S.E. = standard error, CI = confidence interval, OR = odds ratio (odds ratios are only displayed when 0 is not bounded in the respective CI).

consistent. Every control variable is significant in the trust model, and all but two are significant in the satisfaction model (urbanicity and gender). Among those significant relationships, the largest in magnitude is the positive correlations of traditional media trust in both models. The odds ratio is a substantively large 240.09 in the trust model and 123.5 in the satisfaction model. This finding is not surprising, given the landscape of Chinese media, and it lends additional support to our argument. In particular, the traditional media is under the control of the state, and as such, content that is critical of the central government is largely or wholly absent in its programming. It stands to reason that those who place a great deal of trust in such media would have generally positive feelings about the central government. Importantly for our argument is that the coefficient estimate of wall jumping on the trust and satisfaction estimate remains statistically and substantively significant when fully controlling for other such large relationships. Putting it another way, even citizens with an average level of trust in traditional media still tend to be distrusting of and dissatisfied with the central government if they score highly on the wall-jumping propensity measure.

As for the other control variables in the models, none of the estimated relationships are as large as that of traditional media trust, but they are still consequential. For instance, the positive relationship of political interest is substantial in both models—the odds ratio is 4.23 in the trust model and 2.83 in the satisfaction model. Those who are politically interested clearly have largely positive evaluations of the central government. Unsurprisingly, members of the CCP are also generally supportive. The odds ratio indicates that they are on average 1.48 times more likely to be in a higher response category on the trust measure than nonmembers and 1.46 times more likely than nonmembers to be higher on the satisfaction measure. More urban respondents are less likely to be trusting (odds ratio = 0.65), higher-SES respondents are less likely to be trusting of and satisfied with government (odds ratios = 0.27 and 0.40, respectively), women are less likely to be trusting (odds ratio = 0.77), and for every year older, respondents' average odds of being trusting and satisfied decreased, respectively, by 0.36 and 0.28 times. Overall, the fully controlled model adds support to our hypothesis that wall jumping likely exposes users to a counterflow of information that leads to less trust in the central government.

Conclusion

The results presented in this chapter make clear three main points: (1) Many citizens are jumping the wall, in part at least to gather sensitive political information. (2) Distrust in the central government and dissatisfaction with government in general is not uncommon. (3) The more likely citizens are to jump the wall, the less trusting and satisfied they are with the central government. These results have added an empirical twist to the narrative here. We began early in the book demonstrating that digital media consumption was consequential for citizen attitudes about local governments, even the inclination to protest against local governments. This result, we suggest, is driven by exposure to a critical flow of digital information about local governments. This is an acceptable outcome for the central government because it is not a direct threat to their authority. Whether actively or passively, the central government's digital information management strategy seems to be effective. The complicating factor (and key driver for the creation of the firewall) is that, as expected, user exposure to a digital media environment outside the party-state's control engenders less trust and satisfaction in the central government. Here dissidence is not so easy to control and, as the results have shown, can potentially structure citizen attitudes in a way that could pose a threat to central government hegemony.

This result is not surprising for two reasons. The first is that, as has been shown many times in the literature on authoritarian regimes, an uncontrolled counternarrative to that provided by the state is dangerous for an authoritarian regime. We merely extend this finding into the digital realm. Second, it would be somewhat surprising that the regime (and other, similarly controlling autocratic regimes) would expend so much effort on creating a system of blocking external content if that same content had no impact on popular opinion of the central government. If this is the case, further exploration of the prevalence of wall jumping, of the motivations underlying wall jumping, and of the ease with which citizens can do so will help paint a more complete picture of how dangerous a threat this finding actually poses to the regime. Additionally, developing a general profile of wall jumpers will help lay the foundation for understanding the final finding presented in this book, that the Chinese central government has the digital flow and its consequences well managed even in the face of this potential threat. The next empirical chapter proceeds to build this foundation.

6

The Digital Dissident Citizen

Who Are the Wall Jumpers?

In the previous chapter, we provided evidence that many citizens choose to bypass the limited scope of the Chinese internet and venture to the other side of the Great Firewall. In this chapter, we offer a more nuanced description of those who evade government controls. Initially, we examine the awareness of wall jumping. Using a series of questions related to perceptions of wall jumping, we consider whether overcoming censorship is not only something citizens do but, crucially, whether it is a behavior that citizens believe *others* are doing. We used a battery of questions to explore this issue and to uncover how pervasive citizens believe wall jumping may be. We also considered why respondents think people do it and how easy they believe it is, from a technical perspective. We then attempted to construct the picture of what demographic values predict who jumps the firewall and compare the results with the expectations of both our respondents and the previous studies in this area.

To begin to understand citizen perceptions about how many other people are jumping the wall, we first asked respondents to estimate how many people they knew who had accessed blocked websites or other blocked internet services (Q23). This allows us to build an indicator of the pervasiveness of wall jumping while avoiding respondents' reluctance to admit whether they do it themselves. The distribution of responses is presented in figure 6.1. This graph suggests that wall jumping is perceived to be quite pervasive. Well over half of the sample claims to know at least one person who bypasses the Chinese firewall. In fact, slightly more than 12 percent claim to know more than 10 wall jumpers, nearly 17 percent claim to know 5–10, and around 24 percent 2–4. Given the results presented in the previous chapter demonstrating that wall jumping has a clear negative association with both trust in the central government and satisfaction with government generally, widespread wall jumping could threaten the hegemony of the central government if this sentiment ever actualized into resistance.

Directed Digital Dissidence in Autocracies. Jason Gainous, Rongbin Han, Andrew W. MacDonald, and Kevin M. Wagner,
Oxford University Press. © Oxford University Press 2024. DOI: 10.1093/oso/9780197680384.003.0006

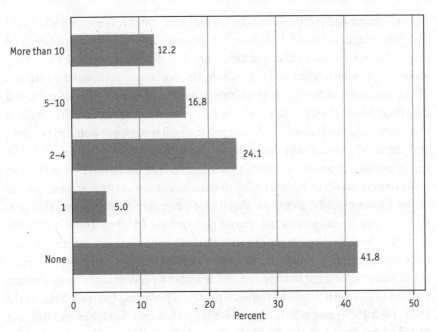

Figure 6.1 Distribution of the Number of People Citizens Claim to Know as Wall Jumpers

Table 6.1 **The Reasons Citizens Believe Their Friends Jump the Wall**

	No	Yes
Foreign Media	64.3%	35.7%
Foreign Entertainment	38.1%	61.9%
Political Content	53.7%	46.3%
	N = 1,325	

That wall jumping is thought to be a common activity also undermines or erodes social stigmas associated with rule breaking and normalizes those who seek to access blocked content. If the perception is that many people are jumping the wall, the obvious question is what respondents consider the reasons for doing so. Belief that other users are jumping the wall simply for entertainment purposes as opposed to accessing political content may impact the contagion effect incentivizing others to do the same.

Consistent with the results presented in figure 5.2 in the previous chapter, those presented in table 6.1 suggest that citizens are most likely to jump the wall to seek out entertainment. Here, though, we asked for the reasons people believed their friends jumped the wall, and along with seeking foreign entertainment and political content, we inquired about foreign media (Q24).[1] The percentages in table 6.1 are based on yes/no responses to each option, and respondents were asked this question only if they indicated in Q23 that they knew people who has jumped the wall. Again, the largest marginal distribution of the options was foreign entertainment, where nearly 62 percent indicated that their friends jumped the wall for this purpose. Slightly less than half, at 46 percent, claimed their friends jumped the wall to seek out political content, and about 36 percent said their friends did so to get foreign media. This last one is perhaps the most interesting. It suggests that many internet users, and wall jumpers in particular, are trying to circumvent central government control of the Chinese media to get an alternative perspective; oftentimes, this perspective may be counter to the central government framing. These results are consistent with findings in other authoritarian countries that government controls and attempts to evade these controls are not always or even principally about political content but are rather attempts to prevent users from viewing content that is what might be termed spiritually polluting (Barrale 2018; Gold 1984; Link 1987; Nagle 2010; Rundle 2018). However, as Hobbs and Roberts (2018) have found, it is very likely that, whatever the initial motivation for jumping the wall, once users are over it, they engage in and seek out other sensitive content.

Related to perceptions of how many other people they know evade internet controls is the question of how difficult users believe it would be to jump the wall themselves. From a technical perspective, there are many free VPN apps and services available for smartphone and desktop in China (of varying quality) that can help users evade the firewall, though the consistency with which they work is relatively low (Roberts 2018). However, users may be unaware that VPN services exist, may be intimidated by their technical nature, or have heard of them but not know where to search themselves. To better understand how users perceive the difficulty of evading controls, we asked respondents how easy it was to access foreign blocked websites (Q21). The distribution of responses to this question are shown in figure 6.2. One of the more surprising results was that about 21 percent of our respondents said that they did not know that foreign websites such as Google were not accessible. We are not sure whether this means that they had never tried to access such sites, or whether they were actually unaware that the government blocked access to foreign websites more specifically (that is, perhaps they were completely unaware of the existence of the Great Firewall). Conversely, nearly 20 percent indicated that it was impossible to access these sites. From a technical perspective, it is relatively easy to find a VPN service if you know where to search and access the sites. However, again emphasizing the importance of the social and word-of-mouth factors, if you are unaware that these services exist, from these respondents' perspective, it would

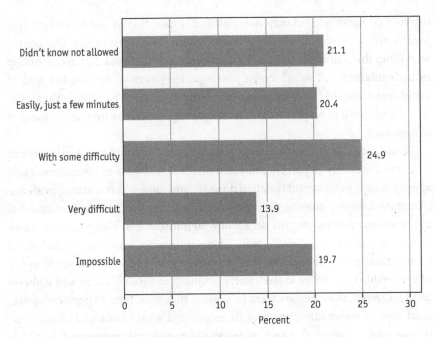

Figure 6.2 How Easy Is It to Access Foreign Websites

seem impossible to access these sites. The population of more aware and technically savvy users is also a significant category; 20 percent claimed that the filters could be easily circumvented in just a few minutes. Others did not agree that it was so easy—24.9 percent said it could be done but with some difficulty, and 13.9 percent claimed that it was very difficult—but nonetheless, they still indicated that it was possible. Taken together, though some users find jumping the wall challenging, overall the results here suggest that most citizens do not seem overly deterred, at least by the technical difficulty.

These results all seem to suggest that awareness is a key factor in whether one jumps the wall. But what motivates users to make the leap from awareness to actually seeking out a VPN-like service? That is to say, we know respondents' self-reported content interest while jumping the wall, and how easy they believe it would be to jump the wall, but what is the breaking point or key event that pushes users to actually download a VPN or proxy service? Our survey does not contain detailed questions in that regard, but we want to highlight another indicator that we believe sheds light on this question. Respondents were asked whether they had ever changed the content of what they intended to write on a blog, Weibo post, WeChat message, forum post, or other online post so as to avoid being censored (Q22). This question's intent was to understand how much pressure users felt to conform to the central government's desired thought control. Respondents who feel compelled to delete or tailor their posts to avoid censorship are clearly aware of, and responding to, the central government's management of the digital information flow. Presumably, the people who jump the wall are same people who would seek to avoid digital censorship in their internet and social media postings. They may go beyond the wall to avoid censorship not only in consumption of information but also in sharing it. The distribution of responses on the censorship avoidance item are presented in figure 6.3.

While about 62 percent claimed to have never done this, the startling result here was that nearly 25 percent indicated that they had done so several times and approaching 7 percent said they had done it many times. This is strong evidence that many Chinese internet users are well aware that the central government is monitoring and managing the digital flow of information. This awareness likely motivates citizens to jump the wall. These results are again consistent with a finding that having content blocked or posts removed (i.e., being made aware of censorship) can serve as the catalyst to jump the wall (Hobbs and Roberts 2018). Overall, these results seem to suggest that what type of person you are, what type of information you seek to access, and what your social characteristics are relate significantly to whether you can consistently get around the Great Firewall. How these relate to demographic factors is an issue we explore further in the following section.

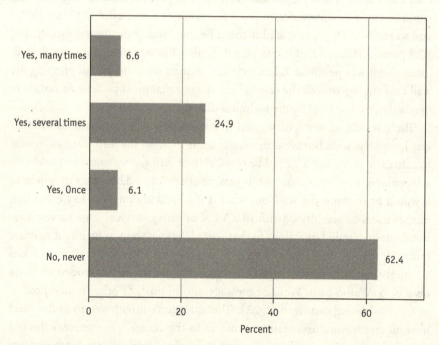

Figure 6.3 Changed the Content of a Post to Avoid Censorship

A Profile of Wall Jumpers

To better understand who is jumping the wall, in this section we attempt to develop a richer profile of those who evade government controls. In the existing literature, little is known, in the aggregate, about what kind of people evade controls. Most work has been anecdotal and emphasized profiles of young digital activists (Mou, Wu, and Atkin 2016; Shen and Zhang 2018; Yang and Liu 2014), though the prevalence of those jumping the wall primarily for entertainment reasons seems to suggest that such activists may not be the modal wall hopper.

Who is trying to avoid censorship, who are these wall jumpers, and why do they do both these things? Clearly, citizens try to avoid consequences by avoiding censorship, and they jump because they want to get something that is not available on the Chinese internet. That said, the characteristics of who is most likely to avoid censorship and jump the wall such as demographic variables are less clear. Further, some of the behavioral variables are uncertain as well. Are those who use both the internet generally and social media more frequently likelier to avoid censorship and jump the wall? Do those who avoid censorship also jump the wall? We address all these questions by, first, looking at the bivariate relationship between potential demographic and behavioral variables of censorship avoidance and wall jumping, and second, we model each, including all variables, to get a sense of how these factors may work together to explain why citizens engage in these dissident behaviors. This also allows us to test whether those who attempt to avoid censorship are also wall jumpers.

We begin with a look at the bivariate relationship between avoiding censorship and general internet use, social media use, political interest, CCP membership, urbanicity, SES, gender, and age. We do so by examining the conditional distributions. Because general internet use, social media use, and SES are distributed continuously, we collapsed them by creating mean-based dummy variables (0 = at or below the mean, 1 = above the mean). This allowed us to get a better sense of the conditional distributions by reducing the number of categories. Likewise, we collapsed urbanicity into three categories (countryside/village and small city, midsized city, and suburban area of a big city and big city). Finally, age is broken into quintiles to make it manageable for the analysis.

The results presented in table 6.2 are the all the conditional distributions of each of the abovementioned variables across the frequency with which respondents said they changed their posts' content in an attempt to avoid censorship. With the exception of the conditional distributions across urbanicity and gender, all of the others are statistically significant (we rely on a X^2 test of cell independence for all the bivariate tests here). Again, these are only bivariate comparisons, so we cannot assume that these relationships will all hold up

Table 6.2 **Who Is Avoiding Censorship?**

	Many Times	Several Times	Once	Never	Total N
Internet Use					
≤ Mean %	4.2	13.8	6.6	75.4	1,043
>Mean %	8.6	34.3	5.7	51.5	1,238
		$X^2 = 164.5$, p-value = .00			
Social Media Use					
≤ Mean %	3.3	18.1	7.3	71.3	790
>Mean %	8.3	28.6	5.4	57.7	1,491
		$X^2 = 60.89$, p-value = .00			
Political Interest					
Very interested %	13.5	24.7	4.4	57.5	637
Somewhat interested %	3.7	28.6	6.1	61.2	1,226
Somewhat uninterested %	3.9	15.2	9.7	71.2	330
Very uninterested %	6.0	13.3	3.6	77.1	83
		$X^2 = 110.43$, p-value = .00			
CCP Membership					
Yes %	5.6	23.6	6.4	64.5	1,731
No %	9.5	29.3	5.3	55.9	546
		$X^2 = 20.89$, p-value = .00			
Urbanicity					
Countryside/Small City %	6.5	20.4	5.5	67.7	476
Mid-sized City %	6.1	25.9	6.4	61.6	607
Suburban/Big City %	6.9	26.8	6.0	60.4	1,174
		$X^2 = 9.35$, p-value = .16			
SES					
≤ Mean %	5.2	18.3	7.0	69.5	1,091
>Mean %	7.8	31.0	5.3	55.9	1,190
		$X^2 = 61.95$, p-value = .00			
Gender					
Male %	7.2	26.0	6.0	60.8	1,195
Female %	5.9	23.8	6.2	64.1	1,084
		$X^2 = 3.62$, p-value = .31			

Table 6.2 **Continued**

	Many Times	Several Times	Once	Never	Total N
Age					
1st Quintile %	5.9	27.0	7.7	59.4	492
2nd Quintile %	9.9	29.4	7.2	53.6	487
3rd Quintile %	6.5	26.1	5.8	61.6	417
4th Quintile %	5.9	23.7	5.9	64.4	455
5th Quintile %	4.4	17.5	3.3	74.8	428
			$X^2 = 52.65$, p-value = .00		

when controlling for each, but nonetheless, it helps us to start building a profile of those who seek to avoid censorship. The next important observation we can make here is that the relationship between both digital information consumption items and avoidance of censorship is quite strong. This will become very important as we move toward the ultimate finding of our research in the next chapter; that is, that frequency of consumption seems to counter the potential effects of wall jumping on the inclination to protest. We will demonstrate shortly that wall jumpers also tend to attempt to avoid censorship, in line with our previous supposition that what may be motivating them is direct experience contemplating censorship.

Perhaps the most telling cell comparison across internet use and censorship avoidance in table 6.2 is between those who claim to never seek to avoid censorship across low ($\leq$) and high ($>$) internet use. Here roughly 75 percent of low internet users said they never alter their posts to avoid censorship while only 51.5 percent of high users claimed the same. Further, 34.3 percent of high users indicated that they had done this several times, relative to only 13.8 percent of low users. It is important to remember that our sample consists entirely of internet users, so this is not a comparison of nonusers to users. These results are mirrored when looking at social media use and censorship avoidance. This is a particularly meaningful result, as research has suggested that social media may be the primary outlet for the exchange of critical or dissident information in authoritarian contexts (Gainous, Wagner, and Gray 2016; Gainous, Wagner, and Ziegler 2018) and postings of the sort that one might feel compelled to alter to avoid censorship. Only 18.1 percent of low social media users claimed to have altered their posts to avoid censorship, while 28.6 percent of high users claimed to do so. In addition, 71.3 percent of low users said they had never done so, relative to 57.7 percent of high users. Taken altogether, it is evident that those who are more digitally active are also more likely to attempt to avoid censorship.

The results also suggest that the more politically interested among our sample are more likely to attempt to avoid censorship. It is clear when looking at table 6.2 that the percentage of those who claim to never alter their posts to avoid censorship goes up as political interest goes down, and the opposite is generally true for those who claim have done so many times and several times. As one would expect, CCP members are significantly less likely to alter posts to avoid censorship; the percentages of those who claim to frequently do so are higher for non-members, and the percentage who claim to never do so are significantly higher for members. Likewise, those living in more urban settings are more likely to alter their posts than those who do not, but again, this relationship is not statistically significant. The relationship between SES and censorship avoidance is statistically significant, indicating that high-SES respondents are more likely to alter their posts to avoid censorship. Again, there is no apparent gender difference. Finally, there is a clear, and statistically significant, relationship between age and censorship avoidance. As one would expect, younger respondents are much more likely to do so, and among the oldest in the sample (the fifth quintile), close to 75 percent claim to never have done so, while only 59.4 percent of those in the first quintile fall in this category. In summary, the results in table 6.2 suggest that those who consume digital information frequently, the politically interested, those not affiliated with the CCP, higher-SES respondents, and young people are more likely to alter their digital posts to avoid censorship, exposing themselves to a possible motivation for jumping the wall.

The next set of bivariate analyses examine the potential relationship between all the same variables as those in table 6.2 but across the propensity to jump the wall. Because our measure of wall jumping is a two-item index (refer back to chapter 5 to the details), it can be treated as a continuous measure here, and thus, we rely on t-tests to examine the relationships between it and our dichotomous variables and one-way analysis of variance (ANOVA) tests when the variable includes more than two categories. These results are presented in table 6.3. The first observation we make here is that every single test is statistically significant. The next, and perhaps most important, foundation to our developing argument here is that the raw difference in wall jumping across both internet use measures, general and social media, is quite large. Those who are at or below the mean on our internet use measure average 0.22 on the wall jumping measure, and those above the mean internet use average 0.40. Likewise, those at or beneath the mean on the social media use indicator average 0.24 on the wall jumping measure, and those above the mean average 0.36. Both results lay the foundation for the findings presented in the next chapter that suggest the influence of digital exposure beyond the wall may be partially mitigated by exposure to the digital flow on the Chinese internet. The people who are more likely to jump the wall are also the people who use the internet more and, as such, are more likely

Table 6.3 **Average Propensity to Jump the Wall**

	Mean	S.D.	P-Value
Internet Use			
≤ Mean	0.22	0.28	
>Mean	0.40	0.33	.00
Social Media Use			
≤ Mean	0.24	0.29	
>Mean	0.36	0.33	.00
Political Interest			
Very interested	0.40	0.36	
Somewhat interested	0.31	0.31	
Somewhat uninterested	0.23	0.27	
Very uninterested	0.17	0.30	.00
CCP Membership			
Yes	0.31	0.32	
No	0.35	0.34	.01
Urbanicity			
Countryside / Small City	0.29	0.33	
Midsized City	0.31	0.31	
Suburban / Big City	0.34	0.33	.03
SES			
≤ Mean	0.27	0.31	
>Mean	0.36	0.33	.00
Gender			
Male	0.36	0.33	
Female	0.27	0.31	.00
Age			
1st Quintile	0.33	0.32	
2nd Quintile	0.38	0.34	
3rd Quintile	0.32	0.33	
4th Quintile	0.31	0.31	
5th Quintile	0.23	0.29	.00

Note: P-values are based on t-tests (difference ≠ 0) for dichotomous variables and on one-way ANOVA tests (probability > F) for other categorical variables.

to also be exposed to the flow on the Chinese internet relative to those who are less likely to jump the wall.

The raw difference in wall jumping across the political interest indicator is significant and large as well. Those who are very uninterested average only 0.17 on the wall jumping index, and those who are very interested average 0.40. This is a telling result when it comes to building a profile of wall jumpers. Those who are more engaged in politics are considerably more likely to venture over the wall to see beyond the Chinese internet. Although not as large a difference, nonetheless, as expected, CCP members were less likely to jump the wall (or admit doing so)—0.31 relative 0.35. Also as anticipated, those living in an urban setting were more likely to jump the wall (see the gradual increase from 0.29 in the countryside / small city category to 0.34 in the suburban / big city category). Those at or below the mean SES were less likely to jump the wall than those above the mean—0.27 and 0.36, respectively. Men were more likely to do so than women, 0.36 to 0.27. Finally, generally speaking, those who were older were less likely to jump the wall. The average of the lower two quintiles was 0.36, the middle or third quintile was 0.32, and the upper two quintiles averaged was only 0.27.

While the bivariate analysis gives us an initial look at the profile of the average wall jumper—a high-SES, politically interested young man without affiliation to the party, who lives in the city and uses the internet frequently—it does not tell us whether the variables hold up when controlling for each. Doing so can indicate whether there is some crossover here. Perhaps, some of these relationships are spurious. Estimating a multivariate model gives us a clear sense of the stronger relationships, building a more accurate profile. The same is true for the profile of those who seek to avoid censorship. Both models are presented in table 6.4.[2]

General internet use is clearly the strongest relationship in the model of our measure of censorship avoidance. Every one-unit increase in internet use boosts the odds of claiming to have changed one's posts seeking to avoid censorship by 30 times. This is astounding. It is also consistent with our earlier foreshadowing of the results to come in the next chapter. Those who engage with the digital environment in any dissident way are also those who use the internet most frequently. Resultantly, they also are more likely to be subject to the pro-China counterflow. We argue that this underlying condition may mitigate the potential effects of a dissident flow of information. The result additionally suggests that using social media increases the odds of claiming to avoid censorship by approximately two times. While not as strong a relationship as that of general internet use, this result is still sizeable. Some of the results from the bivariate analysis in table 6.2 did not hold up in this controlled model. Political interest and CCP membership were significant there but are not here. Urbanicity remains insignificant. Interestingly, while the odds ratio is small (0.53), gender becomes

Table 6.4 **Modeling Censorship Avoidance and Wall Jumpers**

	Avoid Censorship			
	Estimate	S.E.	95% CI	OR
General Internet Use	3.41	0.33	2.75 4.06	30.18
General Social Media	0.76	0.32	0.12 1.40	2.14
Political Interest	−0.16	0.22	−0.59 0.27	—
CCP Member	0.18	0.10	−0.02 0.39	—
Urbanicity	−0.04	0.20	−0.43 0.34	—
SES	1.02	0.39	0.25 1.79	2.78
Female	−0.24	0.09	−0.43 −0.06	0.78
Age	−1.89	0.34	−2.57 −1.22	0.15
Pseudo R^2 = 0.06				
N = 2121				
	Wall Jumpers			
Avoid Censorship	3.25	0.15	2.95 3.54	25.73
General Internet Use	2.25	0.32	1.61 2.88	9.47
Social Media	0.12	0.30	−0.47 0.71	—
Political Interest	0.40	0.22	−0.03 0.82	—
CCP Member	−0.10	0.10	−0.30 0.10	—
Urbanicity	0.04	0.19	−0.34 0.41	—
SES	0.80	0.37	0.06 1.53	2.22
Female	−0.63	0.09	−0.81 −0.45	0.53
Age	−1.52	0.32	−2.16 −0.89	0.22
Pseudo R^2 = 0.14				
N = 1842				

Note: Estimates are derived using ordered logit. S.E. = standard error, CI = confidence interval, OR = odds ratio (odds ratios are only displayed when 0 is not bounded in the respective CI).

significant in the controlled model, suggesting that women are less likely to seek to avoid censorship. Finally, consistent with the bivariate results, older internet users are less likely to alter their posts to try to avoid censorship.

Not surprisingly, those who claim to have changed their posts to avoid censorship are considerably more likely to have also claimed to have jumped the wall (odds ratio = 25.73). We can assume that changing one's post is an indicator that one has opinions or ideas that are critical of the government, or else there would be no need to self-censor. What is interesting here is that the model suggests that this dissident citizen is also peering over the wall. Consistent with the model of censorship avoidance, general internet use has a substantial relationship with wall jumping—a one-unit increase in general internet use increases the odds of being higher on the wall jumping index by 9.47 times. Recalling that all of the bivariate relationships between wall jumping and the set of variables in table 6.3 were statistically significant, that is clearly not the case here. Social media use, political interest, CCP membership, and urbanicity are not significant. This indicates that these relationships were spurious, perhaps driven by the relationship between each and general internet use.[3] That said, SES remains positive and significant (odds ratio = 2.22), and women are still less likely to jump the wall (odds ratio = 0.53), as are older internet users (odds ratio = 0.22).

Conclusion

This chapter has made clear that there are substantial number of wall jumpers and that they do it for a multitude of reasons. Citizens jump the wall for entertainment, to consume foreign media, and to gather political content. These latter two purposes are likely rooted in a passive, at the least, and an active, at the most, desire to seek out dissident information. Further, a significant proportion of Chinese internet users attest that jumping the wall is relatively easy. The data also suggest that many internet users tailor their digital posts to avoid censorship from the central government. We then examined the profile of the users who both actively try to avoid censorship and jump the wall. There was a strong relationship between these two actions, and undergirding both was the fact that those who use the internet most frequently are also the most likely to engage in these behaviors.

It is this last point that the chapter that follows addresses. First, we argue that jumping the wall should stimulate negative attitudes about the central government. The logic here is not complicated. In a closed media environment, exposure to the dissident flow of information on the other side of the wall should encourage dissident attitudes. This claim is not a bold one—researchers have found similar results in many other contexts. As we laid out in earlier chapters, there is quite a bit of research suggesting that the internet can serve as a conduit for a flow of dissident information stimulating protest behavior (see among others Howard et al. 2011; Scherman, Arriagada, and Valenzuela 2015; Tufekci and Wilson 2012; Valenzuela, Arriagada, and Scherman 2012). This, too, is not the first research to evidence both a relationship between internet use and attitudes about government as well as protest in the Asian context (see Gainous, Wagner, and Abbott 2015). Where our final chapter makes a theoretical and empirical contribution is in the fact that wall jumping appears to be correlated with high levels of internet use. The import of this is that heavy internet users are exposed to a large pro-government flow of information in a context where the digital environment is filtered and controlled. This flow, we argue, may counter the effects of being exposed to a dissident flow that exists beyond the confines of the controlled digital environment. The data analysis in chapter 7 supports this theory.

7

Managing the Information War

Voices Heard from Beyond the Wall Are Lost

The effect of the internet is often seen as being independent from existing media. In some work, the internet is framed as a competitive forum that exists beside and outside traditional media (Gainous and Wagner 2011). However, a more in-depth view of the digital sphere is that it interacts and engages with traditional media as well as with the consumers of its content. This hybrid view of the online universe gives a much more nuanced view the digital sphere (Chadwick 2017). The same limitations often structure the view of the Chinese internet. Many are looking to see whether the information on the external internet that is accessed by Chinese users can affect attitudes and lead to more dissidence. In fact, we do some of that work in this book. Nevertheless, that is a narrow and limiting view because it assumes that the outside internet is always competing with the walled garden that exists inside China. However, this is at best an incomplete and narrow picture. The competing narratives interact with each other and the political actors, especially the Chinese state, are well informed of that interaction. Even a walled off internet does not exist in a vacuum.

The Chinese state is aware of the dissident flows of information, and its actions go far beyond the simple and blunt attempts to limit access to contrary sources of information. In this chapter, we explore how China can mediate and limit the potential threat of a competing digital information flow. In particular, we illustrate that the flow existing outside the confines of the Chinese internet is, perhaps, not as significant a threat to the central government's authority as it is sometimes supposed, despite the large number of wall jumpers. Exposure to dissident flows can negatively influence a person's evaluations of the Chinese central government. However, that is only part of the larger picture. While these wall jumpers are being exposed to the dissident information, they are also consuming state narratives as well. Exposure to dissident information can be overcome with competing information. The digital exposure citizens are getting is

---

Directed Digital Dissidence in Autocracies. Jason Gainous, Rongbin Han, Andrew W. MacDonald, and Kevin M. Wagner, Oxford University Press. © Oxford University Press 2024. DOI: 10.1093/oso/9780197680384.003.0007

not limited to the information outside the wall. The Chinese government is actively managing the information flow not only by funding pro-government posters but also more broadly via the maintenance and management of the internal flows of information.

Indeed, as we have observed earlier, the Chinese government is very capable of channeling, deflecting, and reinterpreting narratives. In many ways, the Chinese authorities are far more sophisticated in their approach. Some regimes play a game of simply trying to find and eliminate digital opposition with mixed success. This game of cat and mouse between internet users and monitoring agencies can, at times, be successful, but it is often hard to sustain over extended periods. This is a difficult, though not entirely impossible, strategy to implement continuously. Russia has proven more effective at limiting access to platforms and news outside of the control of the regime over an extended period (Gainous, Wagner, and Ziegler 2018). Less able and more frustrated governments will often take drastic measures to close all access during times of unrest, as Iran does periodically.

China recognizes the danger. More than 11 percent of Chinese internet users have used circumvention tools. Unsurprisingly, an earlier study of them found them to be largely young, well-educated, less trusting in media, and opposed to censorship (Shen and Zhang 2018). More interesting, though, these wall jumpers tended to hold more politically conservative attitudes than nonusers (Shen and Zhang 2018). This is where the effectiveness of the Chinese approach becomes more apparent. Consumers of outside content are consumers of internal content as well. China combines its ability to limit domestic content with a more subtle manipulation of content meant to vitiate competing information when it inevitably is found by wall jumpers and disseminated. As we observed earlier, part of this is accomplished by shifting blame to local governments. However, part of it is the pro–central government narrative that is effectively marketed and disseminated by the state. Below, we consider how that active management technique mitigates the potential negative effects that exposure to dissidence may bring to bear on citizen attitudes, if not behavior.

The Dampening Effect of the Chinese Internet

Our empirical strategy is to examine how individual exposure to multiple conflicting flows may shape opinion. Our argument is that many internet users are exposed to both a pro–central government flow on the Chinese internet and informationally discordant counterflows on the other side of the wall. The former may mitigate or swamp the effects of the latter. Our key empirical observation is that the technological skills required to be a wall jumper are most likely to exist among those who are frequent internet users, likely due to increased awareness of the wall-jumping possibilities and increased technical knowledge. As we detailed earlier, the results do indicate that frequent internet users are more likely to be exposed not only to both critical flows (that of the local government and the central government) but also to the pro–central government flow. This heightened exposure to the latter may counter the effects of the critical flow for wall jumpers. Our results bear out these hypotheses. The negative effect of jumping the wall on citizen attitudes about the government, central and generally, diminishes to a statistical no effect for those who frequently use the internet.

Before getting to those results demonstrating the dampening effect of the Chinese internet on distrust of the central government, we first examine several relationships of internet use and things seen on the internet that are also conditional on wall jumping. Our first finding is that wall jumping is correlated with perceived awareness of paid pro-government posters, that is, the so-called 50 Cent Party (Han 2015b; King, Pan, and Roberts 2017; Miller 2016). A standard assumption might be that those who frequently encounter, or are at least aware of, paid government posters, should be more negative about the government—they have become aware of attempts at manipulating public opinion. However, interestingly, the relationship between perceived awareness of paid posters on support for the central government appears to be conditional on the level of internet use. For high internet users, awareness of paid government posters is positively associated with support for the central government, while for low internet users the reverse is true. Even for those aware of online opinion manipulation, the effects of that awareness appear to be swamped by their heavy (largely domestic) internet use. If we combine this finding with our previous finding showing that exposure to a pro–central government information flow is strongest among heavy internet users we arrive at a result suggesting that the central government is winning the information war in China—exposure to new negative pieces of information (paid government posters) cannot overcome the effect of exposure to pro-government messaging and framing.

Our additional important finding, that wall jumping also cannot overcome the effect of heavy internet use, relies on a finding that wall jumping is associated with high levels of internet use. To provide additional confidence in our results, we next disaggregated our wall-jumping index and compared the bivariate relationship between the subcomponents and levels of internet use. These bivariate relationships are presented in figure 7.1. In particular, examining the bivariate relationship should help us understand whether the relationship between wall jumping and internet use was driven primarily by those seeking entertainment (part of the wall jumping index) or was robust to alternative index specifications. The evidence suggests the addition of entertainment seeking to the index is not a concern for our overall finding. Although the positive relationship is statistically significant for both, that between internet use and wall jumping for political

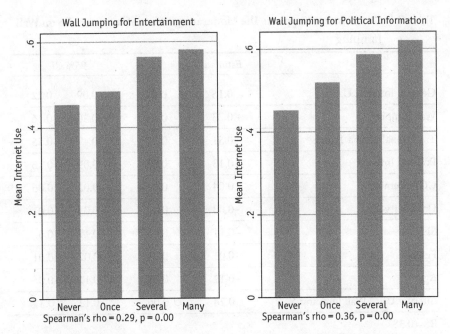

Figure 7.1 The Bivariate Relationship between Internet Use and Wall Jumping

information is slightly stronger (Spearman's rho = 0.36) than that between internet use and jumping the wall for entertainment (Spearman's rho =.29).

This stronger relationship is also clear in the visual representation in figure 7.1. Not only is the mean internet use higher for those who claim to have jumped the wall for political information many times compared those who claimed to have jumped the wall for entertainment many times, but the linear increase in internet use across the ordinal indicator of wall jumping for political information is much clearer. This provides a solid descriptive foundation for our contention that those who jump the wall to get sensitive political information are likely to be exposed to the flow on the Chinese side of the wall.

Referring back to table 5.1, we demonstrated that wall jumping was clearly related to both trust in the central government and general satisfaction with it. In both instances, this effect was, as expected, negative. The more frequently citizens jumped the wall, the less trusting they were of the central government and the less satisfied they were with government. This suggests the potential for a threat to the central government's authority. If this dynamic of decreased trust and satisfaction resulting from continual wall jumping were to continue to percolate, it could potentially boil over into protest. The interactive model in table 7.1 presents evidence to suggest that the Chinese management of digital flow on the domestic side of the wall may dampen the voices from beyond the wall and limit that potentiality. Here, as with our dependent variable, we constructed

102 DIRECTED DIGITAL DISSIDENCE IN AUTOCRACIES

Table 7.1 **Government Support: The Moderating Effect of Internet Use on Wall Jumping**

	Estimate	S.E.	95% CI	
General Internet Use	0.15	0.03	0.09	0.22
Wall Jumping	−0.23	0.04	−0.30	−0.16
Traditional Media Trust	0.51	0.02	0.47	0.55
Political Interest	0.13	0.02	0.09	0.16
CCP Member	0.04	0.01	0.02	0.06
Urbanicity	−0.03	0.02	−0.06	0.01
SES	−0.11	0.03	−0.17	−0.05
Female	−0.01	0.01	−0.02	0.01
Age	−0.12	0.03	−0.17	−0.06
Internet Use * Wall Jumping	0.24	0.06	0.12	0.37
$R^2 = 0.38$				
$N = 1,888$				

Note: Estimates are derived using OLS. S.E. = standard error, CI = confidence interval.

a two-item additive index of trust in the central government and general satisfaction with government (Q13A and Q7). These items scaled well together ($\alpha = 0.69$), suggesting they are capturing the same underlying concept, support for the central government.

The test here is the interaction between internet use and wall jumping. We can presume that those who use the internet more are not spending all of their time jumping the wall but are also spending much or most of their time the Chinese side of the wall. As such, they have more exposure to the pro-government flow than those who use the internet less frequently. As we have argued in this chapter, we suspect that wall jumping and a decrease in support for the central government (table 5.1) is likely moderated by general internet use—that is, for low levels of internet use, we expect the relationship between wall jumping and government trust to be strongly negative, while for high levels of internet use we expect this relationship to moderate.[1] As evidenced in table 7.1, the interaction is statistically significant. Also, the substantive relationships of the control variables do not meaningfully change from those in table 5.1; they are completely consistent with the control estimates of the trust measure there, but where gender and urbanicity were significant correlates of satisfaction in the ordered logit model in table 5.1, they are not here.

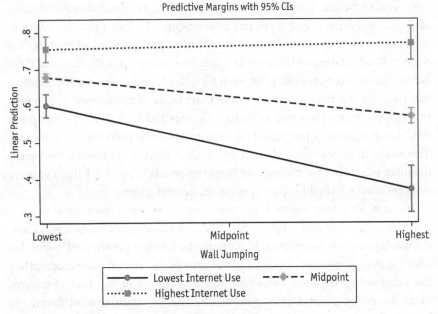

Figure 7.2 Plotting the Moderating Effect from Table 7.1

Further, this moderating effect presented in figure 7.2 is consistent with the above expectations. The results here are quite stark; for those with the lowest internet use, the relationship between wall jumping and support for the central government is strong and negative. For those at the midpoint on the internet use scale, the negative relationship is weaker. Finally, and rather revealing, there is a slight positive relationship of wall jumping for those who use the internet most frequently. This suggests that the potential threat of wall jumping to the Chinese central government may, in fact, be completely mitigated by the pro-government flow on the Chinese side of the wall.

The model results presented in table 7.2 provide further evidence that this, indeed, may be the case.[2] If more frequent internet users are more likely to be exposed to the pro-government flow on the Chinese side of the wall, we would expect their awareness of government-sponsored posters (the 50 Cent Party) to be heightened as they consume more pro-regime information flows, and for these effects to hold up when controlling for wall jumping as well as controlling for other political and demographic factors. The results confirm this expectation. The odds of claiming to be more aware of pro-government posters increases by 1.39 times for every one-unit increase on our wall-jumping index. Likewise, the odds of doing the same increase by 5.59 times for every one-unit increase in the general internet use index.

Again, it is important to note that the statistical significance of the wall jumping and internet use indicators holds up while controlling for other potentially confounding factors. Traditional media trust had the expected negative relationship, political interest had a positive relationship, SES had a positive relationship, and women were less likely to be aware of pro-government posters. The respective odds ratios for these control variables were 0.25, 1.98, 9.39, and 0.82. Notice the strong relationship between SES, the largest in the model, a finding that suggests that the economic elite are most aware of and attuned to potential propaganda forces. However, as Barbara Geddes and John Zaller (1989) point out, elite awareness of propaganda does not necessarily hinder its effectiveness. This model does not tell us whether the 50 Cent Party propaganda is having the intended effect, but we can assume from the results in table 7.1 that exposure does encourage favorable opinion about the central government.

We can also test whether the relationship between awareness of pro-government posters and support for the central government varies across internet use. If pro-government posting is having the Chinese government's intended effect, that is, to promote positive evaluations of the central government, then the relationship between awareness and evaluations of the central government should be positive among those who use the internet most frequently because they are more likely to be exposed to the pro-government propaganda.

Table 7.2 **Wall Jumping and Awareness of Pro-government Posters (50 Cent Party)**

	Estimate	S.E.	95% CI		OR
Wall Jumping	0.33	0.15	0.04	0.62	1.39
General Internet Use	1.74	0.29	1.17	2.31	5.69
Traditional Media Trust	−1.37	0.25	−1.86	−0.89	0.25
Political Interest	0.68	0.20	0.28	1.08	1.98
CCP Member	0.01	0.10	−0.19	0.21	—
Urbanicity	−0.09	0.18	−0.45	0.28	—
SES	2.24	0.37	1.51	2.97	9.39
Female	−0.19	0.09	−0.37	−0.02	0.82
Age	−0.58	0.30	−1.18	0.01	—
Pseudo R^2 = 0.05					
N = 1,889					

Note: Estimates are derived using ordered logit. S.E. = standard error, CI = confidence interval, OR = odds ratio (odds ratios are only displayed when 0 is not bounded in the respective CI).

Concurrently, the positive relationship between internet use and support for the central government should be weakest among those with low awareness and stronger among those with high awareness. These tests can be performed by adding an interaction between internet use and awareness of pro-government posters to the model presented in table 7.1. Because we have already presented multiple additive and interactive models of support for the central government, for the sake of brevity, we present in figure 7.3 only the results of that interaction.

Again, the results confirm our expectations. The interaction was statistically significant (p = .01). The graph on the left-hand side of figure 7.3 demonstrates clearly that the relationship between awareness of pro-government posters and support for the central government is positive only for those who use the internet most frequently. In fact, the relationship is negative for moderate and low users. In addition, it becomes clear when looking at the graph on the right-hand side of figure 7.3 that the positive relationship between internet use and support for the central government is strongest for those with highest awareness of pro-government posters. Both results taken together suggest that exposure to the pro-government flow, as measured by awareness of it, is consequential. They suggest that the Chinese government's management and shaping of the online information flow is effective.

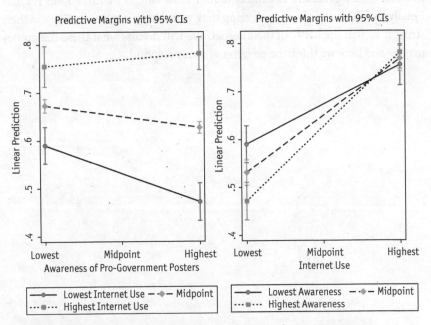

Figure 7.3 Government Support: The Interplay between the Pro-government Information Flow and Internet Use

Conclusion

This chapter has provided empirical evidence that the potential threat of a digital information flow, in particular, that flow existing outside the confines of the Chinese internet is, perhaps, not as significant a threat to the central government's authority as it is sometimes supposed. Yes, there are many wall jumpers. Yes, they are being exposed to dissident information. Yes, this exposure can negatively influence their evaluations of the Chinese central government. These findings would be troubling for the central government if the only digital exposure citizens were getting were on the other side of the wall. This is simply not the case. The Chinese government is actively managing the information flow not only by funding pro-government posters but also more broadly via the maintenance and management of the internal flows of information. The results presented in this chapter have shown that this active management tech mitigates the potential negative effects that exposure to dissidence may bring to bear on citizen attitudes, if not behavior.

Our final chapter will summarize the theoretical argument and empirical evidence that has been laid out thus far. We will provide examples of how the Chinese government is effectively managing the information war and winning. We will also talk about how this case may help us understand autocracies' digital political reality generally. Is China unique? How far can we extend our results? Finally, as China continues to develop they will clearly face new hurdles in their struggle to win the battle of the internet. We will discuss what these difficulties may be and how we think the government may respond.

8

Digital Directed Dissidence in Action

Applications and Its Limits

In this chapter, we consider some of the applications of directed digital dissidence. By reviewing some specific examples of when DDD was employed, we can explore the scope and limits of this governing strategy. In particular, we illuminate the theoretical argument by examining who is targeted and how the individuals engaging in online discourse responded to the state employment of DDD. The examples in this chapter are mostly drawn from the Chinese government's information strategy concerning the COVID-19 pandemic, which is as close to an existential threat as the Chinese government has faced in the past several decades. Indeed, the outbreak and handling of COVID-19 threatened the government's own self-narrative of technocratic competency. The online discourse over it included many examples of credit taking and blame shifting by netizens and government sources, making the government's employment of DDD especially significant. Among the many examples of online discourse over government performance during the epidemic, we highlight two episodes: response to the initial outbreak and online discourse during the Shanghai lockdown. In addition, and as a comparison, we review the online fervor surrounding the boycott of Western brands that refused to use Xinjiang-sourced cotton in 2019. These cases provide a window into how DDD typically works, how it can be used in novel ways, and what may be the limits to its effective employment.

The first and most significant example that of the government redirection of blame for the initial handling of the COVID-19 outbreak is prototypical of how DDD operates in practice. In particular, the central government's strategy of the public shaming of local officials for failure to manage the initial outbreak fits very well within our expectations and supports the survey results developed in previous chapters. This employment of DDD was particularly helpful in redirecting

Directed Digital Dissidence in Autocracies. Jason Gainous, Rongbin Han, Andrew W. MacDonald, and Kevin M. Wagner, Oxford University Press. © Oxford University Press 2024. DOI: 10.1093/oso/9780197680384.003.0008

the online outrage away from the central government and instead focusing it on inevitable missteps made by local officials as they faced difficult choices. Several online incidents associated with the initial outbreak highlight how DDD is implemented in practice, including the case of Dr. Li Wenliang and the online castigation of the mayor of Wuhan. The second case, of the boycott of brands that refused to use Xinjiang cotton, expands these findings outward by looking at how DDD might be aimed at a wider variety of targets, foreign corporations, in response to negative international news. One of the interesting dynamics this case highlights is the signal-boosting relationship between state media accounts and organic user-generated content, indicating how the state may refine and hone its use of DDD.

The final case of the online dynamics of the Shanghai lockdown of 2022 specifically highlights the limits of DDD. In particular, because users had direct personal experience with the events and the central government was too closely tied with the policy choices that led to the lockdown, the use of DDD was not a prominent feature of discourse management. However, situations with these specific features are relatively rare in China; it is perhaps the exception that proves the rule. Taken together, these cases help illustrate the dynamics at play in online political engagement in China. Each case adds important context to the statistical results developed in previous chapters. Combined, the incidents described in this chapter all lend support to our overall argument that social media is an important conduit for dissidence, but this dissidence has mostly been successfully redirected toward alternative targets that do not threaten the central government.

DDD in Action: Initial COVID-19 Response

The outbreak of COVID-19 in Wuhan, Hubei Province, in China presented a national crisis for both emergency services and the state. The government's initial mishandling of the pandemic in January and February 2020 invited widespread criticism in online and offline venues, both inside and outside of China. While many pro-liberal Chinese and foreigners initially attributed the poor response to China's lack of democracy and freedom (e.g., Zhang 2020), the Chinese state worked hard to spin the discourse to its own advantage. In particular, the state mobilized online discourse leaders and online propaganda outlets to argue that the anti-COVID campaign exemplified China's institutional strength and to portray the Chinese Communist Party as representing the best interest of the people while shifting the blame to local officials and hostile foreign forces.

Refocusing the Narrative from Initial Failures to Party Mobilization

The first part of the government's strategy was to change the online discourse from one of state weakness to strength, in part by relying on existing state narrative frames to make the claims more digestible for the average citizen. The Chinese party-state has always claimed, through its education system and propaganda apparatus, that it represents the best interests of the people. China is a big socialist family in which everyone takes care of everyone else (*shehuizhuyi da jiating; yifang younan, bafang zhiyuan*), and the regime is able to "concentrate resources and capabilities to accomplish major undertakings" (*jizhong liliang ban dashi*). During the pandemic, the Chinese state has made considerable efforts to link its actions to these preexisting narratives. For example, state media intensively covered how the government mobilized all provinces across the country to support Hubei, the epicenter of the COVID outbreak, pointing out that all hands, especially the party's grassroots cadres and agencies, mobilized in a total war against the virus and to help those in need. Such a propaganda campaign aims at validating the state's claim of its "institutional strength" (*zhidu youshi*),[1] manifesting that the party-state can and will pull resources and its capacity to serve the people (Tian et al. 2020). The following intercept from a commentary in the *People's Daily* set the tone quite explicitly (bold in the original text) (*People's Daily* 2020).

> **Hubei and Wuhan are the most important and decisive places in this epidemic prevention and control struggle. The entire party, the army, and people of all ethnic groups in the country have always stood with the people of Hubei and Wuhan.** The Party Central Committee sent a steering group to Wuhan to strengthen the guidance of the front-line work of epidemic prevention and control, and fought side by side with the people of Hubei and Wuhan. The People's Liberation Army, the central and national ministries and commissions, all provinces, autonomous regions, and municipalities tried their best to help, and rushed to the front line to wage the all-out people's war of epidemic prevention and control. In this serious struggle, Party organizations at all levels in Hubei and all party members and cadres charged ahead and fought bravely. Medical workers from Hubei and teams dispatched from across the country headed for the front line against the virus, heedless of their own safety. Commanders and soldiers of the PLA charged at the order and bravely undertook the heavy responsibilities. Many community workers, public security officers, grassroots

cadres, squatting cadres,[2] and volunteers are not afraid of wind and rain, and stick to the front line. The masses are united and have actively participated [in the anti-pandemic war], among whom many evocative models and touching deeds emerged, demonstrating the Chinese power of national unity in a difficult time.

On September 17, 2020, a commentary in the *People's Daily* (Fang 2020) directly boasted in its headline that "the anti-pandemic war demonstrates China's institutional strength." The article quoted President Xi Jinping's speech (2020) on September 8 at a national commendation meeting, claiming, "The fight against the COVID-19 epidemic has achieved major strategic results, fully demonstrating the significant advantages of the leadership of the Chinese Communist Party and the socialist system of our country."

In addition to all regular means of reporting, CCTV, *People's Daily Online*, and many other media and online platforms livestreamed the entire process, showing how the two hospitals were constructed from scratch. Viewership reportedly exceeded 200 million people within three days (Zuo 2020), and during peak hours, more than 100 million viewers were simultaneously online (*My Drivers* 2020). This online spectacle successfully showcased in real time how the party-state was delivering on its promises—two brand-new fully equipped hospitals with more than 2,000 beds in about two weeks—with millions of citizens witnessing and supervising it together throughout the process via the internet. Indeed, it is fair to say that even this collective experience of "cloud supervision" (*yun jiangong*) among netizens is part of the state's propaganda effort. The fact that tens of millions of Chinese were constantly watching the construction of the two hospitals indicated not only social media users' interest in COVID stories but also suggests that the attempt to reframe the narrative had fertile ground to work with. This is how an official report tried to convey the rationale (Zuo 2020):

> Little Yang who lives in Chaoyang District, Beijing tells the reporter that the first thing he does every day after getting out of bed is click on the livestreaming. "While I cannot contribute [to the construction] myself, watching the images live streamed from the site makes me feel that I am also participating in the whole process of construction."

In addition to official media coverage, video clips and social media postings of medical teams arriving in and leaving Hubei flooded the online and offline media sphere, further substantiating the state's claims. Thus, it is not surprising that trust in the government increased rather than eroded months into the pandemic (Ma 2021). The Chinese government was able to combine late, but significant, action with effective messaging (Ang 2020), so that the central government was seen as successfully combating the pandemic. The state messaging strategy was effective in this time frame but faced a competing narrative as the pandemic spread.

FINDING NEW TARGETS FOR DDD: LOCAL OFFICIALS

The second part of the central government's strategy was to deflect online anger away from it and toward unsympathetic targets. Quickly after the outbreak of COVID-19, failures in government responsiveness were appearing frequently in social media, such as Weibo (Li, Chandra, and Kapucu 2020). As a result, the full structure of the DDD strategy began to manifest. In addition to glorifying the CCP as a whole and its top leadership, state information strategy during the pandemic also involved starting to publicize the punishment of officials deemed corrupt and incompetent. As early as January 21, 2020, the party's Central Political and Legal Affairs Commission published an article condemning local authorities for concealing information, warning, "Whoever deliberately delays and conceals reports of the information will forever be nailed to history's pillar of shame" (Wang 2020). And immediately following the lockdown of Wuhan, the State Council issued a circular on January 24 soliciting evidence from the public about issues such as local authorities omitting and concealing information regarding the prevention and control of the epidemic (*People's Daily Online* 2020).

Subsequently, many local officials across the country were punished for concealing information or failing to effectively contain the virus. In February 2020, the central government dismissed both the CCP secretary and the director of Hubei's provincial health commission, and then sacked the party secretaries of Hubei Province and Wuhan municipality. Thousands of lower-level officials were punished. By the end of the month, more than 630 cadres were disciplined in Wuhan alone, and Shaanxi's Xi'an had held accountable 338 local cadres. In June, a cluster infection happened in Beijing's Fengtai District, costing the careers of six local officials (Hao 2021; *Yicai Global* 2020).

This targeting of local officials helped obscure the responsibility of the central government in creating underlying structural incentives to which local leaders were responding. Local leaders faced an incentive structure in which personnel decisions allow no negative marks in certain categories, which often includes matters like social stability and enforcement of national priorities (Teets, Hasmath, and Lewis 2017). Even modest but openly reported failures in these categories can be enough to generate a negative personnel dossier. Thus, officials are heavily incentivized to hide negative information, a classic example of the dictator's dilemma (Wintrobe 2000).

Although local officials who hide information are not particularly sympathetic characters, their existence is a predictable consequence of Chinese officials' incentive structure and institutional context. The central government strategy also muted coverage concerning how local areas were often underresourced in fighting the virus. Further, because information was tightly controlled, local officials needed permission to share important relevant information regarding fighting COVID-19. Wuhan mayor Zhou Xianwang noted he was limited by his lack of authorization (Ang 2020). Even those who were willing to disregard the incentive structure were limited in what they could accomplish, given the nature of the virus and the meager testing resources initially available to local officials. Many of the failures of virus containment post-Wuhan can also be traced to the failure to properly implement virus containment by poorly trained and paid front-line workers, staff who must be paid out of limited local government revenues. Given all of these institutional handicaps, it is therefore not surprising that local officials had difficulties in monitoring and controlling outbreaks, a situation that was not permitted to be discussed online (*Wall Street Journal* 2022).

Punishing local officials, in addition to motivating them to fight the virus more effectively (Mei 2020), directly served the DDD purpose by using them as scapegoats. This approach signaled to citizens that the central government cared about its citizens and was responsive to popular anger. The importance and success of this part of the strategy is indicated by the frequent mentions of official discipline on state social media channels and the engagement that such posts generated. For instance, when Hubei and Wuhan party secretaries were replaced, major state media outlets posted the news on their Weibo accounts. The numbers of retweets, comments, and likes demonstrated the massive public interest in these narratives. As of October 7, 2020, the tweet by the *People's Daily* was retweeted 26,656 times, commented upon 37,786 times, and liked 574,763 times; the *Chinese News* tweet was retweeted 2,002 times, commented upon 15,334 times, and liked 207,674 times; for *Global Times*, the counts were 7,636, 12,999, and 157,657 times, respectively (see appendixes C, D, and E). These numbers were substantially higher than typical interactions on a normal post from these sources. For example, a regular tweet by the *Global Times* would typically receive only a few dozen retweets or comments and a few hundred likes. These reports punishing local officials, together with those championing the party's role and President Xi's leadership, conveyed the message that the central government and the regime as a whole care about the people, and their anger should be directed at local officials. The engagement of these posts indicates that the strategy seems to have largely been accepted by social media users.

As an additional benefit, by shifting blame to the local governing structures, China was able to blunt criticism that the nation lacked democratic accountability, because state targets were disciplined after public anger. This message is further validated when compared with what happened in Western liberal democracies, where, according to many Chinese, no officials were promptly punished for mishandling the pandemic. In a post that received more than 1,000 upvotes on the popular social media Zhihu, a netizen asked, "It is already 2021, why are all officials being dismissed because of the COVID-19 pandemic in China?" (Haizhongqingmu 2021). The same poster then argued that this was all because China, unlike other countries, has one ultimate political rule, which is "putting the people at the center of everything" and making it the "aspiration and mission of all government officials." The underlying message of the post was that the Chinese government is accountable and responsive to the public. Punishing local officials not only helps shift blame to local governments and local officials but also improves the image of the central government and the regime as a whole, serving as an often-effective response to pro-liberal Chinese and Western media's criticism of China's democratic deficits.

HARD CASES: DR. LI WENLIANG

Though we identify DDD as a general information strategy of the Chinese government, it is important to note that its implementation can be customized and carefully calibrated. How the party-state handled Dr. Li Wenliang, one of the earliest whistleblowers during the COVID-19 pandemic, is a case in point. This evolving situation shows how the strategy can be adjusted as the context changes. In this case, we focus on how the Chinese party-state can and does adjust DDD messaging strategy during a crisis.

Dr. Li was an ophthalmologist working at the Central Hospital of Wuhan. Upon learning from an internal diagnostic report about a suspected severe acute respiratory syndrome (SARS) case on December 30, 2019, he shared the news with his fellow alumni via WeChat. Despite his request not to further spread the information, the "rumor" soon went public via social media. Dr. Li was subsequently summoned to a local police station in Wuhan on January 3, 2020, and was issued an admonition for spreading "untrue discussions" (*bushi yanlun*). After his reprimand, Dr. Li was then swept up in the all-hands effort to treat early COVID-19 cases and, during that work, tragically caught the disease himself and subsequently died on February 7. His death triggered a huge wave of mourning and protest, especially in cyberspace, where millions of netizens flooded his Weibo account to voice their condolences and dissatisfaction with the authorities (Green 2020).[3]

Dr. Li's experiences as one of the earliest whistleblowers are of interest for several reasons. First, on January 1, 2020, even before Dr. Li was summoned by the local police, the Wuhan Police Bureau's official Weibo account Pingan Wuhan tweeted about eight citizens being reprimanded for rumor mongering. The news was further disseminated by other mainstream local and national media outlets or their social media platforms (such as the official Weibo accounts of the *People's Daily* and Xinhua News Agency) and was aired on CCTV's *Live News* the next day. Considering that Dr. Li was summoned on January 3, he was probably not one of the eight reprimanded citizens. However, the fact that China's three most authoritative official news outlets—the *People's Daily*, Xinhua News Agency, and CCTV—were all involved in the coverage of this specific piece of news suggests that the central government was acting in the same mode as the local authorities in Wuhan. Both appeared to be covering it up, probably with the intention of avoiding mass social panic. The punishment of Li was consistent with this approach.

However, this approach did not hold. As the outbreak grew and escaped state control, more people learned about Dr. Li's treatment and the repercussions he suffered for telling the truth. Dr. Li went from a punished local official to one who was admired for his efforts. Indeed, Dr. Li Wenliang became a focal point for those concerned about the information struggle in China and illustrated a weak point in state propaganda and information control (*China Digital Times* n.d.). The state response was uneven. Dr. Li was interviewed by *Beijing Youth Daily* on January 27, but the report that came out on the same day was removed by the state from the web.[4] State censorship only escalated upon Dr. Li's death. Numerous articles that commemorated him were censored and deleted. And according to a report by the Citizen's Lab, "As a narrative depicting Dr. Li as a martyr grew amongst the public, references to him were blocked on WeChat" (Crete-Nishihata et al. 2020). For the state, Dr. Li Wenliang was the source of a propaganda crisis, and the primary coping strategy was heavy-handed suppression.

As a strategy, censorship is of limited value, especially after a story is spread broadly. The state started to make adjustments by January 2020 to avoid the backlash from its early propaganda mistakes. On January 21, then–*Global Times* chief editor Hu Xijin called upon authorities in Wuhan to reinvestigate the earlier rumor-mongering case in which eight citizens were punished, arguing that correcting wrongful reprimands will only enhance the government's credibility and popular support (Hu, 2020). On January 29, Pingan Wuhan issued a correction notice, claiming that local police apparatus checked and verified information with the eight citizens because "multiple netizens reported that there are people spreading untrue information online," and local police only "educated" and "criticized" these people but did not impose any punishments such as "warning, fine, or detainment" (*Nddaily* 2020). Shifts were also made in handling Dr. Li Wenliang. As mentioned above, upon his death, a huge wave of online activism targeting the state emerged, which in turn triggered heightened state censorship. Yet Weibo did not remove Dr. Li's account but allowed millions of netizens to leave comments on his entries, turning his Weibo into the "Chinese Wailing Wall" (Tan 2020). Although this suggests that the state was fearful of the potential backlash to blocking public access to Li's Weibo, it also shows the state was carefully weighing the options of both suppression and accommodation. The state was moving to adopt a more nuanced approach, using DDD to most effectively channel the online opinion and emotions generated by Dr. Li's treatment away from the central government.

Indeed, as soon as Dr. Li died on February 7, the National Supervisory Commission sent an investigation team to Wuhan to examine the case (Fu 2020). On March 19, the team held a press conference, arguing that Dr. Li was not really punished in any form other than the admonition. However, the investigation team did deem the admonition to be improper and urged local police to revoke it and hold those involved accountable (CCDI 2020). What is particularly worth mentioning is that the press conference concluded by highlighting that Dr. Li was a member of the CCP, not an anti-regime champion:

> It is worth noting that in order to attack the Chinese Communist Party and the Chinese government, some hostile forces have labeled Dr. Li Wenliang as an anti-establishment "hero" and "the awakened." This is totally untrue. Li Wenliang is a CCP member, not a so-called "anti-establishment figure." Those with ulterior motives who want to fan the flames, deceive people, and stir up social emotions are doomed to fail.

The party-state's motive for the investigation seems fairly clear in this passage. Wuhan police immediately followed the instruction from the National Supervisory Commission investigation team and revoked the admonition, apologized to Dr. Li's family, and punished two local police officers for issuing "improper instructions" and failing to follow regular law enforcement procedures (CGTN 2020; China *Net News* 2020). The moves by the state again blamed local officials but did little to address the incentives faced by these local bureaucrats as part of their role in the censorship apparatus. By sending in a central inspection team and punishing two low-level police officers, the state signaled to the public that they should blame the moral failing of local officials. The central government cemented their image as a benevolent check on local malfeasance.

While we have no insider information to verify the state's intention, we believe our interpretation of Dr. Li's case is well grounded, as the evidence suggests that the state, despite its reversal of judgment in Dr. Li's case, continues to carefully monitor and delete any other critical information related to the official response to COVID-19 (Crete-Nishihata et al. 2020). A case in point is Dr. Li Wenliang's colleague Dr. Ai Fen, from whom Li first learned about the outbreak of the virus.

Dr. Ai was featured in a report by the Chinese magazine *Renwu* (People), titled "The One Who Handed Out the Whistles." Despite the magazine's official status as a state-run publication, the article was promptly censored within a day, triggering a massive anti-censorship mobilization, with angry citizens repeatedly trying to get the article back online in creative ways, especially in their social media circles. Although the state was more strategic with DDD in the case of Dr. Li, the censorship approach was not abandoned. In this case, DDD was the fallback position when more heavy-handed measures failed. Information was contained where possible and shaped to the state's advantage through DDD when needed.

DDD against Foreign Forces

In the previous examples and chapters, DDD has primarily been defined as an attempt by the central government to deflect critical online discourse and channel it toward blaming local officials. However, this is not the only target available to the government. Historically, and consistent with the literature on authoritarian regimes (Anderson, Regan, and Ostergard 2002; Kuran 1991; Policzer 2009), the Chinese government has only selectively discussed international criticisms of its conduct. Given that, as discussed in chapter 5, most netizens cannot freely access news on the other side of the Great Firewall, minimizing negative news from international sources has a relatively low cost. Additionally, as Jamie Gruffydd-Jones (2019) finds, when the Chinese media does discuss foreign criticism, it frames it as part of a narrative of international actors and "hostile foreign forces" conspiring against China. In this common framing, China is a long-suffering upstart that foreign firms and governments treat unfairly. Given the availability and shared adoption of this framing by most internet users, it is common for social media users to organically drive the discussion of international affairs in a way that is conducive to employing DDD (Fang and Repnikova 2018; Hyun and Kim 2015). In these situations, the central government needs only to nurture and amplify existing voices, not create a new narrative out of whole cloth.

One of the clearest examples of this strategy comes from the debate regarding the origins of the COVID-19 virus. In 2020 and 2021, the Chinese state came under continual domestic and international pressure to provide an explanation of how the pandemic started. For example, reacting to the blame from US president Donald Trump, Zhao Lijian, spokesperson for the Ministry of Foreign Affairs, posted five times on Twitter on March 12, 2020, in both English and Chinese, accusing the United States of bringing the virus to Wuhan and demanding an apology from the Americans (BBC Chinese 2020). The tweets, in addition to triggering a diplomatic dispute between the two countries, were widely circulated in the Chinese mediasphere and applauded by the more nationalist elements of the Chinese public. In addition, the Chinese state also tolerated, if not encouraged, conspiracy theories or semi-conspiracy theories that suggested the virus originated from other countries, especially the United States. On January 13, 2021, the *People Daily*, amid its busy vaccine diplomacy campaign, published an article claiming that researchers from Italy had found a female COVID case as early as in November 2019. The implication was that the virus did not originate in Wuhan (Xu 2021).

To examine how common this strategy was, we conducted a review of *People's Daily* articles from January 1, 2021, to March 25, 2022, that mentioned COVID-19.[5] This review located 470 articles. Most of the articles consisted of breaking news on COVID-19 events. When we examined the subset of articles that discussed blame and responsibility for the virus, the strategy to point away from China was clear. Seven articles implicitly or explicitly suggested that the virus started somewhere other than China, primarily Italy and the United States. Another seven attempted to rebut the allegations of the lab origin of the virus. Nineteen argued against "politicizing the origin tracing of the virus" or criticized the United States or its allies for doing so. Eighteen criticized other countries, especially the United States, for mishandling the pandemic domestically or highlighted how the pandemic had revealed other nations' domestic problems such as failures of democracy or human rights concerns. In short, when the question of accountability for the virus arose, state media focused on foreign forces rather than responding to criticisms of China's initial handling of the outbreak or theories regarding Wuhan Institute of Virology's role. Online misdirection rather than direct response seemed to be the central government's strategy.

One extreme example of this misdirection and the lengths to which mainstream Chinese media would go to redirect blame was the case of the fake Swiss biologist Wilson Edwards. Media outlets including the *People's Daily*, *Global Times*, China News Net, and CGTN broke news that Swiss biologist Wilson Edwards criticized the United States for unfairly attacking China on the origin of the virus: "Over the past 6 months, especially after the phase I study [of the origins of the virus], WHO sources and a number of fellow researchers complained that they had endured enormous pressure and even intimidation from the U.S. side as well as certain media outlets" (*China Digital Times* 2021b). This style of blame-shifting report, heavily promoted on Chinese social media channels, moves the discussion from whether the virus originated in labs in Wuhan to whether the United States is unfairly attacking China. However, online commentators quickly discovered that Dr. Edwards had only a small online footprint and his social media profiles had been active for only a few weeks. Others pointed out that Wilson Edwards is not a very Swiss-sounding name and that no pictures could be located of the biologist. These investigations strongly suggested that either a Chinese reporter or a sympathetic nationalist user created the account and forwarded it to reporters who did not fact-check the claim. In the end, the Swiss Embassy in Beijing had to respond by clarifying on both Weibo and Twitter that the quote was almost certainly fake news, and the Chinese outlets were then forced to retract all articles in which the supposed source was cited (*Deutsche Welle* 2021; Taylor 2021; Yan 2021). The incident highlights the lengths government sources were willing to go to invest in this particular narrative.

The strategy of directing internal anger at foreign governments is not new in China, but the effectiveness of using online platforms and outlets to engage in the practice adds a new dimension to the strategy. In particular, it also allows the message to seem more organic and unplanned. The online component can complement the more overt government strategy. The Chinese government has often focused on the motives of foreign media rather than responding to their criticisms, suggesting that Western media is biased against China. The *New York Times* has been called out by Chinese media and citizens for holding a double standard about lockdowns in Wuhan and Italy (*Xinhua Baoye Net* 2020). *Der Spiegel* was also widely criticized for its coverage, including an issue with a cover declaring "Corona-Virus Made in China" and an article by a Chinese reporter who criticized China's undemocratic regime and media censorship as the reasons that caused the virus to spread beyond control (Pan 2020).

All such cases were cited and often distorted to show domestic consumers of online information the anti-China bias of the West. This strategy serves the DDD model well, since it indicates that foreign outlets are untrustworthy and thus increases the value of domestic sources, where the state can more easily control and direct the consumption of state-approved narratives. When the pandemic exploded in Europe and North America, anti-Western reports were frequently raised in Chinese social media, with not just state tolerance but also an encouragement to mock the Western media and democracy. The underlying message was clear. Because these foreign news sources were so blinded by distrust of China and biased in their coverage, their criticisms of China could be easily dismissed.

XINJIANG COTTON CASE

Another example of DDD employed against foreign targets is the Chinese online protest movement centered on the refusal of foreign firms to use Xinjiang-produced cotton. Various governments and international bodies have been increasingly forceful in their criticism of China's treatment of Uyghurs in Western China. The Chinese government has been accused of rounding up more than 1 million Uyghurs in a bid to stamp out Islamic radicalism. Satellite evidence shows that China has constructed large-scale detention camps in

Western China, and anecdotal evidence has trickled out that these camps hold the Uyghurs in prison-like conditions. Chinese spokespeople have routinely minimized the number of Uyghurs involved and stated that the camps are simply vocational schools (PRC Embassy 2021). International criticism of China's policies toward Muslim minorities in Xinjiang are heavily censored and are rarely discussed openly on the Chinese internet, even to mention official Chinese rebuttals of such criticism (*China Digital Times* 2021a). One prong of Western interest-group pressure to oppose perceived mistreatment of the Uyghurs is to encourage companies to divest themselves from working with any state-owned enterprises operating out of Xinjiang. This includes divesting from any agricultural products made from what the interest groups claim is forced labor.

After the announcement of joint sanctions on Chinese officials who set policy in Xinjiang by the United States, European Union, Britain, and Canada on March 21, 2021, the Chinese government responded forcefully. Rather than ignore or downplay the criticism, groups associated with the government took a more aggressive tack. A several-months-old statement by the Swedish clothing retailer H&M expressing "serious concerns" over the use of forced labor to harvest cotton in Xinjiang began circulating and attracting criticism online in China (Friedman and Paton 2021). The online criticism of H&M broadened into a broader attack on many Western brands that had previously committed to boycotting Xinjiang cotton, including Nike, Adidas, and Burberry. The attacks on these brands were boosted by official state social media channels such as the *People's Daily* and the Communist Youth League. The initial Communist Youth League post stated (*Sohu News* 2021):

> On one hand you [H&M] cook up a story to boycott Xinjiang cotton, on the other hand you want to make money in China. Truly delusional! @HMChina #xinjiangcottonscam

The attacks quickly led to online retailers refusing to stock products from the controversial brands and Chinese spokespeople for these brands cutting ties with the companies. H&M suffered major losses in China, from which the brand has still not recovered (Hall 2022).

This response to international criticism was both a bottom-up and a top-down campaign. Rather than directly set the message, the state let internet users fine-tune the message and then amplified lines of criticism that meshed with the state's overall strategy (Datt 2021). To prevent the discussion from being sidetracked, internet censors monitored it and removed posts that took the campaign in directions the government did not like. This guiding of opinions worked to remove both voices that were critical of the campaign and those that believed it did not go far enough (Chan 2021). Removed posts included those calling for support of the Xinjiang people (inviting a discussion about their true condition) and posts that argued for a wider boycott of all Western goods. Also removed were posts that sought to dig deeper into the original impetus for the companies to boycott cotton from the region.

Using this method, the government successfully turned a foreign criticism of Chinese domestic policy into a regime-strengthening form of dissidence against perceived Western imperialism. It is likely true that many of the Chinese corporate actors who severed ties with the Western brands did so defensively, perceiving the risk of being on the wrong side of the government messaging strategy. However, the online discussion indicated that the movement had a significant appeal among online consumers and thus a real commercial impact. Social media was flooded with videos and images of regular citizens burning or otherwise destroying products from these brands (Teh 2021). The outrage had a level of virality that indicated that it was not solely about toeing the government line for posters. The breadth of the protest indicated that, in this case, DDD was successful at shifting anger away from state actions in Xinjiang and focusing it on Western corporations and brands.

These two cases of DDD used against foreign forces illustrate how the government can flexibly employ the social media strategy against new targets when the need and opportunity arises. It can also be applied in ways to deflect criticism from external sources rather than anger at local governments. To be sure, there are some important differences between these cases and the previous examples of COVID-19. The foreign criticisms of the Wuhan Institute of Virology and the treatment of Uyghurs in Xinjiang are not as accessible to the average social media users when compared to the large number of online complaints about the tragic mistreatment of Dr. Li Wenliang. Moreover, Chinese citizens, after years of nationalist propaganda priming, are more willing to consider outside criticism unfair than criticism from aggrieved citizens (Chen and MacDonald 2020; Weiss 2019). However, the method of steering online discourse shares important similarities with the case of Li Wenliang. The central government did not ban all discussion of a topic that it considered sensitive. Rather, it sought to guide online opinion toward blaming targets that are politically safe.

It is important to pause here to differentiate DDD from simple scapegoating. The goal of the state is not only to change the subject to simply avoid blame though this is part of the motivation. DDD is a more interactive process in which agency is given to some online voices such that those making complaints in line with state goals feel a sense of empowerment. The online conversations on these topics are *directed*, but they are real conversations. The state does not simply tell citizens who is really to blame and then close the discussion. Rather, it channels true organic discourse in a direction that benefits the state's objectives. In this sense, DDD is a strategy that recognizes that heavy-handed stifling of dissent can create long-term resentment toward central government. Redirection of dissent can help maintain state credibility. These cases add some nuance to our understanding of how the government operationalizes DDD. In both cases, it has taken care to not let the online discussion become too heated or begin to target entities that the government would rather it not touch. This level of control echoes the careful calibration of response seen in the Li Wenliang case. Additionally, these cases highlight the interactivity between the state and social media users to develop the most effective DDD frame.

However, our review of the examples provided so far is not meant to imply that DDD can be used in any situation the government wishes. It is not an infinitely flexible strategy. In cases where users have personal experience, events are moving quickly, and the anger is at a policy closely associated with the central government, DDD has a more limited viability as a media strategy and may simply not be employed in the short term. Such was the case during the April–May 2022 lockdown of the city of Shanghai to contain a new COVID-19 outbreak.

Social media activity related to the 2022 COVID-19 lockdown in Shanghai highlights the limits of DDD. This case helps outline those situations DDD in which might not be effective. One of the most predictive variables appears to be individual experiences. More directly, experiences in which online users have a direct personal exposure and high level of interest do not seem to be as amenable to the use of DDD.

In early March 2022, a case imported from overseas initiated a new outbreak of COVID-19 in Shanghai. Initially, the government largely seemed to have the situation under control, as a targeted lockdown of only those who were close contact with a COVID-19 case and their immediate neighbors was enforced (Cheng 2022). Most of the city continued to operate as normal. However, as the number of cases started to climb in late March, rumors started swirling online of an imminent citywide lockdown (Stanway and Liu 2022). At the end of March, with cases clearly rising out of control, city officials, who had previously tried to avoid it, gave in and announced a citywide shutdown. Residents in some cases were only given a few hours to prepare, and even in areas of the city that were given a longer lead time, groceries and other necessities quickly sold out (McCarthy 2022).

During the initial days of the lockdown, the logistical network of the city came apart, with many of the drivers and delivery people either catching COVID, coming in close contact with someone with COVID, or being locked down themselves (Lin and Jie 2022). Many residents, even wealthy ones, pleaded with their local street committees (the first point of government contact in the city) for food (Bloomberg 2022a). Other residents faced difficulty obtaining medicine, and it was very difficult to reach a hospital in case of an emergency (Dou, Chiang, and Li 2022).

During this time, many stories and videos of hardships were shared on social media. One viral video from early in the lockdown showed a resident, positive with COVID-19 and about to be taken away to a quarantine center, turn a dog loose on the street rather than let it starve in their apartment. Shortly afterward, the dog is filmed wandering the street until a local government worker is shown attacking and killing it (Yeung 2022). Similarly, an audio call between an elderly resident and a local street committee leader went viral on social media as well (Bloomberg 2022b). The elderly resident stated that he will soon run out of food and critical medicine and then asked the local government street leader whether there was someone he could contact for emergency supplies. The local street leader sympathized but said it would be pointless to try to call higher levels of government, as they would not accept even his phone calls. Moreover, he himself had an empty refrigerator and therefore had nothing to share with the elderly resident. Similar tales of hardship were widely and frequently shared on social media during the lockdown period.

One particularly viral video was titled "Voices of April" (*siyue zhi sheng*). This video was a compilation of many of the previously shared hardship videos and recordings with melancholy music edited into the background. Although censors quickly blocked the video, netizens began reposting it with minor alterations in an attempt to evade the ban. The video was widely shared, accumulating more than 400 million views on social media, by an estimated half of internet users in China (Austrian China 2022). For many residents of Shanghai, their friends' social media feeds were dozens or hundreds of posts of this video, though most of the links to it were quickly disabled (Kuo 2022).

After it became clear that the video was being aggressively blocked, residents also began to sarcastically share older videos of Chinese government official spokespeople stating that netizens had the freedom to speak their mind in China (an answer given in response to Western reporters' questions regarding whether the Xinjiang cotton movement was truly grassroots). Also widely shared in response was a clip from the movie *Les Miserables* of "Do You Hear the People Sing," a song that is popularly associated around the world with anti-government protest (Gan 2022a).

The popularity of such videos and their frequent and wide distribution indicate the intense social media user interest in the lockdown situation, both in Shanghai and among other domestic social media users. Their volume overwhelmed the relatively infrequent local government news updates and positive central government propaganda stories. DDD had trouble functioning in part because the government could not control the narrative; events were moving too quickly, and residents were too interested in sharing new stories for the government to be able to effectively manage and redirect local resident anger. Indeed, the experiences of the residents made redirecting that emotion more difficult, as the state itself was at the center of the decision to lock down.

In Shanghai, residents had direct personal experience of their own difficulties during the lockdown. Even residents who had sufficient food worried whether their supplies would last. It was a common experience to spend each morning frantically refreshing the food delivery apps, hoping to be one of the lucky few to secure a grocery delivery slot from the few operating large supermarket groups (Huang 2022). Pet owners could easily imagine themselves being sent to the COVID-19 isolation camp and developed anxiety over what would happen to their pet in this situation. Parents with children found it difficult to work and keep their children occupied in small Shanghai apartments (Gan 2022b).

These direct personal experiences limited the ability of the government to employ DDD. Many residents felt directly and personally let down by the government. Since the COVID zero-tolerance policy had been set at the national level, it was therefore hard for the national government to shift the blame to the local level, although many residents were also understandably angry with the local government. In this particular case, the central government did not take any high-profile actions to punish local government officials or force them to make public apologies. The news messaging surrounding the lockdown was relatively muted as well, indicating that the government adopted a deemphasizing strategy rather than a blame-shifting one.

The Shanghai lockdown helped define the limits for directed digital dissidence. DDD is a strategy that works best in a low-information or conflicted-information environment. When the source of the problem is understood broadly, it has far less utility as a media or governing strategy. As it is strategic and requires time to plan and implement, DDD is limited where the interest level and social media discourse are moving quickly. DDD as a social media strategy uses relatively subtle collaboration with sympathetic online posters to be effective. Attempts to redirect blame for COVID would likely not have worked in Shanghai, given residents' direct experience with the policy failure—attempts to shift blame would be too obvious given residents' lived experiences. The cause of the policy failure was too closely identified with national-level policy to allow for space to redirect online dissonance. This case serves as a useful contrast to the online strategy employed in the case of Li Wenliang and the Xinjiang cotton protests, and it suggests when DDD may not be a success. However, we believe that such events, while perhaps highly threatening to the regime, are also rare. In most cases, the space and conditions are present for DDD to at least be partially employed.

Conclusion

This chapter adds to our understanding of online critical discourse in China by providing specific examples of the process and dynamics of DDD. The social media strategies the government employed in COVID-19 are examples of how the government seeks to manage, contain, and ultimately benefit from online social media flows. The examples show the strategy is effective and flexible, but not limitless.

During the early days of the epidemic, the regime sought to redirect criticism of its handling of the outbreak onto local officials in a way that is consistent with the data in previous chapters. DDD explains how there can be critical flows of information on social media and low levels of trust in local governments but high levels of trust in the central government. The power of redirecting popular dissatisfaction is made even more vivid in the case of Dr. Li Wenliang. The central government worked with social media tools to change the subject and blame his arrest on overzealous local officials, while removing scrutiny from national-level directed censorship and repression.

The regime-led actions during the investigation of the outbreak of the virus and during the Xinjiang cotton boycott highlight the flexibility of the DDD strategy. These cases show that DDD can be applied to international targets instead of local officials. Although our survey does not test the effectiveness of this international strategy, given their similarity to questions asked in the survey, DDD likely affects social media users' attitudes in a similar way (if not more effectively) as compared to when local governments are targeted. An additional element of flexibility demonstrated by these two cases is the incorporation of frames and issues raised organically on social media into official narratives. Rather than relying on a reactive top-down messaging strategy, these two cases demonstrate the power of co-option and cooperation between nationalist-minded social media users and official sources in strengthening the effectiveness of DDD. The strategy works best when there are natural targets that are both credible and emotionally satisfying to the online audience.

Finally, this chapter outlines, through a review of the social media engagement during the Shanghai COVID-19 lockdown, the types of cases in which DDD may not be effective. When there are no credible deflections and personal experiences are visible and widespread, DDD is less effective. However, because these situations are uncommon online, DDD can be viewed as a largely effective type of everyday discourse-shaping strategy. It is those widely shared exceptional events with special characteristics that likely will prove challenging for the government to employ this strategy. Such moments likely highlight some of the highest points of danger for central government censors. Misinformation and misdirection are harder when the facts are constantly in front of the consuming audience. Even the Wizard of Oz could tell when the illusion was done.

9
Will Directed Digital Dissidence Keep Working?

In this book, we considered and measured the role of the internet in shaping political attitudes and the ability of the elite actors in China to manipulate that process to help sustain support for the state. The internet, through social media and related platforms, facilitates the flow of dissident information in authoritarian regimes, and that government direction of this flow is critical for the maintenance of their hegemony. While some states have acted to bluntly constrain the internet to curtail the flow of information, China has been effectively limiting opposition by engaging and directing the discourse. Indeed, the more citizens use the internet generally, the more trusting they are of the central government. Further, internet use, specifically exposure to critical information via the internet, encourages activist- and protest-centered sentiment focused on dissatisfaction with the local governments.

The Chinese government is quite successful at channeling the flow of information in a way that solidifies their hegemony while simultaneously providing a sense of empowerment to citizens. Directed digital dissidence during the height of the COVID-19 pandemic explains how there can be critical flows of information on social media and low levels of trust in local governments but high levels of trust in the central government. Ultimately, the expansion of the internet simultaneously stimulates dissent while providing the central government an avenue to direct that dissent toward local governments or other targets and away from the central government. This allows the government to give citizens a voice while maintaining their largely unchallenged central authority. China has very effectively marshaled the technique of directed digital dissidence and in that sense has transformed the internet into a mechanism that helps sustain the government rather than challenge it.

Part of the success of this strategy rests on the existing social structures. For China, the strategy is rooted in the notion of "rightful resistance," where citizens

Directed Digital Dissidence in Autocracies. Jason Gainous, Rongbin Han, Andrew W. MacDonald, and Kevin M. Wagner, Oxford University Press. © Oxford University Press 2024. DOI: 10.1093/oso/9780197680384.003.0009

can lodge complaints and defend rights (O'Brien and Li 2006). By using the rhetoric and commitments of the central government, protestors effectively exploit institutionalized channels of dissent while avoiding repression. In rightful resistance, protesters actively seek the attention of higher levels of government or the public to enhance the effectiveness of protest directed at local officials. The rightful resistance framework explains how citizens in authoritarian regimes may exploit the slim political opportunity structure and negotiate with the state for better governance. The institution's own commitment to oppose corruption and graft allows an avenue to narrowly resist, but it also presents an opportunity for the state to engage with the dissent and shape the discourse and outcome.

It is in this space that the Chinese state has proven so effective. Although there is a fair amount of research exploring how social media has empowered social actors to challenge authoritarian regimes, there is much less addressing whether and how the state can actively shape the flow of information to its advantage, because few have done it so effectively. While rightful resistance provides opportunity, it also confirms and reinforces the legitimacy of the state. When engaging in rightful resistance, citizens are conferring on the state both trust and the legitimacy to mediate the conflict and resolve the dispute. Rightful resistance explains the paradoxical coexistence of the authoritarian regime and the rise of popular contention in China. Indeed, China not only provides the venue for rightful resistance; the state is able to enter the discourse and shape public opinion through public and sometimes not-so-public engagement.

Our original data provide empirical support for both the existence and effectiveness of directed digital dissidence in China. As noted above, our original survey data show that internet use correlates with trust in the state and government. The more online one is, the greater the trust in the central government. We show that internet use, specifically exposure to critical information via the internet, does appear to encourage activists, and that protest-centered sentiment focused on dissatisfaction with the local government. All our findings are consistent with the premise that the Chinese government is quite successful at guiding the flow of information in a way that solidifies their hegemony while simultaneously providing a sense of empowerment to citizens. Such findings suggest that the "strategic censorship"—optimally tolerating criticism of lower-level officials and adjusting the permissible level of criticism according to social tensions—is working in the Chinese context, allowing the regime to harness the benefits of freer information without risking overthrow (Lorentzen 2014).

Rethinking the Democratic Deficits in the Digital Age

Wide adoption of the internet still presents opportunities for democratization through the spread of dissident information and the organization of parties (Barber 2001; Corrado and Firestone 1996; Gainous and Wagner 2011, 2014). Information has become inexpensive to transmit, receive, and share. In the ideal world, the internet could be the driver of a new age of democratic growth around the globe. Indeed, participation rates correlate with online social media use (Boulianne 2015), and there has been evidence of a leveling effect in some developed nations in the areas of campaigning, fundraising, advertising, and even political organization (Bimber 2003; Mossberger, Tolbert, and McNeal 2008; Wagner and Gainous 2009).

Yet the online path does not necessarily lead to democratization and openness. Indeed, even in nations with an open online environment, political actors are particular adept at manipulating content (Gainous, Segal, and Wagner 2018). In the United States and other Western democracies, the online public sphere is an opaque and increasingly toxic brew of information and misinformation authored by not just internal domestic adversaries but foreign ones as well. Democracies rely on open engagement of the people, but the people are dependent on information, and the internet, it turns out, has no ideology other than the ones provided and promoted. It is not inherently democratizing. Indeed, policing misinformation with the help of the platforms themselves and a presumed neutral bureaucracy has proven challenging, as social media provides information at a scale and speed that is unmatched in human history.

Further, even in these largely stable democracies, the political leaders have their own agendas that are not always supportive of a transparent internet. The online space is dynamic, and it is increasingly accessible by large portions of the population as mobile devices become more sophisticated and more ubiquitous. As networks expand and the cost of devices declines, the penetration rate of the internet and social media has grown rapidly across nations (Wagner, Gray, and Gainous, 2017). More people are reachable, incentivizing political actors to compete to dominate the messaging through this new medium. We can build new and inexpensive digital lanes for information to travel, but familiar voices are often driving the vehicles. Even in open Western democracies, traditional political actors are still the most significant players online or offline (Gainous, Segal, and Wagner 2018). In the end, the players are familiar, and the sophistication of the actors is a driver of control and success.

Even in the most generous view, the democratizing effect of the internet has been at best limited and uneven. Although, as noted above, much of this is driven by the sophistication of political actors, much is possible because human nature is predictable. Cheap information and online forums have led to connections with like-minded users, which reinforces users' opinions while making them feel better about themselves (Park and Lee 2014). People are content with their preexisting views and are resistant to change. Even when trying to be active, many are content engaging online as opposed to offline because of the relative low cost. This participation has come to be derogatorily called "slacktivism" (Gladwell 2010). This malaise combined with effective messaging has established that the online forum is susceptible to manipulation from traditional political players, stifling significant change in the basic power balance of the political systems (Bimber and Davis 2003; Hindman 2008; Margolis and Resnick 2000; Stromer-Galley 2014; Ward, Gibson, and Lusoli 2003).

A similar disappointing pattern has emerged in more closed states. Early work on the role of the digital sphere in closed nations suggested that it would give new opportunities for dissident narratives and challenge the stability of autocracies. The media was quick to trumpet this narrative by assigning credit to internet platforms for providing the political space for democratic movements in Russia, the Middle East, and Asia (See, e.g., Alhindi, Talha, and Sulong 2012). But, increasingly, the results of the digital movements in many nations have proven far less significant and durable than initially assumed. Russia's Snow Revolution has been largely vitiated (Gainous, Wagner, and Ziegler 2018; Oates 2013). The Arab Spring has yet to transform nations in the Middle East into budding democracies (Wagner and Gainous 2013). In Asia, China has led the way in illustrating that the internet can not only be mediated and limited but can also be captured to actually sustain the regime by directing and redirecting dissidence in ways that serve the state. China has shown that the internet does not have to be blocked in its entirety if the state can ably direct it by competing and winning control of the narrative. The messaging surrounding the COVID-19 pandemic is a prominent example of where the information wars will be fought and the advantage state actors have with a tightly controlled messaging strategy.

Even with the dubious evidence to support the role of the internet in democratization, China's success is particularly impressive. For all the discussion in the literature about how this new digital reality could threaten the hegemony of the Chinese government over its citizens, it appears that the state's complex strategy of managing the information war is remarkably successful. They limit opposition, but since that has diminishing returns, they compete in information market and, as our results indicate, regularly win. The Chinese state is one of the main drivers of public opinion. It is constantly monitoring actions and engaging in a variety of actions intended to eliminate or co-opt the opposition. It should not be surprising that a well-financed state can spin its own narrative to great effect. The flaw in the democratizing view of the internet was not in the failure to understand the power of the medium to move information but rather in over-estimating people's ability to discard misinformation and underestimating state actors' effectiveness in manipulating political and cultural narratives.

Although the focus of this book has been on the efforts to control and limit the internet, the truth is that the scope of the Chinese state's behaviors is broad and connected. China is able to stockpile vast amounts of information on its own people, which fuels its ability to limit opposition and direct dissidence across multiple mediums and modalities. China is one of the most invasive nations when it comes to the surveillance of its people. By 2018, more than 200 million cameras were placed across the nation watching people walking, shopping, working, and going about nearly every aspect of daily life (Mozur 2018). Even considering the sizable population of China, that comes out to about one camera for every seven people, with a goal perhaps to double or even triple that surveillance (Economy 2019). The state is not only talking with you online; it is following you home offline (Xiao 2019).

The Chinese state has married population control to technology far beyond what most other nations have managed. The government has returned to using informants who are tasked with reporting "incorrect" thoughts or suspicious political behavior of others in classrooms, neighborhoods, and workplaces. However, digital tools take reporting to a new level. China's Social Credit System calculates the aggregate "trustworthiness" of citizens based on such considerations as whether they have outstanding loans, jaywalked, or otherwise misbehaved in public places (Economy 2019; Kostka 2019). Some of the pilot programs account for how many hours of video games a citizen plays. In theory, the state could grade people on purchasing Chinese as opposed to foreign-made goods. Social shaming is not a new concept in China, but new technologies increase the areas that the state can monitor, and the results are far easier to share. Failing to repay one's debts can be a particular black mark in China, and the state armed with new data is reviving public shaming by displaying the faces of debt defaulters on large billboards (Economy 2019; Liang et al. 2018)).

Indeed, the amount of data that the state is able to marshal and use presents a unique challenge to opposition movements. The digital sphere is part of a larger narrative of control that is made possible by the amount of personal data that is increasingly easy to obtain in the absence of strict limits on its gathering and use. This is a troubling prospect in open democracies but increasingly disturbing in closed states. China's success might well provide a blueprint to other closed states as they obtain access to these technologies. The mechanisms to monitor the population and observe behavior are decreasing in cost and increasing in efficacy. The addition of these data will link well with China's internet strategy

130 DIRECTED DIGITAL DISSIDENCE IN AUTOCRACIES

and allow the state to play an even more intrusive and likely effective role in smoothing and removing dissidence. The same strategies that have proven so effective in limiting opposition become both easier and less expensive to implement with increasingly detailed understandings of individual behavior and the mountains of available data. Combined with real-time video, facial recognition software, and predictive algorithms, the tools the state may implement are substantial. With these opportunities, the Chinese state is likely to increase its control over discourse.

However, nothing is static. Technology changes and people adapt. The Chinese state has proven effective in the current environment, but people can learn how the state intervenes in public discourse, and opposition leaders are likely to be a bit more nimble as they grasp the various ways to counter state tools. Creative circumvention of technology is the hallmark of effective counter-messaging. Indeed, although we cannot predict how opposition will manage in this high surveillance society, they will likely be creative in ways we did not anticipate. Citizens in nations with intrusive internet limitations have managed to organize by repurposing dating and business applications or other creative strategies (Howard 2010). Control mechanisms are difficult to maintain over long periods, and assumptions about future control is precarious at best. This is especially true considering the growing digital world and the shifting population, as older citizens are gradually be replaced by the younger, more tech savvy generation. This will ultimately result in the state racing to stay ahead of the citizens so that the technology can be used to sustain the governing coalition. History suggests that the state's approach cannot succeed indefinitely, though it might persist for some time.

Further, the strategy of directed digital dissidence itself does present some opportunities to change the state. The idea of directing unrest toward state institutions is premised on the idea that the citizens accept the state as a proper venue for the resolution of conflict. This means that the state is forced to hold at least some institutions of government accountable or risk directing their dissatisfaction through less controlled channels at the very state itself and its apparatus. We noted previously that the approach now in China is to scapegoat local government so that the national state avoids scrutiny. However, as scholars of critical legal theory have long established, venues created to limit or blunt popular will through the appearance of objectivity can evolve over time to more closely resemble their image than the designers intended (Thompson 1975). People come to believe that the institutions are fair, and the citizens who operate the institutions start to reflect that belief. If the Chinese state continues to provide a venue for the resolution of dissatisfaction with governance, at some point those venues may act in ways that provide actual recourse. However, in the case of China, such a possibility is more theoretical than substantive at this point.

Indeed, the state has been so effective at channeling and manipulating unrest that there is likely little concern about the risks associated with losing control of the institutions or the process.

The story of China and the digital sphere is a sound lesson about the limitations of technology and the importance of the individual. The belief that technology is or was the solution to democratic deficits was clearly more aspirational than empirical. The fear that technology will sharply curtail discursive or opposition discourse is worrisome and disturbing but far from definitive. Technology is neither the cure nor the disease. It is an opportunity structure, which presents both promising and troubling avenues on which to journey. In the end, the most important question lands again at the feet of society and the choices that must be made collectively about the role technology should play and what we are willing to accept. The answers, it seems, are not online; they are within us.

APPENDIX A

Survey Questions

Q1 About how many hours a **day** would you estimate you spend checking email, reading websites, or using social media (social media means applications like Weibo, QQ, Renren, Kaixin001, Douban, WeChat, or other sites and services that allow users to interact with each other) either with a computer or on a mobile device?
1. 0–1
2. 1–2
3. 2–3
4. 3–4
5. 4–5
6. 5–6
7. 6–7
8. 7–8
9. 8–9
10. More than 9

Q2 About how many hours a **day** would you estimate you spend using only social media? Social media means applications like Weibo, QQ, Renren, Kaixin001, Douban, WeChat, or other sites and services that allow users to interact with each other.
1. 0–1
2. 1–2
3. 2–3
4. 3–4
5. 4–5
6. 5–6
7. 6–7

133

134   APPENDIX A

8. 7–8
9. 8–9
10. More than 9

Q3 About how long have you been using the internet, either via computer or via your phone?

_____Years

Q4 How often do you use computer or applications on your phone to get news about political events? Political events include news about politicians, local governments, international relations, and government plans and policies.
1. Many times during the day (more than 5 times a day)
2. A few times a day (3–5 times a day)
3. About once a day (1–2 times a day)
4. Three to five days a week
5. Once a week
6. Less often
7. Never

Q5 How often do you read news stories about political events that have been posted on social media (social media means applications like Weibo, QQ, Renren, Kaixin001, Douban, WeChat, or other sites and services that allow users to interact with each other)?
1. More than once a day
2. Everyday
3. Three to five days per week
4. One to two days per week
5. Less often
6. Never

Q6 Do you check email, read websites, and use social media (social media means applications like Weibo, QQ, Renren, Kaixin001, Douban, WeChat, or other sites and services that allow users to interact with each other) more than you did five years ago?
1. Yes
2. No

Q7 On the whole, how satisfied or dissatisfied are you with the way the government works in China? Are you . . .
1. Very satisfied

Survey Questions   135

    2. Fairly satisfied
    3. Not very satisfied
    4. Not at all satisfied

Q8 Do you ever see stories posted on the internet, including on applications on your phone, that are critical about local governments or government officials?
    1. Yes, very often
    2. Yes, often
    3. Yes, occasionally
    4. No, never

Q9 Do you or people you know ever post comments on the internet, including on applications on your phone, that are critical about local governments or government officials?
    1. Yes, very often
    2. Yes, often
    3. Yes, occasionally
    4. No, never

Q10 Do you ever use local government websites to gather information about local services available to you?
    1. Yes, many times
    2. Yes, several times
    3. Yes, once
    4. No, never

Q11 Do you ever use local government websites to gather information about government policy?
    1. Yes, many times
    2. Yes, several times
    3. Yes, once
    4. No, never

Q12 Have you ever used your local government website to submit a complaint, suggestion, or comment about local government activities?
    1. Yes, many times
    2. Yes, several times
    3. Yes, once
    4. No, never

136   APPENDIX A

Q13 (A/B/C versions) Here are some institutions. For each one, please indicate how much trust you have in them.

*** A/B versions have question H. On question H, if "4. None at all" not selected on A, survey ends. Any answer allowed on B version.

*** C version has no H.

A. Central government
   1. A great deal
   2. Moderate trust
   3. Not very much trust
   4. None at all

B. The Courts
   1. A great deal
   2. Moderate trust
   3. Not very much trust
   4. None at all

C. My Local Government
   1. A great deal
   2. Moderate trust
   3. Not very much trust
   4. None at all

D. Civil Society (includes NGOs, membership organizations, business organizations, and similar)
   1. A great deal
   2. Moderate trust
   3. Not very much trust
   4. None at all

E. Lawyers
   1. A great deal
   2. Moderate trust
   3. Not very much trust
   4. None at all

F. The *People's Daily* and other party newspapers
   1. A great deal
   2. Moderate trust
   3. Not very much trust
   4. None at all

G. Commercialized media such as *Southern Weekend*, evening newspapers, or city newspapers
1. A great deal
2. Moderate trust
3. Not very much trust
4. None at all

H. On this line, please select "None at all"
1. A great deal
2. Moderate trust
3. Not very much trust
4. None at all

**************** List Questions
Block 1

Q14a1 Below are a number of institutions that people often place trust in. How many of them do you trust? Please note you do not have to answer which specific institutions you trust, just how many.
- Your city's police
- Real estate companies
- Chinese Red Cross
- Your city's newspaper
- Your local government

Q14a2 Below are a number of institutions that people often place trust in. How many of them do you trust? Please note you do not have to answer which specific institutions you trust, just how many.
- Your city's police
- Real estate companies
- Chinese Red Cross
- Your city's newspaper

Q14b1 Below a number of strategies people often use when they believe that they have been wronged by the local government. How many strategies would you use if you were in that situation? Please note you do not have to answer which specific strategies you would use, just how many.
- Work through your personal network
- Speak with a local government official
- Write to a higher level of government about the problem

138   APPENDIX A

- Offer a bribe to a local official
- Participate in a protest against the local government

Q14b2 Below a number of strategies people often use when they believe that they have been wronged by the local government. How many strategies would you use if you were in that situation? Please note you do not have to answer which specific strategies you would use, just how many.
- Work through your personal network
- Speak with a local government official
- Write to a higher level of government about the problem
- Offer a bribe to a local official

Q15a1 I'm going to read to you a number of things people often see on the internet. Please tell me how many you have seen. Please note you do not have to answer which specific things you have seen, just how many.
- Dating website advertisements
- An angry debate between netizens
- Religious or spiritual information
- Negative news about a celebrity
- Politically sensitive information

Q15a2 I'm going to read to you a number of things people often see on the internet. Please tell me how many you have seen. Please note you do not have to answer which specific things you have seen, just how many.
- Dating website advertisements
- An angry debate between netizens
- Religious or spiritual information
- Negative news about a celebrity

****************END LIST QUESTIONS

Q16 How trustworthy do you think each of the following sources of news are:
A. Television
1. Very trustworthy
2. Somewhat trustworthy
3. Somewhat untrustworthy
4. Very untrustworthy

B. Newspapers
1. Very trustworthy
2. Somewhat trustworthy
3. Somewhat untrustworthy
4. Very untrustworthy

C. Internet in General
1. Very trustworthy
2. Somewhat trustworthy
3. Somewhat untrustworthy
4. Very untrustworthy

Q17 Regarding paid online government posters,
1. I've never heard of them.
2. I've heard of them, but I haven't seen any posts from them.
3. I think I've seen posts from them.

*************** only ask if 2 or 3 of Q17 is selected

Q17a Regarding online forum posts, what percentage of comments would you estimate are posted by users paid by the government to post their views?
1. ____ percent

Q18 Regarding posters sponsored by net–spies or other hostile forces,
1. I've never heard of them.
2. I've heard of them, but I haven't seen any posts from them.
3. I think I've seen posts from them.

*************** only ask if 2 or 3 of Q18 is selected

Q18a Regarding online forum posts, what percentage of comments would you estimate are posted by users sponsored by net–spies or other hostile forces?
1. ____ percent

Q19 How interested are you in political news?
1. Very interested
2. Somewhat interested
3. Somewhat uninterested
4. Very uninterested

140 APPENDIX A

Q20 Here's a list of activities some people might do in response to a local government doing something they think is wrong. For each activity, please tell me if you think the action taken in response is always acceptable, sometimes acceptable, only in extreme circumstance acceptable, or never acceptable.

A. Participate in public protests against local government
1. Always acceptable
2. Sometimes acceptable
3. Only in extreme circumstances acceptable
4. Never acceptable

B. Ignoring laws and regulations
1. Always acceptable
2. Sometimes acceptable
3. Only in extreme circumstances acceptable
4. Never acceptable

C. Refuse to pay taxes as an act of protest against government
1. Always acceptable
2. Sometimes acceptable
3. Only in extreme circumstances acceptable
4. Never acceptable

D. Sign a petition letter to the local government
1. Always acceptable
2. Sometimes acceptable
3. Only in extreme circumstances acceptable
4. Never acceptable

E. Join a social group that tries to influence the local government
1. Always acceptable
2. Sometimes acceptable
3. Only in extreme circumstances acceptable
4. Never acceptable

F. Take the story to the press
1. Always acceptable
2. Sometimes acceptable
3. Only in extreme circumstances acceptable
4. Never acceptable

G. Sue the local government 行政诉讼（民告官）
1. Always acceptable
2. Sometimes acceptable
3. Only in extreme circumstances acceptable
4. Never acceptable

Q21 Some foreign websites and internet services such as Google are not accessible in China. How difficult would it be for you to access blocked foreign websites or other blocked internet services?
1. Did not know foreign websites are not accessible
2. Easily—just a few minutes of work
3. With some difficulty—half an hour or more
4. Very difficult—over an hour of work
5. Impossible—don't know how to access

Q22 Have you ever changed the content of what you intended to write on a blog, Weibo post, WeChat message, forum post, or other online post so as to avoid being censored?
1. Yes, many times
2. Yes, several times
3. Yes, once
4. No, never

Q23 How many people do you know who have accessed blocked websites or other blocked internet services?
1. More than 10
2. 5–10
3. 2–4
4. 1
5. None

***************** only ask if 1–4 of Q23 is selected

Q24 Among the people that you know that access blocked internet sites or services, what are some of the reasons for using these sites or services? (check yes to all that apply)
1. Use foreign social media applications to keep in touch with foreign friends
2. Access foreign movies, TV shows, and other entertainment content
3. Read political content

142   APPENDIX A

4. View adult material
5. Other

Q25 Have you tried to access blocked websites or other blocked internet services to read sensitive political information?
1. Yes, many times
2. Yes, several times
3. Yes, once
4. No, never

Q26 Have you tried to access blocked websites or other blocked internet services to watch foreign movies, TV shows, and other entertainment content?
1. Yes, many times
2. Yes, several times
3. Yes, once
4. No, never

Q27 Which of these best describes the place in which you live?
1. Countryside/village
2. Small city
3. Midsized city
4. Suburban area of a big city
5. Big city
6. Other

Q28 Gender
1. Female
2. Male

Q29 Are you a member or probationary member of the CCP?
1. Yes
2. No

Q30 Here is a table showing the range of **monthly** incomes that people have. Which of the letters on this table best represents the total **monthly** income of your household (after tax)?
A. 0–3,000
B. 3,000–6,000
C. 6,000–10,000
D. 10,000–15,000

E. 15,000–25,000

F. 25,000–40,000

F. More than 40,000

_____ Group

Q31 How old are you?

1. ____ Age

Q32 What is the highest level of education that you have obtained?

1. No formal education
2. Primary
3. Middle school (初中)
4. High school (高中)
5. University
6. Advanced studies/graduate school

APPENDIX B

Normality of Residuals for All Models—
Labeled by Associated Table/Figure and
Dependent Variable

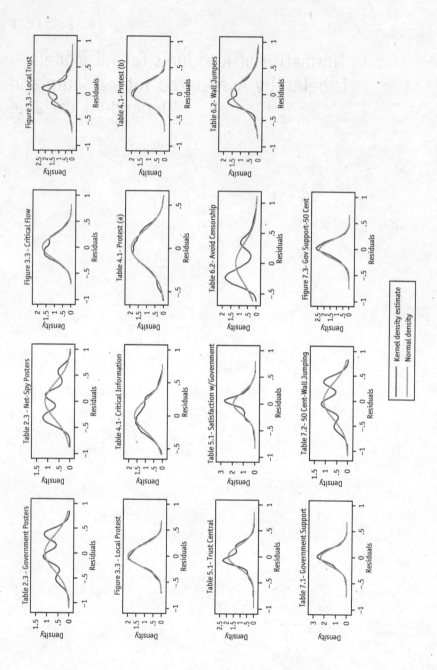

APPENDIX C

Chinese Social Media Posts

人民日报 V

【#应勇任湖北省委书记#】日前,中共中央决定:应勇同志任湖北省委委员、常委、书记,蒋超良同志不再担任湖北省委书记、常委、委员职务。#湖北省委主要负责同志职务调整#

02月13日 11:15 来自 微博 weibo.com

收藏　　　　转发 26656　　　　评论 37786　　　　574763

中国新闻网 V

【#湖北省委主要负责同志职务调整#】#应勇任湖北省委书记# 日前，中共中央决定：应勇同志任湖北省委委员、常委、书记，蒋超良同志不再担任湖北省委书记、常委、委员职务。

应勇简历

应勇，男，1957年11月生，汉族，浙江仙居人，中共党员，1976年12月参加工作，在职大学，法学硕士，二级大法官。现任十 展开全文∨

02月13日 11:17 来自 微博 weibo.com

| 收藏 | 转发 2002 | 评论 15334 | 👍 207674 |

环球时报 V

【#王忠林任武汉市委书记# #马国强不再担任#】新华网武汉2月13日电 日前，中央对湖北省委主要负责同志职务进行了调整。应勇同志任湖北省委委员、常委、书记，蒋超良同志不再担任湖北省委书记、常委、委员职务。

2月13日，湖北省召开领导干部会议，中央组织部副部长吴玉良同志在会上宣布了中央决定，称这 展开全文∨

02月13日 12:00 来自 微博 weibo.com

| 收藏 | 转发 7636 | 评论 12999 | 👍 157657 |

Notes

Chapter 1

1. The term Great Firewall is thought to be coined by Geremie R. Barmie and Sang Ye on June 1, 1997, in their article "The Great Firewall of China" on Wired.com.

Chapter 2

1. For example, the Asian Barometer (http://www.asianbarometer.org/), the Latin Barometer (https://www.latinobarometro.org/lat.jsp), and the World Values Survey (https://www.worldvaluessurvey.org/wvs.jsp) among others.
2. See https://data.worldbank.org/country/china (go to the Country Profile).
3. We reached out to the CNNIC in attempt to get access to the raw data so we could conduct subsample analyses excluding those under 19 from the sample, which would make our samples more comparable, but we received no response.
4. This measure is based on an additive index of several indicators, including the frequency of internet use (Q1), the number of years using the internet (Q3), the frequency of digital political information gathering (Q4), and visiting government websites for various reasons, including using services, policy related reasons, and filing complaints (Q10–Q12). Each was rescaled to range from 0 to 1 with intervals between, then a reliability analysis indicated that these items scaled well together ($\alpha = 0.68$), so we created an additive index and rescaled this index to range from 0 to 1 with associated intervals creating a continuous scale.
5. This measure is based on an additive index of two ordinal items asking respondents, first, how trustworthy they thought television news was and, second, how trustworthy they thought newspapers were (Q16A and Q16B). Each was rescaled to range from 0 to 1, tested for reliability ($\alpha = 0.80$), summed, and again rescaled to range from 0 to 1.
6. This measure is based on an additive index of income (Q30) and education (Q32). Each was rescaled to range from 0 to 1, tested for reliability ($\alpha = 0.39$), summed, and rescaled to range from 0 to 1. Reliability was relatively low here, but although income and education are not strongly related, we decided that the combination of the two was still our best representation of SES in the data.
7. All of our measures, even single-item measures, are rescaled to range from 0 to 1 to make the coefficients in all the models we estimate comparable in size (the number of decimal places before a nonzero value are similar). This facilitates an easier read of the tables. Again, these are linear transformations so none of the intervals are changed, only the scale of the measures.

150 *Notes*

Chapter 3

1. See Constitution of the People's Republic of China (amended in 2004).
2. The total number of government websites in 2016 is actually lower than that in 2014.
3. CCYLCC School Department College Branch, *Wangluo Xuanchuanyuan Duiwu Jianshe Tongzhi* [Circular on Establishing Internet Propaganda Troop], leaked official email communication to Shanghai Communist Youth League School Department, March 20, 2014, 10:52 p.m.
4. We would have also estimated this model with indicators of critical information exposure and protest against the central government, but we decided that social desirability effects would have made survey measures of these concepts difficult. Here we would expect that effect to be smaller than that of the local critical flow if we are correct about the central government strategy. We do have later analysis showing that there is a relationship between jumping the firewall, where we can assume there is a higher likelihood of exposure to dissidence, and trust in the central government.
5. Again we tested whether ordinary least squares (OLS) were suitable for each stage of this mediation model. We estimated each level of the model using OLS and plotted the kernel density estimates against the normal density plot to examine whether the residuals of the model were distributed normally. The results presented in appendix B suggest that the residuals for the models of critical flow and local trust do not distribute normally, so we relied on ordered logit to estimate these levels. That said, the residuals in the model of attitudes about protest do distribute normally; thus, we rely on OLS for the final stage of the model.

Chapter 4

1. It is worth noting that several companies competed in the microblogging market, including IT giants such as Tencent and Netease. In fact, Sina Weibo was not even the first microblogging service site in China. Fanfou.com, the first website that offered a microblogging service, came into being as early as 2007. However, the site was closed in July 2009 because of censorship. Though it was reopened in November 2010, Sina Weibo had already established its dominance. Today, Sina Weibo is the most successful Twitter-like microblogging service in China. Weibo almost by default refers to Sina Weibo.
2. According to *The 37th Statistical Report on Internet Development in China*, by CNNIC, QQ Zone (the blogging and social networking extension of QQ), Weibo, Renren, and Douban had a penetration rate of 65.1 percent, 33.5 percent, 15.6 percent, and 13.6 percent, respectively, in December 2015. The total internet population by December 2015 was 668.26 million, meaning that the four sites respectively had 448.06 million, 230.57 million, 107.37 million, and 93.60 million users. The report does not include data for Kaixin001 or WeChat. *The 39th Statistical Report on Internet Development in China* reveals that WeChat and QQ are the two most frequently used apps, covering 79.6 percent and 60.0 percent of Chinese netizens, respectively.
3. After rescaling these three items to range from 0 to 1, we constructed an additive index from them and rescaled it to range from 0 to 1 as well, for use in the analysis that follows. The reliability estimate was not high ($\alpha = 0.31$), but we nonetheless proceeded with construction of the index because the face validity still holds up. Those who claim to use social media generally more often, claim to read political news more often, and claim to use it more than they did in the past are likely more frequent social media users.
4. We tested again whether OLS was suitable for each of the three models presented in table 4.1. After estimating each of the three models using OLS and plotting the kernel density estimates against the normal density plot, it was evident that the residuals of the critical information model were not distributed normally, but the residuals in both protest models were (see appendix B). Thus, we rely on ordered logit for the former and OLS for both of the latter models.

Notes 151

5. We also estimated this model replacing general social media first with the frequency respondents used the internet generally (Q1) and second with political information gathering other than social media (Q4). The results indicated that social media use was a stronger predictor of critical exposure than either. The respective odds ratios for these estimates were slightly less than 2 and around 1. Thus, social media has a considerably stronger relationship.

6. The relationships are measures based on a Pearson's product-moment point-biserial correlation coefficient, and the positive Spearman's rank-order coefficient, respectively.

7. There is no consensus on the classification of Chinese cities in tiers because different institutions and companies often use different criteria to categorize them. However, it is generally agreed that the first and second tier are composed of megacities such as Beijing and Shanghai and provincial capitals and sub–provincial capital cities. The third tier is made up of prefecture capital cities mostly, which often have an urban population of at least half a million. For a good illustration of the tier-system of Chinese cities, see Dorcas Wong (2019).

Chapter 5

1. Using a nationally representative survey dataset, Fei Shen and Zhi'an Zhang (2018) find that wall jumpers tend to be more likely to oppose censorship, have less trust in news media, and to participate in civic activities, but they also hold more politically conservative attitudes. In addition, Hobbs and Roberts (2018) show that the censorship may counterintuitively increase access to blocked information as it incentivizes citizens to learn methods of censorship evasion, which then can be applied to browse censored sites.

2. Our tests of whether OLS was suitable for the two models presented in table 5.1 suggested that ordered logit was more appropriate for both. The residuals were not distributed normally (see appendix B).

3. These two items scaled well together after being rescaled to range from 0 through 1 and then inverted to run the intuitive direction ($\alpha = 0.77$).

Chapter 6

1. Respondents were asked also about whether their friends had jumped the wall to get pornographic material—about 34 percent said they had.

2. Referring to appendix B, the residuals for the OLS models did not distribute normally for either, so we fit both models using ordered logit.

3. Bivariate correlations between social media use, political interest, CCP membership, and urbanicity with general internet use were significant (social media use—Pearson's r p-value = .00, political interest—Spearman's p-value = .00, CCP member—point-biserial p-value = .08, urbanicity—Spearman's p-value = .00).

Chapter 7

1. Although we relied on ordered logit for both models in table 5.1, as is clear in the graph in appendix B, the residuals normalized for the OLS model once these two items were indexed. Thus, the model results in table 7.1 are based on OLS.

2. We relied on ordered logit here because the residuals did not distribute normally when estimating the model using OLS (see appendix B).

Chapter 8

1. The term "institutional strength" had made way into the party's official ideological construct before the pandemic but has been frequently cited as an explanation to China's success in coping with the crisis. See "Zhonggong Zhongyang guanyu jianchi he wanshan

Zhongguo tese shehuizhuyi zhidu tuijin guojia zhili tixi he zhili nengli xiandaihua ruogan zhongda wenti de jueyi (shuangyu yaodian)" [Decision of the Central Committee of the Communist Party of China on several major issues concerning adhering to and improving the socialist system with Chinese characteristics and promoting the modernization of the national governance system and governance capability (bilingual highlights)] (*China Daily* 2019).

2. This means cadres sent down from upper levels to the community level, mostly to facilitate policy implementation.

3. Also see *China Digital Time's explainer on* Dr. Li Wenliang available at https://chinadigitaltimes.net/space/李文亮 (*China Digital Times* n.d.).

4. The report is still available on platforms beyond the control of the Chinese state. For instance, see Shou xunjie de Wuhan yisheng: 11 Tian hou bei bingren chuanran zhujin geli bingfang" [The disciplined Wuhan doctor: Infected by a patient and admitted to an isolation ward 11 days later], available at , https://www.zaobao.com.sg/wencui/politic/story20200128-1024296 (Zaobao 2020).

5. Specifically, we coded articles from the print version of the paper with either "New Corona" (新冠), "New Coronavirus" (新型冠状病毒), "Epidemic" (疫情), "Fighting the Epidemic" 抗疫 or "Battling the Epidemic" (战疫) in the title.

References

Alhindi, Waheed Ahmed, Muhammad Talha, and Ghazali Bin Sulong. 2012. "The Role of Modern Technology in Arab Spring." *Archives des sciences* 65 (8): 101–12.

Anderson, Christopher J., Patrick M. Regan, and Robert L. Ostergard. 2002. "Political Repression and Public Perceptions of Human Rights." *Political Research Quarterly* 55 (2): 439–56. https://doi.org/10.1177/106591290205500208.

Ang, Yuen Yuen. 2020. "When COVID-19 Meets Centralized, Personalized Power." *Nature Human Behaviour* 4 (5): 445–47.

Austrian China (Substack newsletter). 2022. "Shanghai Video Overwhelms Chinese Censor, Gets 400m Views." April 24, 2022. https://austrianchina.substack.com/p/shanghai-video-gets-400m-views.

Babbie, Earl G. 2021. *The Practice of Social Research*. 15th edition. Boston: Cengage Learning.

Bambauer, Derek E., Ronald J. Deibert, John G. Palfrey, Rafal Rohozinski, Nart Villeneuve, and Jonathan L. Zittrain. "Internet Filtering in China in 2004–2005: A Country Study." April 15, 2005. http://dx.doi.org/10.2139/ssrn.706681.

Bandurski, David, and Martin Hala, eds. 2010. *Investigative Journalism in China: Eight Cases in Chinese Watchdog Journalism*. Hong Kong: Hong Kong University Press.

Barber, Benjamin. 2001. "The Uncertainty of Digital Politics: Democracy's Uneasy Relationship with Information Technology." *Harvard International Review* 23 (1): 42–47.

Barrale, Natascia. 2018. "Foreign Literature as Poison: (Self-)Censorship in the Translation of German Popular Fiction in Italy during the 1930s." *Perspectives: Studies in Translation Theory and Practice* 26 (6): 852–67.

BBC Chinese. 2020. "Feiyan yiqing: 'Tuite fengbo' zhaqi, Meiguo xiang Cui Tiankai ti kangyi" [Pneumonia Epidemic: Outbreak of 'Twitter storm' and US Protests to Cui Tiankai]. March 13, 2020. https://www.bbc.com/zhongwen/simp/world-51872515.

Béja, Jean-Philippe. 2009. "The Massacre's Long Shadow." *Journal of Democracy* 20 (3): 5–16.

Bernstein, Thomas. P, and Xiaobo Lv. 2003. *Taxation without Representation in Rural China*. New York: Cambridge University Press.

Bimber, Bruce. A., and Richard Davis. 2003. *Campaigning Online: The Internet in US Elections*. New York: Oxford University Press.

Bloomberg. 2022a. "Shanghai's Locked-Down Elite Are Joining Hunt for Groceries." April 8, 2022. https://www.bloomberg.com/news/articles/2022-04-08/shanghai-s-locked-down-elite-are-joining-hunt-for-groceries.

Bloomberg. 2022b. "Elderly Shanghai Man's Pleas for Medical Help Censored in China." April 14, 2022. https://www.bloomberg.com/news/articles/2022-04-14/elderly-shanghai-man-s-pleas-for-medical-help-censored-in-china.

154 *References*

Bolsover, Gillian, and Philip Howard. 2019. "Chinese Computational Propaganda: Automation, Algorithms and the Manipulation of Information about Chinese Politics on Twitter and Weibo." *Information, Communication & Society* 22 (14): 2063–80. https://doi.org/10.1080/1369118X.2018.1476576.

Boulianne, Shelley. 2015. "Social Media Use and Participation: A Meta-analysis of Current Research." *Information Communication and Society* 18 (5): 524–38. https://doi.org/10.1080/1369118X.2015.1008542.

Brady, Anne-Marie. 2008. *Marketing Dictatorship: Propaganda and Thought Work in Contemporary China.* Lanham, MD: Rowman & Littlefield.

Brook, Timothy. 1998. *Quelling the People: The Military Suppression of the Beijing Democracy Movement.* Stanford, CA: Stanford University Press.

Cai, Yongshun. 2010. *Collective Resistance in China: Why Popular Protests Succeed or Fail.* Stanford, CA: Stanford University Press.

Cai, Yongshun. 2014. *State and Agents in China: Disciplining Government Officials.* Stanford, CA: Stanford University Press.

Cairns, Christopher. 2017. "China's Weibo Experiment: Social Media (Non-)Censorship and Autocratic Responsiveness." Cornell University.

Campbell, Angus, Philip E. Converse, Warren E. Miller, and Donald E. Stokes. 1960. *The American Voter.* New York: John Wiley and Sons.

Central Commission for Discipline Inspection and National Supervisory Commission [CCDI]. 2020. "Guojia jianwei diaochazu fuzeren da jizhewen" [National Supervisory Commission Inspection Team Head Answers Reporters' Questions]. March 19, 2020. https://www.ccdi.gov.cn/toutiao/202003/t20200319_213887.html.

CGTN. 2020. "Wuhan Police Apologize to Doctor Who Sounded Early Alarm on COVID-19." March 20, 2020. https://news.cgtn.com/news/2020-03-19/Admonition-letter-to-Dr-Li-Wenliang-improper-investigation-OZvG7i94Fa/index.html.

Chadwick, Andrew. 2017. *The Hybrid Media System: Politics and Power.* 2nd edition. Oxford University Press.

Chan, John. 2021. "Netizen Voices: 'Don't Just Support Xinjiang Cotton, Support Xinjiang People.'" *China Digital Times,* March 25, 2021. http://chinadigitaltimes.net/2021/03/netizen-voices-dont-support-xinjiang-cotton-support-xinjiang-people-instead/.

Chao, Loretta. 2012. "Sina, Tencent Shut down Commenting on Microblogs." *The Wall Street Journal,* March 31, 2012, pA10.

Chase, Michael S., and James C. Mulvenon. 2002. *You've Got Dissent.* Santa Monica, CA: RAND Corporation.

Chen, An. 2002. "Capitalist Development, Entrepreneurial Class, and Democratization in China." *Political Science Quarterly* 117 (3): 401–22.

Chen, Dan, and Andrew W. MacDonald. 2020. "Bread and Circuses: Sports and Public Opinion in China." *Journal of Experimental Political Science* 7 (1): 41–55. https://doi.org/10.1017/XPS.2019.15.

Chen, Feng. 2003. "Industrial Restructuring and Workers' Resistance in China." *Modern China* 29 (2): 237–62.

Chen, Jidong, Jennifer Pan, and Yiqing Xu. 2016. "Sources of Authoritarian Responsiveness: A Field Experiment in China." *American Journal of Political Science* 60 (2): 383–400.

Chen, Jidong, and Yiqing Xu. 2017. "Why Do Authoritarian Regimes Allow Citizens to Voice Opinions Publicly?" *Journal of Politics* 79 (3): 792–803. https://doi.org/10.1086/690303.

Chen, Jie. 2004. *Popular Political Support in Urban China.* Stanford, CA: Stanford University Press.

Chen, Jie, and Bruce J. Dickson. 2010. *Allies of the State: China's Private Entrepreneurs and Democratic Change.* Cambridge, MA: Harvard University Press.

Chen, Wenhong, and Barry Wellman. 2004. "The Global Digital Divide—within and between Countries." *IT & Society* 1 (7): 18–25.

Chen, Xi. 2008. "Collective Petitioning and Institutional Conversion." In *Popular Protest in China,* ed. Kevin J. O'Brien, 54–70. Cambridge, MA: Harvard University Press.

Chen, Xi. 2009. "Between Defiance and Obedience: Protest Opportunism in China." In *Grassroots Political Reform in Contemporary China*, eds. Elizabeth J. Perry and Merle Goldman, 253–81. Cambridge, MA: Harvard University Press.

Cheng, Shuwen. 2014. "Woguo Wangluo Fanfu Xian 'Duanyashi Jiangwen'" [Online Anti-corruption Cools Down Dramatically]. *Nanfang Dushibao [Southern Metropolis Daily]*, December 26, 2014.

Cheng, Evelyn. 2022. "China Is Shutting Down Shanghai in Two Phases to Control COVID." *CNBC*, March 28, 2022. https://www.cnbc.com/2022/03/28/china-is-shutting-down-shanghai-in-two-phases.html.

China Daily. 2019. "Zhonggong zhongyang guanyu jianchi he wanshan zhongguo tese shehu-izhuyi zhidu tuijin guojia zhili tixi he zhili nengli xiandaihua ruogan zhongda wenti de jueyi (shuangyu yaodian)" [Decision of the Central Committee of the Communist Party of China on Several Major Issues concerning Adhering to and Improving the Socialist System with Chinese Characteristics and Promoting the Modernization of the National Governance System and Governance Capability (Bilingual Highlights)]. November 6, 2019. https://language.chinadaily.com.cn/a/201911/06/WS5dc229baa310cf3e35575b18.html.

China Digital Times. 2021a. "[*CDT Minganci Zhoubao*] Di 11 Qi: Renren yingshi zimuzu, Xinjiang daguimo xingqin, Club House" [(*CDT Sensitive Words Weekly*) Issue 11: Renren TV and Movie Subtitle Group, Xinjiang Mass Sexual Assault, and Clubhouse. February 9, 2021. https://chinadigitaltimes.net/chinese/662492.html.

China Digital Times. 2021b. "[404 Wenku]: Guanchazhe wang; Ruishi shengwuxue zhuanjia Wilson Edwards baodao de zuizao Zhongwen banben" ([404 Library]: The Observer Net; The Earliest Report on Swiss Biologist Wilson Edwards in Chinese]. August 10, 2021. https://chinadigitaltimes.net/chinese/669506.html.

China Digital Times. n.d. "Li Wenliang." https://chinadigitaltimes.net/space/.

China E-government Council [Dianzi Zhengwu Lishihui], ed. 2015. *China's E-government Yearbook* (2015). Beijing: Social Sciences Academic Press.

China Internet Network Information Center (CNNIC). 1997. *The 1st Statistical Report on China Internet Development*. CNNIC. https://www.cnnic.cn/n4/2022/0401/c88-802.html.

China Internet Network Information Center (CNNIC). 2009. *The 1st Statistical Report on China Internet Development*. CNNIC. http://www.cnnic.cn/hlwfzyj/hlwxzbg/200905/P020120709345374625930.pdf.

China Internet Network Information Center (CNNIC). 2016. *The 37th Statistical Report on Internet Development in China*. CNNIC. https://www.cnnic.com.cn/IDR/ReportDownloads/201604/P020160419390562421055.pdf.

China Internet Network Information Center (CNNIC). 2017. *The 39th Statistical Report on Internet Development in China*. CNNIC. https://www.cnnic.com.cn/IDR/ReportDownloads/201706/P020170608523740585924.pdf.

China News Net. 2020. "Wuhan jingfang tongbao Li Wenliang shijian: chexiao xunjieshu xiang jiashu daoqian" [Wuhan Police Reports on the Li Wenliang Incident: Revoke the Admonition Letter and Apologize to Li's Family]. March 19, 2020. https://www.chinanews.com.cn/gn/2020/03-19/9131338.shtml.

Clark, William A. 1993. *Crime and Punishment in Soviet Officialdom: Combating Corruption in the Political Elite, 1965–1990*. New York: M. E. Sharpe.

Corrado, Anthony, and Charles M. Firestone. 1996. *Elections in Cyberspace: Toward a New Era in American Politics*. Washington, DC: Aspen Institute.

Creemers, Rogier. 2017. "Cyber China: Upgrading Propaganda, Public Opinion Work and Social Management for the Twenty-First Century." *Journal of Contemporary China* 26 (103): 85–100. https://doi.org/10.1080/10670564.2016.1206281.

Crete-Nishihata, Masashi, Jakub Dalek, Jeffrey Knockel, Nicola Lawford, Caroline Wesley, and Mari Zhou. 2020. "Censored Contagion II: A Timeline of Information Control on Chinese Social Media during COVID-19." *Citizen Lab*. https://citizenlab.ca/2020/08/censored-contagion-ii-a-timeline-of-information-control-on-chinese-social-media-during-covid-19/.

Damm, Jens. 2007. "The Internet and the Fragmentation of Chinese Society." *Critical Asian Studies* 39 (2): 273–94.

Datt, Angeli. 2021. "The CCP Hand behind China's Xinjiang Cotton Backlash." *Freedom House*, May 3, 2021. https://freedomhouse.org/article/ccp-hand-behind-chinas-xinjiang-cotton-backlash.

Davis, Sara Meg, and Hai Lin. 2004. "Demolished: Forced Evictions and the Tenants' Rights Movement in China." *Human Rights Watch* 16 (4): 1–43.

Deibert, Ronald. 2015. "Cyberspace under Siege." *Journal of Democracy* 26 (3): 64–78.

Deibert, Ronald, John Palfrey, Rafal Rohozinski, and Jonathan Zittrain. 2008. *Access Denied: The Practice and Policy of Global Internet Filtering*. Cambridge, MA: MIT Press.

Deibert, Ronald, John Palfrey, Rafal Rohozinski, and Jonathan Zittrain. 2010. *Access Controlled: The Shaping of Power, Rights, and Rule in Cyberspace*. Cambridge, MA: MIT Press.

Deng, Yanhua, and Kevin J. O'Brien. 2013. "Relational Repression in China: Using Social Ties to Demobilize Protesters." *China Quarterly*, 215: 533–52.

Deng, Zhong, and Donald J. Treiman. 1997. "The Impact of the Cultural Revolution on Trends in Educational Attainment in the People." *American Journal of Sociology* 103 (2): 391–428.

Deutsche Welle. 2011. "Zhongguo guanmei yinshu xuezhe cheng Meiguo konghe Ruishi: chawu ciren" [Chinese State Media Citing Scholar Claiming that the U.S. Intimidated Switzerland: No Such Person Found]. August 11, 2011. https://p.dw.com/p/3ypPj.

Diamant, Neil J., and Kevin J. O'Brien. 2014. "Veterans' Political Activism in China." *Modern China* 41 (3): 278–312.

Diamant, Neil J., Stanley B. Lubman, and Kevin J. O'Brien, eds. 2005. *Engaging the Law in China: State, Society, and Possibilities for Justice*. Stanford, CA: Stanford University Press.

Dickson, Bruce J. 2003. *Red Capitalists in China: The Party, Private Entrepreneurs, and Prospects for Political Change*. Cambridge: Cambridge University Press.

Dickson, Bruce J. 2021. *The Party and the People: Chinese Politics in the 21st Century*. Princeton, NJ: Princeton University Press.

Dikötter, Frank. 2013. *The Tragedy of Liberation: A History of the Chinese Revolution 1945–1957*. New York: A&C Black.

Dittmer, Lowell, and Guoli Liu. 2006. *China's Deep Reform: Domestic Politics in Transition*. Lanham, MD: Rowman & Littlefield.

Dou, Eva, Vic Chiang, and Lyric Li. 2022. "Medical Emergencies Mount as Shanghai's Lockdown Tightens." *Washington Post*, April 1, 2022. https://www.washingtonpost.com/world/2022/04/01/china-shanghai-medical-emergencies-coronavirus-lockdown/.

Economist. 2017. "Three Kingdoms, Two Empires: China's Internet Giants." 423 (9037): 57.

Economy, Elizabeth. 2019. "30 Years after Tiananmen: Dissent Is Not Dead." *Journal of Democracy* 30 (2): 57–63. https://doi.org/10.1353/jod.2019.0024.

Embassy of the People's Republic of China in the United States of America [PRC Embassy]. 2021. "So-Called 'Re-education Camps.'" June 25, 2021. http://us.china-embassy.gov.cn/eng/zt_120777/dmxj/wjbxinjiang1/zaijiaoyu1/202106/t20210625_9039435.htm.

Esarey, Ashley. 2015. "Winning Hearts and Minds? Cadres as Microbloggers in China." *Journal of Current Chinese Affairs* 44 (2): 69–103.

Esarey, Ashley, and Qiang Xiao. 2008. "Political Expression in the Chinese Blogosphere." *Asian Survey* 48 (5): 752–72.

Esarey, Ashley, and Qiang Xiao. 2011. "Digital Communication and Political Change in China." *International Journal of Communication* 5: 298–319.

Fang, Kecheng, and Maria Repnikova. 2018. "Demystifying 'Little Pink': The Creation and Evolution of a Gendered Label for Nationalistic Activists in China." *New Media & Society* 20 (6): 2162–85. https://doi.org/10.1177/1461444817731923.

Fang, Ning. 2020. "Renmin yaolun: Kangyi douzheng zhangxian zhongguo zhidu youshi" [People Daily Key Comments: The Fight against the Epidemic Demonstrates China's Institutional Advantages]. *People's Daily*, September 17, 2020. http://theory.people.com.cn/n1/2020/0917/c40531-31864467.html.

Friedman, Vanessa, and Elizabeth Paton. 2021. "What Is Going On with China, Cotton and All of These Clothing Brands?" *New York Times*, March 29, 2021. https://www.nytimes.com/2021/03/29/style/china-cotton-uyghur-hm-nike.html.

Fu, Jingying. 2020. "Guojia jianwei jueding pai diaochazu jiu sheji Li Wenliang yisheng youguan wenti zuo quanmian diaocha" [National Supervisory Commission Decides to Send Inspection Team to Comprehensively Investigate Issues Related to Dr. Li Wenliang]. *People's Daily Online*, February 7, 2020. http://fanfu.people.com.cn/n1/2020/0207/c64371-31576267.html.

Fu, King Wa, Chung Hong Chan, and Michael Chau. 2013a. "Assessing Censorship on Microblogs in China: Discriminatory Keyword Analysis and the Real-Name Registration Policy." *IEEE Internet Computing* 17 (3): 42–50.

Fu, King-wa, Chung-hong Chan, and Michael Chau. 2013b. "FP Assessing Censorship on Microblogs in China." *IEEE Internet Computing* 17 (3): 2–10. https://doi.org/10.1109/MIC.2013.28.

Gainous, Jason, Adam David Marlowe, and Kevin M. Wagner. 2013. Traditional Cleavages or a New World: Does Online Social Networking Bridge the Political Participation Divide?. *International Journal of Politics, Culture, and Society* 26 (2): 145–58.

Gainous, Jason, Andrew Segal, and Kevin Wagner. 2018. "Is the Equalization/Normalization Lens Dead? Social Media Campaigning in US Congressional Elections." *Online Information Review* 42 (5): 718–31.

Gainous, Jason, and Kevin M. Wagner. 2011. Rebooting American *Politics*: The *Internet Revolution*. Rowman & Littlefield.

Gainous, Jason, and Kevin M. Wagner. 2014. Tweeting to Power: The Social Media Revolution in American Politics. New York: Oxford University Press.

Gainous, Jason, Kevin M. Wagner, and Jason P. Abbott. 2015. "Civic Disobedience: Does Internet Use Stimulate Political Unrest in East Asia?" *Journal of Information Technology & Politics* 12 (2): 219–36. https://doi.org/10.1080/19331681.2015.1034909.

Gainous, Jason, Kevin M. Wagner, and Tricia Gray. 2016. "Internet Freedom and Social Media Effects: Democracy and Citizen Attitudes in Latin America." *Online Information Review* 40 (5): 712–38.

Gainous, Jason, Kevin M. Wagner, and Charles E. Ziegler. 2018. "Digital Media and Political Opposition in Authoritarian Systems: Russia's 2011 and 2016 Duma Elections." *Democratization* 25 (2): 209–26. https://doi.org/10.1080/13510347.2017.1315566.

Gallagher, Mary E. 2002. "'Reform and Openness': Why China's Economic Reforms Have Delayed Democracy." *World Politics* 54 (3): 338–72. https://doi.org/10.1353/wp.2002.0009.

Gallagher, Mary E. 2011. *Contagious Capitalism: Globalization and the Politics of Labor in China*. Princeton, NJ: Princeton University Press.

Gan, Nectar. 2022a. "'Voices of April': China's Internet Erupts in Protest against Censorship of Shanghai Lockdown Video." *CNN*, April 25, 2022. https://www.cnn.com/2022/04/25/china/china-covid-beijing-shanghai-mic-intl-hnk/index.html.

Gan, Nectar. 2022b. "'We Are the Last Generation': China's Harsh Lockdowns Could Exacerbate Population Crisis." *CNN*, May 16, 2022. https://www.cnn.com/2022/05/16/china/china-population-crisis-shanghai-lockdown-intl-hnk-mic/index.html.

Gao, Jie. 2015. "Political Rationality vs. Technical Rationality in China's Target-Based Performance Measurement System: The Case of Social Stability Maintenance." *Policy and Society* 34 (1): 37–48.

Gao, Li, and James Stanyer. 2014. "Hunting Corrupt Officials Online: The Human Flesh Search Engine and the Search for Justice in China." *Information, Communication, & Society* 17 (7): 814–29.

Geddes, Barbara, and John Zaller. 1989. "Sources of Popular Support for Authoritarian Regimes." *American Journal of Political Science* 33 (2): 319–47.

Gladwell, Malcolm. 2010. "Small Change: Why the Revolution Will Not Be Tweeted." *The New Yorker* 4: 42–49. https://www.newyorker.com/magazine/2010/10/04/small-change-malcolm-gladwell.

Gold, Thomas B. 1984. "'Just in Time!' China Battles Spiritual Pollution on the Eve of 1984." *Asian Survey* 24 (9): 947–74.

Göbel, Christian. 2021. "The Political Logic of Protest Repression in China." *Journal of Contemporary China* 30 (128): 169–85. https://doi.org/10.1080/10670564.2020.1790 897.

Granville, Johanna. 2005. "'Caught with Jam on Our Fingers': Radio Free Europe and the Hungarian Revolution of 1956." *Diplomatic History* 29 (5): 811–39. https://doi.org/ 10.1111/j.1467-7709.2005.00519.x.

Gray, Tricia, Jason Gainous, and Kevin M. Wagner. 2017. "Gender and the Digital Divide in Latin America." *Social Science Quarterly* 98 (1): 326–40.

Green, Andrew. 2020. "Li Wenliang." *Lancet* 395 (10225): 682. http://www.thelancet.com/arti cle/S0140673620303822/fulltext.

Gruffydd-Jones, Jamie J. 2019. "Citizens and Condemnation: Strategic Uses of International Human Rights Pressure in Authoritarian States." *Comparative Political Studies* 52 (4): 579–612. https://doi.org/10.1177/0010414018784066.

Guo, Shaohua. 2018. "'Occupying' the Internet: State Media and the Reinvention of Official Culture Online." *Communication and the Public* 3 (1): 19–33. https://doi.org/10.1177/ 2057047318755166.

Habermas, Jürgen. 1991. *The Structural Transformation of the Public Sphere: An Inquiry into a Category of Bourgeois Society (Studies in Contemporary German Social Thought)*. Boston: The MIT Press.

Haizhongqingmu. 2021. "Dou 2021 nian le, zenme yin xinguan yiqing bei chezhi de guanyuan haishi quanzai Zhongguo" [It's Already 2021, Why Only in China Are Officials Dismissed for Mishandling the Pandemic?]. *Zhihu*, May 23, 2021. https://zhuanlan.zhihu.com/p/ 374692338.

Hall, Casey. 2022. "H&M Returns to Alibaba's Tmall, 16 Months after Xinjiang Controversy." *Reuters, Retail & Consumer*, August 16, 2022. https://www.reuters.com/business/ret ail-consumer/hm-returns-alibabas-tmall-16-months-after-xinjiang-controversy-2022-08-16/.

Han, Rongbin. 2015a. "Cyberactivism in China: Empowerment, Control, and Beyond." In *The Routledge Companion to Social Media and Politics*, eds. Axel Bruns, Gunn Enli, Eli Skogerbo, Anders Olof Larsson, and Christian Christensen, 268–80. Routledge.

Han, Rongbin. 2015b. "Manufacturing Consent in Cyberspace: China's 'Fifty-Cent Army.'" *Journal of Current Chinese Affairs* 44 (2): 105–34.

Han, Rongbin. 2018a. *Contesting Cyberspace in China: Online Expression and Authoritarian Resilience*. New York: Columbia University Press.

Han, Rongbin. 2018b. "Withering Gongzhi: Cyber Criticism of Chinese Public Intellectuals." *International Journal of Communication* 12: 1966–87.

Han, Rongbin. 2019. "Patriotism without State Blessing: Chinese Cyber Nationalists in a Predicament." In *Handbook of Dissent and Protest in China*, ed. Teresa Wright, 346–60. Northampton, MA: Edward Elgar.

Han, Rongbin, and Li Shao. 2022. "Scaling Authoritarian Information Control: How China Adjusts the Level of Online Censorship." *Political Research Quarterly* 75 (4): 1345–59.

Han, Rongbin, and Linan Jia. 2018. "Governing by the Internet: Local Governance in the Digital Age." *Journal of Chinese Governance* 3 (1): 67–85.

Hao, Qianyu. 2021. "Yiqing fasheng yilai, quanguo wenze chuli geji ganbu chao qianren" [Since the Epidemic Started, over One Thousand Cadres at Different Levels Have Been Held Accountable across the Nation]. *Jiankang shibao* [Health Times], May 24, 2021. http://www.jksb.com.cn/html/xinwen/2021/0524/170947.html.

Hartford, Kathleen. 2005. "Dear Mayor: Online Communications with Local Governments in Hangzhou and Nanjing." *China Information* 19 (2): 217–60.

Harwit, Eric. 1998. "China's Telecommunications Industry: Development Patterns and Policies." *Pacific Affairs* 71 (2): 175–94. https://doi.org/10.2307/2760975.

Harwit, Eric, and Duncan Clark. 2001. "Shaping the Internet in China: Evolution of Political Control over Network Infrastructure and Content." *Asian Survey* 41 (3): 377–408.

Hassid, Jonathan. 2012. "Safety Valve or Pressure Cooker? Blogs in Chinese Political Life." *Journal of Communication* 62 (2): 212–30.

Hassid, Jonathan. 2015. *China's Unruly Journalists: How Committed Professionals Are Changing the People's Republic.* New York: Routledge.

Hassid, Jonathan, and Wanning Sun. 2015. "Stability Maintenance and Chinese Media: Beyond Political Communication?" *Journal of Current Chinese Affairs* 44 (2): 3–15.

Heberer, Thomas, and Gunter Schubert, eds. 2008. *Regime Legitimacy in Contemporary China: Institutional Change and Stability.* New York: Routledge.

Hess, Steve. 2013. "From the Arab Spring to the Chinese Winter: The Institutional Sources of Authoritarian Vulnerability and Resilience in Egypt, Tunisia, and China." *International Political Science Review* 34 (3): 254–72.

Hindman, Matthew. 2008. *The Myth of Digital Democracy.* Princeton: Princeton University Press.

Hobbs, William R., and Margaret E. Roberts. 2018. "How Sudden Censorship Can Increase Access to Information." *American Political Science Review* 112 (3): 621–36. https://doi.org/10.1017/S0003055418000084.

Hou, Rui. 2017. "Neoliberal Governance or Digitalized Autocracy? The Rising Market for Online Opinion Surveillance in China." *Surveillance & Society* 15 (3/4): 418–24.

Hou, Rui. 2020. "The Commercialisation of Internet-Opinion Management: How the Market Is Engaged in State Control in China." *New Media & Society* 22 (12): 2238–56. https://doi.org/10.1177/1461444819889959.

Howard, Philip N. 2010. *The Digital Origins of Dictatorship and Democracy: Information Technology and Political Islam.* New York: Oxford University Press.

Howard, Philip N., Sheetal D. Agarwal, and Muzammil M. Hussain. 2011. "When Do States Disconnect Their Digital Networks? Regime Responses to the Political Uses of Social Media." *Communication Review* 14 (3): 216–32. https://doi.org/10.1080/10714421.2011.597254.

Hu, Xujin. 2020. "About Wuhan Police System . . ." *Weibo*, January 21, 2020, https://www.weibo.com/1989660417/IqvfedDd2.

Huang, Carol. 2011. "Facebook and Twitter Key to Arab Spring Uprisings: Report." thenational.ae. May 17, 2015.

Huang, Haifeng. 2015. "Propaganda as Signaling." *Comparative Politics* 47 (4): 419–44.

Huang, Zheping. 2022. "Shanghai Lockdown Throws Food Delivery Apps into Disarray." *Bloomberg*, April 13, 2022. https://www.bloomberg.com/news/newsletters/2022-04-13/shanghai-lockdown-throws-food-delivery-apps-into-disarray.

Human Rights Watch. 2008. *"Walking on Thin Ice": Control, Intimidation, and Harassment of Lawyers in China.* New York: Human Rights Watch.

Hung, Chin-Fu. 2010. "China's Propaganda in the Information Age: Internet Commentators and the Weng'an Incident." *Issues & Studies* 46 (4): 149–81.

Hurst, William. 2009. *The Chinese Worker after Socialism.* New York: Cambridge University Press.

Hyun, Ki Deuk, and Jinhee Kim. 2015. "The Role of New Media in Sustaining the Status Quo: Online Political Expression, Nationalism, and System Support in China." *Information, Communication & Society* 18 (7): 766–81. https://doi.org/10.1080/1369118X.2014.994543.

Iacus, Stefano M., Gary King, and Giuseppe Porro. 2012. "Causal Inference without Balance Checking: Coarsened Exact Matching." *Political Analysis* 20 (1): 1–24.

Jacobs, Andrew. 2011. "Chinese Authorities Keep Unrest at Bay." *New York Times*, March 1, 2011. https://www.nytimes.com/2011/03/01/world/asia/01china.html.

Jiang, Junyan, Tianguang Meng, and Qing Zhang. 2019. "From Internet to Social Safety Net: The Policy Consequences of Online Participation in China." *Governance* 32 (3): 531–46. https://doi.org/10.1111/gove.12391.

Jiang, Min. 2016. "The Coevolution of the Internet, (Un)Civil Society, and Authoritarianism in China." In *The Internet, Social Media, and a Changing China*, eds. Jacques DeLisle, Avery Goldstein, and Guobin Yang, 28–48. Philadelphia, PA: University of Pennsylvania Press.

160 References

Kadivar, Mohammad Ali. 2019. "Iran Shut Down the Internet to Stop Protests. But for How Long?" *Washington Post*, November 27. https://www.washingtonpost.com/politics/2019/11/27/iran-shut-down-internet-stop-protests-how-long/.

Kan, Karita. 2013. "Whither Weiwen? Stability Maintenance in the 18th Party Congress Era." *China Perspectives* 2013 (1): 87–93.

Kelly, David. 2006. "Citizen Movements and China's Public Intellectuals in the Hu-Wen Era." *Pacific Affairs* 79 (2): 183–204.

Kennedy, John James. 2009. "Maintaining Popular Support for the Chinese Communist Party: The Influence of Education and the State-Controlled Media." *Political Studies* 57 (3): 517–36. https://doi.org/10.1111/j.1467-9248.2008.00740.x.

Kennedy, John James, and Yaojiang Shi. 2015. "Rule by Virtue, the Mass Line Model and Cadre-Mass Relations." In *East Asian Development Model: The 21st Century Perspectives*, ed. Shiping Hua, 217–33. New York: Routledge.

King, Gary, Jennifer Pan, and Margaret E. Roberts. 2013. "How Censorship in China Allows Government Criticism but Silences Collective Expression." *American Political Science Review* 107 (2): 1–18.

King, Gary, Jennifer Pan, and Margaret E. Roberts. 2014. "Reverse-Engineering Censorship in China: Randomized Experimentation and Participant Observation." *Science* 345 (6199): 1–10.

King, Gary, Jennifer Pan, and Margaret E. Roberts. 2017. "How the Chinese Government Fabricates Social Media Posts for Strategic Distraction, Not Engaged Argument." *American Political Science Review* 111 (3): 484–501. https://doi.org/10.1017/S0003055417000144.

Kostka, Genia. 2019. "China's Social Credit Systems and Public Opinion: Explaining High Levels of Approval." *New Media & Society* 21 (7): 1565–93. http://journals.sagepub.com/doi/10.1177/1461444819826402.

Kuo, Lily. 2022. "China Shuts Down Talk of COVID Hardship; Users Strike Back." *Washington Post*, May 12, 2022. https://www.washingtonpost.com/world/interactive/2022/china-coronavirus-voices-of-april-shanghai/.

Kuran, Timur. 1991. "Now out of Never: The Element of Surprise in the East European Revolution of 1989." *World Politics* 44 (1): 7–48. https://doi.org/10.2307/2010422.

Lagerkvist, Johan. 2007. *The Internet in China: Unlocking and Containing the Public Sphere*. Lund: Lund University.

Lagerkvist, Johan. 2008. "Internet Ideotainment in the PRC: National Responses to Cultural Globalization." *Journal of Contemporary China* 17 (54): 121–40.

Lagerkvist, Johan. 2010. *After the Internet, Before Democracy: Competing Norms in Chinese Media and Society*. Bern, Switzerland: Peter Lang.

Lee, Ching Kwan, and Guobin Yang. 2007. *Re-envisioning the Chinese Revolution: The Politics and Poetics of Collective Memories in Reform China*. Washington, DC: Stanford University Press.

Lee, Ching Kwan, and Yonghong Zhang. 2013. "The Power of Instability: Unraveling the Microfoundations of Bargained Authoritarianism in China." *American Journal of Sociology* 118 (6): 1475–508.

Lei, Ya-wen. 2011. "The Political Consequences of the Rise of the Internet: Political Beliefs and Practices of Chinese Netizens." *Political Communication* 28 (3): 291–322.

Leibold, James. 2011. "Blogging Alone: China, the Internet, and the Democratic Illusion?" *Journal of Asian Studies* 70 (4): 1023–41.

Li, Cheng. 2009. "Intra-party Democracy in China: Should We Take It Seriously?" *China Leadership Monitor* 30 (3): 1–14.

Li, Cheng. 2012. "The End of the CCP's Resilient Authoritarianism? A Tripartite Assessment of Shifting Power in China." *China Quarterly* 211: 595–623.

Li, Lianjiang. 2004. "Political Trust in Rural China." *Modern China* 30 (2): 228–58.

Li, Lianjiang. 2008. "Political Trust and Petitioning in the Chinese Countryside." *Comparative Politics* 40 (2): 209–26.

Li, Lianjiang. 2013. "The Magnitude and Resilience of Trust in the Center: Evidence from Interviews with Petitioners in Beijing and a Local Survey in Rural China." *Modern China* 39 (1): 3–36.

Li, Lianjiang. 2016. "Reassessing Trust in the Central Government: Evidence from Five National Surveys." *The China Quarterly* 225: 100–21.

Li, Lianjiang, and Kevin J. O'Brien. 2008. "Protest Leadership in Rural China." *China Quarterly* 193 (March): 1–23. https://doi.org/10.1017/S0305741008000015.

Li, Lianjiang, Mingxing Liu, and Kevin J. O'Brien. 2012. "Petitioning Beijing: The High Tide of 2003–2006." *The China Quarterly* 210: 313–34.

Li, Ling. 2019. "Politics of Anticorruption in China: Paradigm Change of the Party's Disciplinary Regime 2012–2017." *Journal of Contemporary China* 28 (115): 47–63. https://doi.org/10.1080/10670564.2018.1497911.

Li, Xiaoping. 2002. "'Focus' (Jiaodian Fangtan) and the Changes in the Chinese Television Industry." *Journal of Contemporary China* 11 (30): 17–34.

Li, Yiran, Yanto Chandra, and Naim Kapucu. 2020. "Crisis Coordination and the Role of Social Media in Response to COVID-19 in Wuhan, China." *American Review of Public Administration* 50 (6–7): 698–705. doi:10.1177/0275074020942105.

Li, Yonggang. 2009. *Women de Fanghuoqiang: Wangluo shidai de biaoda yu jianguan* [Our Great Firewall: Expression and governance in the era of the internet]. Nanning: Guangxi Normal University Press.

Liang, F., V. Das, N. Kostyuk, and M. M. Hussain. 2018. "Constructing a Data-Driven Society: China's Social Credit System as a State Surveillance Infrastructure." *Policy & Internet* 10 (4): 415–53.

Liebman, Benjamin L. 2012. "The Media and the Courts: Towards Competitive Supervision?" *China Quarterly* 208 (January): 833–50.

Lin, Gang. 2004. "Leadership Transition, Intra-party Democracy, and Institution Building in China." *Asian Survey* 44 (2): 255–75.

Lin, Liza, and Jie, Yang. 2022. "Shanghai's COVID Lockdown Leads to Logistics Disarray, with Quarantined Truckers, Piled-Up Containers." *Wall Street Journal*, April 21, 2022. https://www.wsj.com/articles/shanghai-lockdown-leads-to-logistics-disarray-with-quarantined-truckers-piled-up-containers-11650537303.

Link, Perry. 1987. "The Limits of Cultural Reform in Deng Xiaoping's China." *Modern China* 13 (2): 115–76. http://journals.sagepub.com/doi/10.1177/009770048701300201.

Lollar, Xia Li. 2006. "Assessing China's E-government: Information, Service, Transparency and Citizen Outreach of Government Websites." *Journal of Contemporary China* 15 (46): 31–41.

Lorentzen, Peter. 2013. "Regularizing Rioting: Permitting Public Protest in an Authoritarian Regime." *Quarterly Journal of Political Science* 8 (2): 127–58.

Lorentzen, Peter. 2014. "China's Strategic Censorship." *American Journal of Political Science* 58 (2): 402–14.

Lorentzen, Peter. 2017. "Designing Contentious Politics in Post-1989 China." *Modern China* 43 (5): 459–93. https://doi.org/10.1177/0097700416688895.

Lotan, G., E. Graeff, M. Ananny, D. Gaffney, and I. Pearce. 2011. "The Revolutions Were Tweeted: Information Flows during the 2011 Tunisian and Egyptian Revolutions." *International Journal of Communication* 31 (5): 1375–405.

Ma, Josephine. 2021. "Chinese More Trusting of Government Months into Pandemic, Survey Finds." *South China Morning Post*, May 11, 2021. https://www.scmp.com/news/china/politics/article/3132965/chinese-more-trusting-government-months-pandemic-survey-finds.

Ma, Yan. 2000. "Chinese Online Presence: Tiananmen Square and Beyond." In *Technology and Resistance: Digital Communications and New Coalitions around the World*, eds. Ann De Vaney, Stephen Gance, and Yan Ma, 139–51. New York: Peter Lang.

MacFarquhar, Roderick, and Michael Schoenhals. 2006. *Mao's Last Revolution*. Cambridge, MA: Harvard University Press.

References

MacKinnon, Rebecca. 2009. "China's Censorship 2.0: How Companies Censor Bloggers." *First Monday* 14 (2). https://firstmonday.org/ojs/index.php/fm/article/download/2378/2089.

MacKinnon, Rebecca. 2011. "China's 'Networked Authoritarianism.'" *Journal of Democracy* 22 (2): 32–46. https://doi.org/10.1353/jod.2011.0033.

Manion, Melanie. 2004. *Corruption by Design: Building Clean Government in Mainland China and Hong Kong*. Cambridge, MA: Harvard University Press.

Manion, Melanie. 2006. "Democracy, Community, Trust: The Impact of Elections in Rural China." *Comparative Political Studies* 39 (3): 301–24.

Margolis, Michael, and David Resnick. 2000. *Politics as Usual: The Cyberspace Revolution*. London: Sage Publications, Inc.

McCarthy, Simone. 2022. "Panic at the Supermarket as Shanghai Forces Residents into Lockdown." *CNN*, March 28, 2022, https://www.cnn.com/2022/03/28/china/shanghai-lockdown-china-covid-19-outbreak-intl-hnk/index.html.

Mei, Ciqi. 2020. "Policy Style, Consistency and the Effectiveness of the Policy Mix in China's Fight against COVID-19." *Policy and Society* 39 (3): 309–25.

Meng, Bingchun. 2016. "Political Scandal at the End of Ideology? The Mediatized Politics of the Bo Xilai Case." *Media, Culture & Society* 38 (6): 811–26.

Miller, Blake. 2016. "Automatic Detection of Comment Propaganda in Chinese Media." *SSRN Electronic Journal*, 1–38. https://doi.org/10.2139/ssrn.2738325.

Millward, Steven. 2013. "Sina Weibo Punishes or Deletes over 100,000 Accounts that Violated New Government Rules." *Yahoo News*, November 13.https://sg.news.yahoo.com/sina-weibo-punishes-deletes-over-140058761.html.

Minzner, Carl F. 2006. "Xinfang: An Alternative to Formal Chinese Legal Institutions." *Stanford Journal of International Law* 42 (1): 103–80.

Montinola, Gabriella, Yingyi Qian, and Barry R. Weingast. 1995. "Federalism, Chinese Style: The Political Basis for Economic Success in China." *World Politics* 48 (1): 50–81.

Mossberger, Karen, Caroline J. Tolbert, and Ramona S. McNeal. 2008. *Digital Citizenship: The Internet, Society, and Participation*. Cambridge, MA: The MIT Press.

Mou, Yi, Kevin Wu, and David Atkin. 2016 . "Understanding the Use of Circumvention Tools to Bypass Online Censorship." *New Media & Society* 18 (5): 837–56.

Mozur, Paul. 2018. "Inside China's Dystopian Dreams: A.I., Shame and Lots of Cameras." *New York Times*, July 8, 2018. Accessed April 25, 2023. https://www.nytimes.com/2018/07/08/business/china-surveillance-technology.html.

Mu, Qing, and Keun Lee. 2005. "Knowledge Diffusion, Market Segmentation and Technological Catch-up: The Case of the Telecommunication Industry in China." *Research Policy* 34 (6): 759–83. https://doi.org/10.1016/j.respol.2005.02.007.

Mulaik, Stanley A. 2009. *Linear Causal Modeling with Structural Equations*. New York: Chapman and Hall/CRC.

My Drivers. 2020. "Huoshenshan, Leishenshan jianshe 24 xiaoshi zhibo: Yun jiangong po yi yi" [24-Hour Live Broadcasting of Huoshenshan and Leishenshan Hospitals Construction: Cloud Construction Supervisors Exceed 100 Million]. January 31, 2020. https://news.mydrivers.com/1/669/669555.htm.

Nagle, John. 2011. "Pornography as Pollution." *Maryland Law Review* 70 (4): 939–84. https://dig italcommons.law.umaryland.edu/mlr/vol70/iss4/4.

Nathan, Andrew. 2003. "Authoritarian Resilience." *Journal of Democracy* 14 (1): 6–17.

Naughton, Barry. 1996. *Growing Out of the Plan: Chinese Economic Reform, 1978–1993*. Cambridge: Cambridge University Press.

Naughton, Barry. 2007. *The Chinese Economy: Transitions and Growth*. Cambridge, MA: MIT Press.

Nddaily WeChat public account. 2020. "Ganggang, Wuhan jingfang huiying 'Ba ren chuanyao bei chuli'" [Just Now, Wuhan Police Responded to News on "8 People Disciplined for Spreading Rumors"]. January 29, 2020. https://mp.weixin.qq.com/s/WRiGyb7jdwM b1qzhHtlZiQ.

References 163

Norris, Pippa. 2001. *Digital Divide: Civic Engagement, Information Poverty, and the Internet Worldwide*. New York: Cambridge University Press.

Oates, Sarah. 2013. *Revolution Stalled: The Political Limits of the Internet in the Post-Soviet Sphere*. New York: Oxford University Press.

O'Brien, Kevin J. 1996. "Rightful Resistance." *World Politics* 49 (1): 31–55.

O'Brien, Kevin J. 2001. "Villagers, Elections, and Citizenship in Contemporary China." *Modern China* 27 (4): 407–35.

O'Brien, Kevin J., and Yanhua Deng. 2015. "The Reach of the State: Work Units, Family Ties and 'Harmonious Demolition.'" *China Journal*, no. 74: 1–17.

O'Brien, Kevin J., and Neil J. Diamant. 2014. "Contentious Veterans: China's Retired Officers Speak Out." *Armed Forces & Society* 41 (3): 563–81.

O'Brien, Kevin J., and Rongbin Han. 2009. "Path to Democracy? Assessing Village Elections in China." *Journal of Contemporary China* 18 (60): 359–78.

O'Brien, Kevin J., and Lianjiang Li. 2004. "Suing the Local State: Administrative Litigation in Rural China." *The China Journal* 51: 75–96.

O'Brien, Kevin J., and Lianjiang Li. 2006. *Rightful Resistance in Rural China*. New York: Cambridge University Press.

Pan, Gongyu. 2020. "Feiyan yiqing xia de 'meiti bingdu,' Deguo zhizao" [The 'Media Virus' during the Pneumonia Epidemic, Made in Germany]. *Guanchazhe* [Observer], February 23, 2020. https://www.guancha.cn/pangongyu/2020_02_03_534248.shtml.

Park, Namkee, and Seungyoon Lee. 2014. "College Students' Motivations for Facebook Use and Psychological Outcomes." *Journal of Broadcasting and Electronic Media* 58 (4): 601–20. https://www.tandfonline.com/doi/abs/10.1080/08838151.2014.966355.

Pearl, Judea. 2014. "Interpretation and Identification of Causal Mediation." *Psychological Methods* 19 (4): 459–81.

Peerenboom, Randall. 2001. "Globalization, Path Dependency and the Limits of Law: Administrative Law Reform and Rule of Law in the People's Republic of China." *Berkeley Journal of International Law* 19 (2): 161–264.

Peerenboom, Randall. 2003. "A Government of Laws: Democracy, Rule of Law and Administrative Law Reform in the PRC." *Journal of Contemporary China* 34 (12): 45–67.

Pei, Minxin. 1997. "Citizens v. Mandarins: Administrative Litigation in China." *China Quarterly*, no. 152: 832–62.

Pei, Minxin. 2009. *China's Trapped Transition: The Limits of Developmental Autocracy*. Cambridge, MA: Harvard University Press.

Penney, Joel. 2017. *The Citizen Marketer: Promoting Political Opinion in the Social Media Age*. New York: Oxford University Press.

People's Daily Commentator. 2020. "Yingxiong de chengshi, yingxiong de renmin" [Wuhan: The Heroic City and the Heroic People]. *People's Daily*, March 12, 2020: 1.

People's Daily Online. 2020. "Guowuyuan zhengji loubao manbao yiqing wenti xiansuo: Yijing chashi, yansu chuli" [The State Council Collects Clues about Underreporting or Concealing the Epidemic Situation: Once Verified, It Will Be Dealt with Seriously]. January 24, 2020. http://politics.people.com.cn/n1/2020/0124/c1001-31561932.html.

Perry, Elizabeth J. 2015. *Challenging the Mandate of Heaven: Social Protest and State Power in China; Social Protest and State Power in China*. New York: Taylor & Francis.

Perry, Elizabeth J., and Mark Selden. 2003. "Chinese Society: Change, Conflict and Resistance." In *Asia's Transformations*, eds. Elizabeth J. Perry and Mark Selden, 2nd edition. London: RoutledgeCurzon.

Policzer, Pablo. 2009. *The Rise and Fall of Repression in Chile*. South Bend, IN: University of Notre Dame Press.

Qin, Bei, David Strömberg, and Yanhui Wu. 2017. "Why Does China Allow Freer Social Media? Protests versus Surveillance and Propaganda." *Journal of Economic Perspectives* 31 (1): 117–40. https://doi.org/10.1257/jep.31.1.117.

References

Qiu, Jack Linchuan. 2004. "The Internet in China: Technologies of Freedom in a Statist Society." In *The Network Society*, ed. Manuel Castells, 99–124. Northampton, MA: Edward Elgar. https://ideas.repec.org/h/elg/eechap/3203_4.html.

Reilly, James. 2013. *Strong Society, Smart State: The Rise of Public Opinion in China's Japan Policy*. New York: Columbia University Press.

Repnikova, Maria. 2017. *Media Politics in China: Improvising Power under Authoritarianism*. Cambridge, UK: Cambridge University Press. https://doi.org/10.1017/9781108164474.

Roberts, Margaret E. 2018. *Censored: Distraction and Diversion inside China's Great Firewall*. Princeton, NJ: Princeton University Press.

Robison, Joshua, Randy T. Stevenson, James N. Druckman, Simon Jackman, Jonathan N. Katz, and Lynn Vavreck. 2018. "An Audit of Political Behavior Research." *SAGE Open* 8 (3): 1–14.

Rundle, Christopher. 2018. "Stemming the Flood: The Censorship of Translated Popular Fiction in Fascist Italy." *Perspectives: Studies in Translation Theory and Practice* 26 (6): 838–51. https://www.tandfonline.com/doi/abs/10.1080/0907676X.2018.1444646.

Saich, Tony. 2007. "Citizens' Perceptions of Governance in Rural and Urban China." *Journal of Chinese Political Science* 12 (1): 1–28.

Sande, Jon Bingen, and Mrinal Ghosh. 2018. "Endogeneity in Survey Research." *International Journal of Research in Marketing* 35 (2): 185–204.

Scherman, Andrés, Arturo Arriagada, and Sebastián Valenzuela. 2015. "Student and Environmental Protests in Chile: The Role of Social Media." *Politics* 35 (2): 151–71. http://journals.sage pub.com/doi/10.1111/1467-9256.12072.

Schlæger, Jesper. 2013. *E-government in China: Technology, Power and Local Government Reform*. Abingdon: Routledge.

Schlæger, Jesper, and Min Jiang. 2014. "Official Microblogging and Social Management by Local Governments in China." *China Information* 28 (2): 189–213.

Schneider, Florian. 2018. *China's Digital Nationalism*. Oxford and New York: Oxford University Press. https://doi.org/10.1093/oso/9780190876791.001.0001.

Seligson, Mitchell A. 2002. "The Impact of Corruption on Regime Legitimacy: A Comparative Study of Four Latin American Countries." *Journal of Politics* 64 (2): 408–33. https://doi.org/10.1111/1468-2508.00132.

Shambaugh, David L. 2008. *China's Communist Party: Atrophy and Adaptation*. Oakland, CA: University of California Press.

Shen, Fei, and Zhi'an Zhang. 2018. "Do Circumvention Tools Promote Democratic Values? Exploring the Correlates of Anticensorship Technology Adoption in China." *Journal of Information Technology & Politics* 15 (2): 106–21. https://doi.org/10.1080/19331 681.2018.1449700.

Shi, Tianjian. 2001. "Cultural Values and Political Trust: A Comparison of the People's Republic of China and Taiwan." *Comparative Politics* 33 (4): 401–19.

Shi, Tianjian. 2008. "China: Democratic Values Supporting an Authoritarian System." In *How East Asians View Democracy*, eds. Larry Diamond, Andrew J Nathan, and Doh Chull Shin, 209–37. New York: Columbia University Press.

Shirk, Susan. 2007. *China: Fragile Superpower*. Oxford: Oxford University Press.

Shirky, Clay. 2011. "The Political Power of Social Media: Technology, the Public Sphere, and Political Change." *Foreign Affairs* 90 (1): 28–41.

So, Alvin Y. 2013. *Class and Class Conflict in Post-socialist China*. Singapore: World Scientific.

Sohu News. 2021. "H&M xuanbu dizhi Xinjiang mian, wangyou jiti nule! Gongqingtuan zhongyang: Xinjiang mianhua buchi zheyitao! Huang Xuan, Song Qian jinji fasheng zhongzhi hezuo" [H&M Announced Boycott of Xinjiang Cotton, and Netizens Are Infuriated! Central Committee of the Communist Youth League: Xinjiang Cotton Does Not Buy It! Huang Xuan and Song Qian Urgently Voiced Termination of Cooperation]. March 24, 2021. https://www.sohu.com/a/457143540_119666.

South China Morning Post. n.d. 2023. "Urban Legend: China's Tiered City System Explained." Accessed April 25, 2023. http://multimedia.scmp.com/2016/cities/.

Spalding, Elizabeth E. 2006. "True Believers." *The Wilson Quarterly* 30 (2): 40–48.

Stanway, David, and Roxanne Liu. 2022. "Shanghai Denies Lockdown Rumours as Daily COVID Infections near 1,000." *Reuters China*, March 23, 2022. https://www.reuters.com/world/china/china-reports-2667-new-covid-cases-march-22-vs-2338-day-earlier-2022-03-23/.

State Council Information Office, and Ministry of Information Industry. 2005. *Hulianwang Xinwen Xinxi Fuwu Guanli Guiding* [*Administrative Provisions of Internet News Information Services*]. September 25. http://www.gov.cn/flfg/2005-09/29/content_73270.htm.

Steinhardt, H. Christoph. 2017. "Discursive Accommodation: Popular Protest and Strategic Elite Communication in China." *European Political Science Review* 9 (4): 539–60. https://doi.org/10.1017/S1755773916000102.

Stern, Rachel E., and Jonathan Hassid. 2012. "Amplifying Silence: Uncertainty and Control Parables in Contemporary China." *Comparative Political Studies* 45 (10): 1230–54.

Stockmann, Daniela. 2013. *Media Commercialization and Authoritarian Rule in China.* Cambridge: Cambridge University Press.

Stockmann, Daniela, and Mary E. Gallagher. 2011. "Remote Control: How the Media Sustain Authoritarian Rule in China." *Comparative Political Studies* 44 (4): 436–67.

Stromer-Galley, J. 2019. *Presidential Campaigning in the Internet Age.* New York: Oxford University Press.

Su, Yang, and Xin He. 2010. "Street as Courtroom: State Accommodation of Labor Protest in South China." *Law and Society Review* 44 (1): 157–84.

Su, Zheng, and Tianguang Meng. 2016. "Selective Responsiveness: Online Public Demands and Government Responsiveness in Authoritarian China." *Social Science Research* 59 (September): 52–67. https://doi.org/10.1016/J.SSRESEARCH.2016.04.017.

Sullivan, Jonathan, and Lei Xie. 2009. "Environmental Activism, Social Networks and the Internet." *China Quarterly* 198 (198): 422. https://doi.org/10.1017/S0305741009000381.

Sun, Yanfei, and Dingxin Zhao. 2008. "Popular Protest in China." In *Popular Protest in China*, ed. Kevin J. O'Brien, 144–62. Cambridge, MA: Harvard University Press.

Tai, Yun, and King-wa Fu. 2020. "Specificity, Conflict, and Focal Point: A Systematic Investigation into Social Media Censorship in China." *Journal of Communication* 70 (6): 842–67. https://doi.org/10.1093/joc/jqaa032.

Tai, Zixue. 2006. *The Internet in China: Cyberspace and Civil Society.* London: Routledge.

Tan, Yvette. 2020. "Li Wenliang: 'Wailing Wall' for China's Virus Whistleblowing Doctor." *BBC News*, June 23. https://www.bbc.com/news/world-asia-china-53077072

Tang, Min, and Narisong Huhe. 2013. "Alternative Framing: The Effect of the Internet on Political Support in Authoritarian China." *International Political Science Review* 35 (5): 559–76. https://doi.org/10.1177/0192512113501971.

Tang, Wenfang. 2016. *Populist Authoritarianism: Chinese Political Culture and Regime Sustainability.* New York: Oxford University Press.

Teets, Jessica C., Reza Hasmath, and Orion A. Lewis. 2017. "The Incentive to Innovate? The Behavior of Local Policymakers in China." *Journal of Chinese Political Science* 22 (4): 505–17. https://doi.org/10.1007/s11366-017-9512-9.

Teh, Cheryl. 2021. "Chinese Social-Media Users Burn Their Nikes after the Company Says It's 'Concerned' about Forced Labor of Uyghurs in Xinjiang." *Insider*, March 24, 2021. https://www.insider.com/chinese-weibo-angry-xinjiang-burning-nike-shoes-2021-3.

Thompson, E. P. 1975. *Whigs and Hunters: The Origins of the Black Act.* New York: Pantheon.

Tian, Doudou, Yuanzhou Cheng, Haotian Fan, and Jun Wu. 2020. "Wuhan: Fenmiao bizheng kang yiqing" [Wuhan: Every Second Counts against the Pandemic]. *People's Daily*, January 25, 2020. http://health.people.com.cn/n1/2020/0125/c14739-31562097.html.

Toepfl, Florian. 2011. "Managing Public Outrage: Power, Scandal, and New Media in Contemporary Russia." *New Media & Society* 13 (8): 1301–19.

Tong, Yanqi, and Shaohua Lei. 2013. "War of Position and Microblogging in China." *Journal of Contemporary China* 22 (80): 292–311.

Tsai, Kellee S. 2007. *Capitalism Without Democracy: The Private Sector in Contemporary China.* Ithaca, NY: Cornell University Press.

Tsai, Lily L. 2015. "Constructive Noncompliance." *Comparative Politics* 47 (3): 253–79.

Tufekci, Zeynep, and Christopher Wilson. 2012. "Social Media and the Decision to Participate in Political Protest: Observations from Tahrir Square." *Journal of Communication* 62 (2): 363–79.

Valenzuela, Sebastián, Arturo Arriagada, and Andrés Scherman. 2012. "The Social Media Basis of Youth Protest Behavior: The Case of Chile." *Journal of Communication* 62 (2): 299–314.

Wagner, Kevin M., and Jason Gainous. 2009. "Electronic Grassroots: Does Online Campaigning Work?" *Journal of Legislative Studies* 15 (4): 502–20.

Wagner, Kevin M., and Jason Gainous. 2013. "Digital Uprising: The Internet Revolution in the Middle East." *Journal of Information Technology and Politics* 10 (3): 261–75.

Wagner, Kevin M., Jason Gainous, and Jason P. Abbott. 2019. "Gender Differences in Critical Digital Political Engagement in China: The Consequences for Protest Attitudes." *Social Science Computer Review* 39 (2): 211–25.

Wagner, Kevin M., Tricia J. Gray, and Jason Gainous. 2017. "Digital Information Consumption and External Political Efficacy in Latin America: Does Institutional Context Matter?" *Journal of Information Technology and Politics* 14 (3): 277–91.

Wall Street Journal. 2022. "China's Economy Tested by Strained City Finances." July 31, 2022. https://www.wsj.com/articles/chinas-economy-tested-by-strained-city-finances-1165 9261600.

Walton, Greg. 2001. "China's Golden Shield: Corporations and the Development of Surveillance Technology in the People's Republic of China." Montreal: International Centre for Human Rights and Democratic Development. http://www.dd-rd.ca/site/_PDF/publications/globalization/CGS_ENG.PDF.

Wang, Gang, Liyun Wu, and Rongbin Han. 2015. "College Education and Attitudes toward Democracy in China: An Empirical Study." *Asia Pacific Education Review* 16 (3): 399–412. https://doi.org/10.1007/s12564-015-9386-5.

Wang, Lingyu, Weina Qu, and Xianghong Sun. 2013. "An Analysis of Microblogging Behavior on Sina Weibo: Personality, Network Size and Demographics." In *Lecture Notes in Computer Science (Including Subseries Lecture Notes in Artificial Intelligence and Lecture Notes in Bioinformatics).* 8023 LNCS:486–92. https://doi.org/10.1007/978-3-642-39143-9-54.

Wang, Yanan. 2020. "Years after SARS, a More Confident China Faces a New Virus." *AP News*, January 22, 2020. https://apnews.com/article/wuhan-health-international-news-china-xi-jinping-0bf5cd116c250483a8232533d41edc69.

Wang, Yuan, and Rongbin Han. 2023. "Cosmetic Responsiveness: Why and How Local Authorities Respond to Mundane Online Complaints in China." *Journal of Chinese Political Science* 28 (2): 187–207.

Wang, Yuhua. 2018. "Are College Graduates Agents of Change? Education and Political Participation in China." *SSRN*, February 13, 2018. http://dx.doi.org/10.2139/ssrn.2905288.

Wang, Yuhua, and Carl Minzner. 2015. "The Rise of the Chinese Security State." *China Quarterly*, 222 (May): 339–59.

Ward, Stephen, Rachel Gibson, and Wainer Lusoli. 2003. "Online Participation and Mobilization in Britain: Hype, Hope and Reality." *Parliamentary Affairs* 56 (4): 652–68.

Wedeman, Andrew. 2012. *Double Paradox: Rapid Growth and Rising Corruption in China.* Ithaca, NY: Cornell University Press.

Weibo Data Center. 2017. *Weibo Yonghu Fazhan Baogao (Weibo User Development Report).* February 6. https://www.wesdom.me/weibo-pdf/.

Weiss, Jessica Chen. 2019. "How Hawkish Is the Chinese Public? Another Look at 'Rising Nationalism' and Chinese Foreign Policy." *Journal of Contemporary China* 28 (119): 679–95. https://doi.org/10.1080/10670564.2019.1580427.

Weller, Robert P. 2012. "Responsive Authoritarianism and Blind-Eye Governance in China." In *Socialism Vanquished, Socialism Challenged: Eastern Europe and China, 1989–2009*, eds. Nina Bandelj and Dorothy J. Solinger, 83–102. New York: Oxford University Press.

Wintrobe, Ronald. 2000. *The Political Economy of Dictatorship*. Cambridge: Cambridge University Press.

Wong, Dorcas. 2019. "China's City-Tier Classification: How Does It Work?" *China Briefing*, February 27. https://www.china-briefing.com/news/chinas-city-tier-classification-defined/.

Xi, Jinping. 2020. "Zai quanguo kangji xinguan feiyan yiqing biaozhang dahui shang de jianghua" [Speech at the National Commendation Conference for Fighting the COVID-19 Epidemic]. *Xinhua Net*, September 8, 2020. http://www.xinhuanet.com/politics/leaders/2020-10/15/c_1126614978.htm.

Xiao, Qiang. 2011. "The Battle for the Chinese Internet." *Journal of Democracy* 22 (2): 47–61. https://doi.org/10.1353/jod.2011.0020.

Xiao, Qiang. 2019. "The Road to Digital Unfreedom: President Xi's Surveillance State." *Journal of Democracy* 30 (1): 53–67.

Xie, Yue. 2013. "Rising Central Spending on Public Security and the Dilemma Facing Grassroots." *Journal of Current Chinese Affairs* 42 (2): 79–109.

Xie, Yue, and Wei Shan. 2012. "China Struggles to Maintain Stability: Strengthening Its Public Security Apparatus." In *China: Development and Governance*, eds. Gungwu Wang and Yongnian Zheng, 55–62. Singapore: World Scientific.

Xinhua Baoye Net. 2020. "Zan Yidali, mengcai Zhongguo, Niuyue Shibao de shuangbiao sale shui de lian" [Praising Italy while Heavily Criticizing China, *New York Times'* Double Standard Practice Slapped Whose Face]. March 12, 2020. http://www.xhby.net/zt/zzccfkyq/pl/202003/t20200312_6554099.shtml.

Xu, Liqun. 2021. "Yi yanjian faxian gaiguo Yiming nvxing 2019 nian 11 yue yi ganran xinguan bingdu" [Italian Study Finds One Woman in Italy Infected with Coronavirus in November 2019], *People's Daily*, January 13, 2021. http://paper.people.com.cn/rmrbhwb/html/2021-01/13/content_2028637.htm.

Xu, Xu. 2020. "To Repress or to Co-opt? Authoritarian Control in the Age of Digital Surveillance." *American Journal of Political Science* 65 (2): 309–25. https://doi.org/10.1111/ajps.12514.

Yan, Sophia. 2021. "Chinese State Media Called Out for Inventing Fake Swiss Scientist to Bolster COVID Origin Dispute: Biologist Wilson Edwards Had Allegedly Criticised the US for Attacking China—but Turned Out not to Exist." *Telegraph*, August 11, 2021. https://www.telegraph.co.uk/world-news/2021/08/11/chinese-state-media-called-inventing-fake-swiss-scientist-bolster/.

Yang, Dali L. 2007. "China's Long March to Freedom." *Journal of Democracy* 18 (3): 58–64.

Yang, Guobin. 2003. "The Internet and Civil Society in China: A Preliminary Assessment." *Journal of Contemporary China* 12 (36): 453–75.

Yang, Guobin. 2009. *The Power of the Internet in China: Citizen Activism Online*. New York: Columbia University Press.

Yang, Guobin, and Shiwen Wu. 2018. "Remembering Disappeared Websites in China: Passion, Community, and Youth." *New Media & Society* 20 (6): 2107–24. https://doi.org/10.1177/1461444817731921.

Yang, Hongxing, and Dingxin Zhao. 2015. "Performance Legitimacy, State Autonomy and China's Economic Miracle." *Journal of Contemporary China* 24 (91): 64–82. https://doi.org/10.1080/10670564.2014.918403.

Yang, Qinghua, and Yu Liu. 2014. "What's on the Other Side of the Great Firewall? Chinese Web Users' Motivations for Bypassing the Internet Censorship." *Computers in Human Behavior* 37 (August): 249–57. https://doi.org/10.1016/j.chb.2014.04.054.

Yao, Yuan, and Rongbin Han. 2016. "Challenging, but Not Trouble-Making: Cultural Elites in China's Urban Heritage Preservation." *Journal of Contemporary China* 25 (98): 292–306.

References

Yeung, Jessie. 2022. "A COVID Worker Beat a Dog to Death in Shanghai after Its Owner Tested Positive." *CNN*, April 8, 2022. https://www.cnn.com/2022/04/08/china/shanghai-corgi-death-china-covid-intl-hnk/index.html.

Yicai Global. 2020. "Shaanxi Xi'an 338 ren yin yiqing fangkong bei zhuize wenze" [Shaanxi Xi'an 338 Cadres Being Held Accountable Due to Problems in Epidemic Prevention and Control]. February 28, 2020. https://m.yicai.com/news/100525939.html.

Yun, Sheng. 2020. "Feiyan yiqing: 'Fashaoren' yinfa fan shencha zhan, Zhongguo ren yong chuangyi jieli fanji" [Pneumonia Epidemic: "The One Who Distributes Whistles" Triggers Anti-censorship War, Chinese Citizens Relay Resistance Effort with Creativity]. *BBC Chinese*, March 11, 2020. https://www.bbc.com/zhongwen/simp/chinese-news-51831652.

Zaller, John R. 1992. *The Nature and Origins of Mass Opinion.* New York: Cambridge University Press.

Zaller, John, and Stanley Feldman. 1992. "A Simple Theory of the Survey Response: Answering Questions versus Revealing Preferences." *American Journal of Political Science* 36 (3): 579–616.

Zaobao. 2020. "Shou xunjie de Wuhan yisheng: 11 Tian hou bei bingren chuanran zhujin geli bingfang" [The Disciplined Wuhan Doctor: Infected by a Patient and Admitted to an Isolation Ward 11 Days Later]. January 28, 2020. https://www.zaobao.com.sg/wencui/politic/story2 0200128-1024296.

Zhang, Qianfan. 2020. "Fangzhi bingdu, Zhongguo xuyao xianzheng minzu" [To prevent and cure coronavirus, China needs constitutional democracy]. *New York Times* (Chinese edition), February 21, 2020. https://cn.nytimes.com/opinion/20200211/zhang-qianfan-constitutio nal-cure-coronavirus-china-democracy/

Zhao, Dingxin. 2001. *The Power of Tiananmen: State-Society Relations and the 1989 Beijing Student Movement.* Chicago: University of Chicago Press.

Zhao, Dingxin. 2009. "The Mandate of Heaven and Performance Legitimation in Historical and Contemporary China." *American Behavioral Scientist* 53 (3): 416–33.

Zhao, Yuezhi. 2012. "The Struggle for Socialism in China." *Monthly Review: An Independent Socialist Magazine* 64: 1–17.

Zheng, Yongnian. 2008. *Technological Empowerment: The Internet, State, and Society in China.* Stanford, CA: Stanford University Press.

Zhou, Yuezhi. 2000. "Watchdogs on Party Leashes? Contexts and Implications of Investigative Journalism in Post-Deng China." *Journalism Studies* 1 (4): 577–97.

Zhu, Jiangnan, Huang Huang, and Dong Zhang. 2019. "'Big Tigers, Big Data': Learning Social Reactions to China's Anticorruption Campaign through Online Feedback." *Public Administration Review* 79 (4): 500–13. https://doi.org/10.1111/puar.12866.

Zhu, Jiangnan, Jie Lu, and Tianjian Shi. 2012. "When Grapevine News Meets Mass Media: Different Information Sources and Popular Perceptions of Government Corruption in Mainland China." *Comparative Political Studies* 46 (8): 920–46.

Zuckerman, Ethan. 2010. "Intermediary Censorship." In *Access Controlled: The Shaping of Power, Rights and Rule in Cyberspace,* eds. Ronald J. Deibert, John G. Palfrey, Rafal Rohozinski, and Jonathan Zittrain, 71–85. Cambridge, MA: MIT Press.

Zuo, Handi. 2020. "Wuhan huoshenshan yiyuan he leishenshan yiyuan jianshe xianchang xiyin wangyou guanzhu, sanri nei chao liangyi renci guankan shigong zhibo" [Construction of Wuhan Huoshenshan and Leishenshan Hospitals Draw Netizens' Attention, with the Live Broadcast Attracting More Than 200 Million Viewers in Three Days]. *Central Commission for Discipline Inspection and National Supervisory Commission,* January 30, 2020. https://www. ccdi.gov.cn/yaowen/202001/t20200130_210448.html.

Index

For the benefit of digital users, indexed terms that span two pages (e.g., 52–53) may, on occasion, appear on only one of those pages.

Tables and figures are indicated by *t* and *f* following the page number

activism online in China, 40–41
Administration Litigation Law, 51
Administrative Provisions of Internet News Information Services, 56–57
Ai Fen, 115–16
anti-corruption campaign in China, 42
Arab Spring riots, 75
astroturfing, 17–18, 29
authoritarian states
  China as (*see* central government)
  control of internet, 1–2, 7–8, 9–10, 74–75
  and flows of information, 2, 73, 83
  impact of internet, 17–19, 58, 75, 128
  protests against, 10–11, 75
  use and control of media, 8
autocratic single-party systems, decline, 1

behavioral theory, research on, 20–21
Bo Xilai, 58–59

Cai, Yongshun, 51
campus forums and message boards, 57–58
censorship in China (online)
  avoidance, 15, 87–88, 88*f*, 89–92, 90*t*, 94–96, 95*t*
  effectiveness of system, 7–8, 43–44, 126
  "strategic censorship," 8–9, 126
  strategy of central government, 8–9, 44–45
  use for COVID, 114–15
  as wall jumping, 75
central government of China
  baselines of the state, 59
  criticism online, 6, 41–42, 43
  dissatisfaction with, 4–5, 14

  existing narrative frames, 109
  monopoly over speech, 39
  online presence and direction of propaganda, 44–45
  population control through technology, 129–30
  power of, 5, 125
  resilience and durability, 1, 3
  shaping of online information, 105–6
  stability from protests, 5–6
  support by citizens, 3–4, 79–83, 80*f*, 81*t*, 104–5, 105*f*
central-local divide, in discontent channeling, 10
central-local relations, citizens' role in, 40–45
Chen, An, 3
China's E-Government Yearbook, 25
China World Value Survey data (2007), 19–20
Chinese authoritarian state. *See* central government
Chinese Census, 25
Chinese Communist Party (CCP), 42–43.
  See also central government
citizens participation principle ("mass line"), 42–43
closed states. *See* authoritarian states
CNNIC (China Internet Network Information Center)
  data on internet in China, 19, 26–27, 37–38
  description and role, 26
  on internet use, 56
  online presence of central government, 44–45
Communist Youth League, 44, 119
Constitution (Article 41) of China, 42–43

169

170 *Index*

COVID-19, response to
overview, 107–8, 124
initial response and mishandling, 108
Li Wenliang as case, 107–8, 113–16, 124
local officials as targets, 107–8, 111–13, 115–16, 124, 125
narrative refocus, 108, 109–16
and origins of virus, 116–18
Shanghai lockdown as case, 107, 108, 121–23
critical flows of information
central government as target, 79–82, 80f, 81t
exposure in general, 51–52
exposure on internet in China, 53–54, 54t, 125
exposure through social media in China, 13, 58, 61–62, 63–66, 64t, 67–68, 70
increase in China, 40–41
local government as target, 45–46, 45t
making of critical posts, 45–46, 45t
model for, 51–54, 52f, 54t
Cyberspace Administration of China, 72

data for survey. *See* survey data
data on citizens. *See* surveillance
democracy, and internet, 127–29
democracy in China, low demand for, 3, 4–5
Deng, Yanhua, 5
Deng Xiaoping, 73
directed digital dissidence (DDD)
description and as concept, 2–3, 8–9
limits of, 121
similar approaches and studies, 9, 10
directed digital dissidence (DDD) in China
alternatives to, 13
application to real events, 15
and central-local divide, 10
future of, 16, 130–31
limits of, 121–23, 124
as relief valve, 2–3, 12
research findings, 10–11, 125, 126
research overview and goals, 10–11
research premise, 12–13
and "rightful resistance," 8–9
as strategy, 2–3, 12, 15, 51–52, 111, 113, 120–21, 123, 128–29, 130–31
survey description, 11–12
survey questions asked, 133–43
as winning strategy of central government, 12–13, 16, 125–26, 128–29, 130–31
directed digital dissidence (DDD) in China – applications and examples
overview, 107–8
COVID (*see* COVID-19, response to)
foreign forces, 116–20, 124
limits of, 121–23, 124
Li Wenliang, 107–8, 113–16, 124
Xinjiang cotton, 107–8, 118–20, 124

dissidence, direction management, 2–3, 41–42
dissident behavior. *See* critical flows; jumping of Great Firewall; protests in China
distrust, and protest behavior, 49–50, 51–53
Douban, 59–60

economic opportunities and internet in China, 17, 38–39
Edwards, Wilson, 117–18
entertainment (foreign), access to, 77–78, 78f, 85–86
entrepreneurs, adaptation to central government, 3

fax machines, 72
50 Cent Party, 28–30, 32, 100, 103–4. *See also* pro-government posters
flows of information
and authoritarian states, 2, 73, 83
awareness of influence from, 31–33, 32t, 34
control and shaping in China, 17–18, 40, 126
counterflow with politically dissident ideas, 28–29, 30
as critical information (*see* critical flows)
in DDD theory, 2–3
and freer access to information, 39–40
influence on public opinion, 45–51
and internet, 7, 12, 39–40
motivations of pro-government posters, 31–33, 32t
pro–central government flow, 28–30, 30t
and success of central government, 10–11, 12, 125, 126
and wall jumping, 14
foreign direct investment, liberalization, 3
foreign forces (firms and governments), in DDD strategy, 116–20, 124
foreign media, 85–86, 85t, 118
Free (Zatan) message board, 40–41

Geddes, Barbara, 103–4
Global Times, narrative on COVID, 112, 114–15
government of China. *See* central government
government posters. *See* pro-government posters
Grassroots Voices (Baixing Shengyin) message board, 40–41
Great Firewall
access to information outside, 72, 73–74, 75, 76–77
cracks in, 13–14, 72
See also jumping of Great Firewall
groups to influence government policies, 51
Gruffydd-Jones, Jamie, 116

Habermas, Jürgen, 8
Han, Rongbin, 10
Hassid, Jonathan, 5

higher education institutions in China, propaganda from, 44–45
H&M (retailer), 119
Hobbs, William, 78, 85–86
hostile forces, 12
hostile posters. *See* net-spies
Huang, Haifeng, 67–68
Hubei Province
  case study of DDD, 108–16
  local officials dismissal and punishment, 111, 112
  official media coverage, 110–11
Hyun, Ki Deuk, 19–20

Internet
  access in controlled states, 74
  control by authoritarian states, 1–2, 7–8, 9–10, 74–75
  and democracy, 127–29
  impact on autocratic governments, 17–19, 58, 75, 128
  limitations, 1–2
  misinformation on, 127
  as positive and politically transformative, 1–2
  for regime support, 2–3
  as tool of governments, 2
  use for protests, 7
internet in China
  adoption, 37–38
  censorship avoidance, 15, 87–88, 88f, 89–92, 90t, 94–96, 95t
  channeling of discontent by government, 9–11
  complaints lodged via government websites, 28, 41
  critical flows and trust in local government, 53–54, 54t, 125
  data scarcity on, 19–20
  data sources, 19–20
  description, 18, 27–34
  disjuncture between online and offline worlds, 18
  exposure to political information, 28f, 28
  general use items, 27–28, 28f
  news providers, 56–57
  online news use, 56–57
  online services used, 38t
  political impact, 17–20, 60–61
  political information exchange by citizens, 38–39
  and "rightful resistance," 7, 8–9, 43–44
  selective censorship by government, 8–9
  shaping of discourse by government, 44–45
  as state-led political tool, 2, 8–9, 128
  structure as two spheres, 73–74, 75
  survey description, 11–12
  and traditional media, 98

use and trust in government, 12–13, 55, 125, 126
use and wall jumping, 96–97, 100–1, 101f, 102–4, 103f, 104t
use frequency, 27, 31, 34, 35–36
users and use, 24–26, 27–28, 28f, 37–38, 38t, 56, 125, 126
Internet in China – and central government
  challenges and opportunities, 17, 38–39
  control effectiveness, 9–10
  control of, 5, 7–8, 17–18, 73–75
  freer flows, 39–40
  state discourse and engagement of citizens, 8, 126
  as threat, 72
Internet propaganda troop (*wangluo xuanchuanyuan*), 44–45

Jinri Toutiao news aggregator, 44
jumping and jumpers of Great Firewall
  awareness of, 84–85, 85f, 87–88
  censorship avoidance, 15, 94–97
  competing effects, 35–36
  consequences, 14, 74, 75–76, 79–83, 81t
  definition and description, 75
  difficulty of, 86–87, 87f
  and flows of information, 14
  motivations, 14, 75–76, 85–86, 85t, 87–88, 96
  numbers and frequency, 15, 76–77, 77f, 78, 96
  political information access, 76–78, 77f, 78f
  profile of jumpers, 14, 89–96
  propensity to, 92–94, 93t
  and use of internet in China, 96–97, 100–1, 101f, 102–4, 103f, 104t
jumping of Great Firewall – and central government
  criticism information, 79
  exposure to government information, 15
  neutralization by central government, 14, 15, 98–105, 106
  and trust, 77f, 101–2, 102t
  views of central government, 96–97

Kaixin001, 59–60
Kim, Jinhee, 19–20
King, Gary, 8–9, 10

Lee, Ching Kwan, 5
Lei, Ya-wen, 19–20
Leibold, James, 18–20
list experiment in survey, 47–49, 48f, 62–63, 63f, 76–77, 77f
Li Wenliang
  in DDD strategy, 107–8, 113–16, 124
  description and role, 113, 115

172   *Index*

local authorities/officials
  channeling of problems and criticisms to, 6–7,
    12–13, 41–42, 79
  citizens' supervision of, 42–43
  complaints lodged via government websites,
    28, 41
  critical flows, 45–46, 45t
  criticisms by citizens, 40–41, 43
  local officials dismissal and punishment,
    111–12
  response to criticism, 40–41
  as targets in COVID-19 response, 107–8,
    111–13, 115–16, 124, 125
local authorities/officials – and trust
  vs. central government, 6, 41, 49, 125
  and DDD, 125
  distribution of, 46–47, 47f, 48f, 48, 53–54, 54t
  and exposure to critical flows, 53–54, 54t, 125
  and use of internet in China, 12–13, 55
  and wall jumping, 79–80
Local Leader Message Board, 41
Lorentzen, Peter, 10
Lu Wei, 59

Mao, 1
"mass line" (citizens participation), 42–43
media. *See* foreign media; state media outlets;
    traditional media,
mediation models, description and use, 53
Meng, Bingchun, 18
middle class, 3
Ministry of Information Industry
    (MII, later MIIT), 56–57

net-spies or hostile posters
  awareness of, 30t, 31–33, 32t
  estimated posts coming from, 33–34, 35t
  evidence of, 30
  posts by, 29
  See also pro-government posters
news providers online, 56–57

O'Brien, Kevin, 5
online information. *See* internet; internet in
    China
ordered logit, use in survey data, 31–33
ordinary least squares (OLS), use in survey
    data, 31

Pan, Jennifer, 8–9, 10
Peking University, 49
People's Daily, narrative on COVID, 109–10, 112,
    116–17
Pingan Wuhan, tweets on COVID, 113–15
political actors, and internet, 127, 128
political interest
  censorship avoidance, 92

and social media in China, 67–69
  in wall jumping, 94
population control through technology, 129–30
"populist authoritarianism," as concept, 3–4
posts, changing of. *See* censorship in China,
    avoidance
pro-government posters
  awareness of, 30t, 31–33, 32t, 100, 103, 104–
    5, 104t
  effectiveness, 103–5
  estimated posts coming from, 33–34, 35t
  motivations, 31–33, 32t
  and wall jumping, 100
  See also 50 Cent Party
protests in China
  acceptability and support for, 49–51, 50t
  channeling of discontent by government for
    own benefits, 9, 10–11
  dissatisfaction channeled to local government,
    6–7
  list experiment in survey, 62–63, 63f
  methods of central government in prevention
    of protests, 5–6
  and opinions about local government, 49–51,
    50t
  and power of central government, 5
  and regime stability, 5–6
  relationship with distrust, 49–50, 51–53
  unrest and "mass incidents," 4–5, 62
  See also "rightful resistance"

QQ, 59–60
Qualtrics, 22–24

reforms in China
  demands for, 4–5
  negative effects, 4–5
  of 1980s, 73–74
  positive impact, 3–4
  and unrest, 4–5
"rightful resistance"
  benefits for both state and protesters, 8
  central government in, 7, 41–42, 43, 125–26
  coexistence of protest and central government,
    7
  and DDD, 8–9
  description as mechanism, 5–6, 125–26
  function, 41–42, 125–26
  and government policies, 42
  and internet in China, 7, 8–9, 43–44
  and local authorities, 6–7, 41–42
  and success of central government, 126
Roberts, Margaret E., 8–9, 10, 78, 85–86

Seven Baselines, 59
Shanghai lockdown, 107, 108, 121–23
Shao, Li, 10

Index

Shirky, Clay, 39
Sina Weibo, 59–60, 61–62
Social Credit System, 129
social desirability bias, 47, 48
social media
  censorship avoidance, 91
  use for protests, 7
social media in China
  COVID information and posts, 111, 113–14
  critical flows on, 61–62, 63–65, 64t, 67
  dissidence on (controlled), 13
  distribution of media items, 60–61, 61f
  examples, 147
  exposure to critical flows, 13, 58, 63–66, 64t, 67–68, 70
  foreign forces criticism, 119–20
  limit and control by central government, 57–59, 70
  local-level critical flows, 13
  news and information on, 57, 58, 60–61
  online campaigns against, 58–59
  online survey by authors, 11–12, 59–63, 61f
  other surveys or measures, 69
  political attitudes impact, 64t, 67–68, 69
  and political interest, 67–69
  political use, 60–61
  protests support on, 62–65, 63f, 64t, 66–67, 70–71
  and Shanghai lockdown, 121, 122–23
  as threat to central government, 57–58, 59
  use and reach in China, 58, 61–62, 65
  use measurement and impact, 59–68, 61f, 70
  user profile, 68–69
  user profile – correlates, 68–69, 68t
State Council Information Office (SCIO), 56–57
state government. *See* central government
state media outlets
  and foreign criticism, 116
  narrative on COVID, 109–10, 112, 113–14, 116–18
  online outlets, 56–57
  in online propaganda, 44–45
  and trust in government, 53–54
  See also traditional media
Statistical Reports on Internet Development in China (37th report), 26–27
Steinhardt, Christoph, 9
Stern, Rachel, 5
"strategic censorship," 8–9, 126
structural equations, description and use, 53
surveillance and data on citizens in China, 129–30
survey by authors
  administration details, 22–24
  age and education in, 25–27, 25t
  and CNNIC survey, 26–27

commentators paid or sponsored by government, 29, 30t
critique of central government by wall jumpers, 79–83, 80f, 81t
data for (*see* survey data)
demographics in, 25–26, 25t
description and goals, 11–12, 20, 22–23
design of, 22–24
findings overview, 34–36, 125–26
and frequency of internet use in China, 27, 31, 34, 35–36
general use items of internet in China, 27–28, 28f
measure of central government response, 11–12
posts (estimated) coming from political actors, 33–34, 35t
protests acceptability and strategies, 49–50, 62
questions asked, 22–24, 133–43
respondents, 23–24
respondents *vs.* Chinese population, 24–26, 25t
social desirability bias and list experiment, 47–49, 48f
social media use in China, 11–12, 59–63, 61f
on wall jumpers, 76–78, 77f, 78f, 84–88, 85f, 85t
survey data
  causal inferences from correlational models, 21–22
  collection, 24
  on information technology–related concepts in China, 23
  introduction, 22–27
  limitations of data, 20–22
  multiple indicators added, 21, 22–23
  regression models and variables, 22
  scarcity and lack of other data, 19–20, 23, 26
surveys, as research tool, 20–21

Tang, Wenfang, 3–4
technology
  population control by central government, 129–30
  as solution to democratic deficits, 131
  as threat to central government, 72, 73–74
Texas A&M University, 49
Tiananmen Square demonstrations, 72, 73
Tianya (tianya.cn), 40–41
traditional media in China, 39, 80–82, 85–86, 98. *See also* state media outlets
Truman, Harry S., 73
Trump, Donald, 116–17
trust in government in China
  central government, 53–54, 79–83, 80f, 81t, 126
  central (high) *vs.* local (low), 6, 41, 49, 125

174   Index

trust in government in China (*cont.*)
 jumping of Great Firewall, 77*f*, 79–80, 101–2, 102*t*
 list experiment in survey, 47–49, 48*f*
 model for, 51–54, 52*f*, 54*t*
 other studies, 49
 and use of internet in China, 12–13, 55, 125, 126
 See also local authorities/officials – and trust
"trustworthiness" of citizens, 129
Tsai, Kellee, 3
Twitter, 116–17

United States
 internet in, 127
 and origins of COVID, 116–18
unrest and "mass incidents" in China, 4–5, 62
Uyghurs. *See* Xinjiang-sourced cotton boycott

"Voices of April" (*siyue zhi sheng*)
 video, 122
VPN services, 86–88

wall jumping. *See* jumping of Great Firewall
WeChat, 44, 59–60, 61–62
Weibo platform
 central government presence, 44
 and COVID, 113–15

 description and use, 59–60
 and government control, 59
 user profile, 69
Weibo User Development Report, 69
Western countries
 anti-China bias, 118
 internet in, 127
Wuhan
 case study of DDD, 108–16
 local officials dismissal and punishment, 111
 and origins of COVID virus, 116–18
 streaming of hospitals building, 110
 See also COVID-19
Wuhan Institute of Virology, 117, 120

Xijin, Hu, 114–15
Xi Jinping, 42, 44–45, 110
Xinjiang-sourced cotton boycott, in DDD
 strategy, 107–8, 118–20, 124
Xue, Charles, 59

YTHT campus forum, 57–58

Zaller, John, 103–4
Zhang, Yonghong, 5
Zhao Lijian, 116–17
Zhiyong, Xu, 51
Zhou Xianwang, 112